Spain and The Netherlands, 1559-1659

Ten Studies

Geoffrey Parker

Enslow Publishers
Short Hills, New Jersey, 07078
1979

First published 1979
© Geoffrey Parker 1979

Library of Congress Cataloging in Publication Data
Parker, Noel Geoffrey.
  Spain and the Netherlands, 1559–1659.

  Includes bibliographical references and index.
  1. Netherlands—History—Wars of Independence,
  1556–1648—Collected works. I. Title.

DH186.5.P285   949.2'03   79–12356
ISBN 0 89490 029 3

Printed in Great Britain

10 9 8 7 6 5 4 3 2 1

For Charles Wilson

Spain and The Netherlands, 1559-1659

Contents

Acknowledgements

All the essays in this volume have already been published, although I have revised them – sometimes extensively – for this edition. I am most grateful to the following for permission to reprint articles originally published elsewhere: the Past and Present Society, Oxford, for Chapters 1 and 5; H. J. Tjeenk Willink, Groningen, for Chapters 3 and 8; the Literary Director of the Royal Historical Society for Chapter 2; the Editor of *History* for Chapter 7; the Editor of the *Journal of Modern History* and the University of Chicago for Chapter 4; the Editor of the *Mariner's Mirror* for Chapter 6; the Editor of the *English Historical Review* and the Longman Group Ltd for Chapter 9; and the Syndics of Cambridge University Press for Chapter 10. In addition, since Chapters 6 and 9 are the fruit of collaboration, I am most grateful to my co-authors for their permission to reprint our joint work here: respectively, Dr I. A. A. Thompson of the University of Keele and Dr Hugo de Schepper of the Department of Dutch Law, University of Amsterdam. I would also like to thank the two people who have done more than anyone else to make this volume possible: Richard Ollard, my editor at Collins, who encouraged and guided my efforts; and Angela Parker, who read and criticized before publication every article printed here and saved me from innumerable errors and ambiguities. Other debts are acknowledged individually in the footnotes.

St Andrews, 10 May 1978

Preface

When I graduated from Cambridge University in June 1965 I had already decided that I wished to undertake research into Spain's reaction to the Dutch Revolt. During the Michaelmas Term of 1964 a number of 'Henry Mellish Scholarships', worth £50 each, were offered by the City of Nottingham to any persons educated in the city's schools who were then at university. The scholarships were intended to assist them to undertake some field work which was connected with their undergraduate courses but was not essential to them. While I was trying to think of a suitable topic to submit to the Scholarship Trustees, I attended the lecture course given by John Elliott on the history of early modern Europe. One morning he pointed to the map of sixteenth-century Europe and observed that a major mystery of Habsburg imperialism was the way in which Spain managed to fight such expensive wars, with so many men, so far from her financial and demographic base. This simple logistical problem fired my imagination; it also convinced the Scholarship Trustees. In the Easter vacation of 1965, my £50 was spent on a journey to find the 'Spanish Road' (as contemporaries called it) by which the Spanish Habsburgs had sent their men, money and munitions to Brussels, Milan and Vienna. This preliminary expedition indicated that there was enough material in the subject for a doctoral thesis, and I produced one, under John Elliott's supervision, in June 1968. After a great deal more work, my research was published as two books: *Guide to the Archives of the Spanish Institutions in or concerned with the Netherlands, 1556-1706* (Brussels, 1971) and *The Army of Flanders and the Spanish Road, 1567-1659. The logistics of Spanish victory and defeat in the Low Countries' Wars* (Cambridge, 1972). Even before these were published, I was invited to produce two further books on the subject of Spain and the Netherlands. The Penguin Press commissioned me to write a new history of the Dutch Revolt (the last one in English being over forty years old), and Little, Brown and Company of Boston asked me to provide a new biography of King Philip II of Spain. The two volumes, *The Dutch Revolt* and *Philip II*, were published in 1977 and 1978 respectively.

11

But apart from these four books, there are also ten articles on the theme of Spain and the Netherlands which have been published at various times and in various places. Some examine aspects of the subject in more detail than was possible in the books; others present a general view of one facet of the revolt; the rest suggest modifications to the general interpretation of the Spanish-Dutch struggle. All of them were composed in response to specific invitations to produce a paper, and some of the invitations were issued in unexpected circumstances (Chapter 10, for example, was commissioned by Dr Jay Winter one sunny afternoon as we pushed my daughter on a swing in a Cambridge playground). I have recorded the circumstances which occasioned the various essays in a short preface attached to each one, since they tend to vindicate the conferences, symposia and 'guest lectures' which loom so large in modern academic life: each invitation challenges the historian to examine familiar evidence in new ways and to extend his research in new directions. But despite the variety of stimuli, the studies printed in this collection have three things in common. First, they all study an aspect of the mechanics whereby Spain managed to maintain its preponderance in Europe from the Peace of Cateau-Cambrésis in 1559 to the Peace of the Pyrenees just a century later. Second, they all emphasize the same outlook on the Dutch Revolt: that it only makes sense when set in a European context; that its outcome was determined more by political than by economic factors (and in particular by the successive decisions to employ Spain's resources outside the Netherlands); and that it retarded the economic growth of the North Netherlands as well as accelerating the decline of Spain and the South Netherlands. Finally, they all share the same outlook on history.

Since my undergraduate days I have always been impressed by the work of the French 'Annales school', with their penchant for writing 'total history' and their delight in measuring trends and quantifying developments. The work of Fernand Braudel and his illustrious pupils from the Ecole Pratique des Hautes Etudes made me dream of producing a work of quantitative history on Habsburg Spain; and, in 1967, on a visit on the Ecole Pratique, Braudel himself encouraged me to do this and supplied me with invaluable guidance to suitable archives. But two considerations deterred me. First, it soon became clear that to write the 'total history' of anything more than a solitary (and perhaps atypical) village is excessively demanding. To be meaningful, history *au style Annales* requires a team of expert, experienced and docile researchers, a vast reservoir of patience (for many French theses take two decades to complete), prolonged leisure from teaching, and financial resources on a scale which no British historian – least of all one in his twenties – can ever hope to command. Perhaps it was sour grapes which made me wonder whether this unattainable dream had in fact been a good idea in the first place: were those enormous theses, sometimes running to over 1000 pages even on relatively minor topics, really the best way of presenting history to the public? 'Total history', it has been observed, can easily become 'endless history'. And in truth, for the early modern period, it is also doomed to be incomplete: until the nineteenth century at least, there is simply not enough surviving data to permit the historian, however devoted his team of colleagues and however generous his financial resources, to study with confidence every group of people, let alone every person, in a given period or society, however minute. Not even for a single village can the entire population be 'reconstituted' for the purpose of historical description and analysis. And where copious data does survive, it is often flawed because the reasons for its compilation were different from the interests of the modern researcher: the questions which he wants to ask did not always occur to his early modern forebears, and the questions which his forebears did ask were often aimed at other objectives. This basic difference of outlook appears with charming but absolute finality in a letter written by a Turkish official to an English scholar early in the nineteenth century:

My illustrious friend and joy of my liver: The thing you ask of me is both difficult and useless. Although I have passed all my days in this place, I have neither counted the houses nor have I inquired into the number of the inhabitants; and as to what one person loads on his mules and the other stows away in the bottom of his ship, that is no business of mine . . . It were unprofitable for us to inquire into it. O my soul! O my lamb! Seek not after the things which concern thee not . . . Thou art learned in

13

the things I care not for; and as for that which thou hast seen, I defile it.[1]

The anxious enquiries of modern quantitative historians about vital statistics, trade figures and other serial data would have been met with just the same bland surprise and unhelpful dismissal by the officials of most early modern states, and we cannot pretend otherwise. The materials for writing 'total history' were simply not generated in the sixteenth and seventeenth centuries. It does not matter how much we may want to know something about the past: if the sources are not there, we cannot invent them.

Taking all these considerations into account, the articles reprinted in this volume are therefore deliberately confined to a limited problem and they equally deliberately make use of quantitative techniques and serial data only when such things help to place the events and conditions of the time in a clearer perspective or a wider context. What I learned in Paris from Fernand Braudel and his colleagues has been married with what I was taught in Cambridge by Christopher Cheney, John Elliott, Geoffrey Elton, Philip Grierson, Jack Plumb, Brian Pullan and Quentin Skinner. And in this symbiosis, the historian whose approach to the past has most influenced me, as I hope will be apparent, is Charles Wilson, who has combined in all his work the quantitative approach of Braudel with the qualitative approach of Ranke. It is to mark my long-standing debt to his friendship, his teaching and his writings that this volume is dedicated to him.

I

The Dutch Revolt
in its European Setting

1

It has sometimes been observed with surprise that Philip II, with all his vast dominions, never produced, nor caused to be produced, a 'blueprint for empire'. Certainly his father, Charles V, had intended to create a Christian world monarchy guided by the plans drawn up by two of his ministers, Gattinara and Guevara; but both Philip II and his advisers failed to evolve a comprehensive theory of empire to take the place of the outmoded ideas of earlier days. 'For this failure,' Professor H. G. Koenigsberger has written, 'there can be only one reasonable explanation: they had no such plan or programme.'

Some French historians have argued from this failure that Philip II's imperialism was purely pragmatic, empirical and opportunist, reacting to the ebb and flow of the economy, and especially to the rhythm of the trade between Spain and America, with Spain's foreign policy reduced to the shuttle-cock of the Seville trade. This seems highly improbable. It is clear that there existed certain guiding principles, or maxims, which governed the development of the Prudent King's imperialism. Professor Koenigsberger has established the importance of three of them: the defence of the king's dominions against all attacks from the outside or subversion from the inside; the preservation of the Roman Catholic faith; and the provision of equal justice for all his subjects. 'There remained, however, the vital question of what he meant by them and how he was going to act on them in practice.' (See Koenigsberger's masterly article: 'The state-craft of Philip II', *European Studies Review*, I, 1971, pp. 1-21.)

This paper attempts to answer the 'vital question', for if Philip II did not have an 'overall political plan', at least he had a set of priorities which determined how his resources should be deployed at any given moment; and these priorities remained largely the same until at least the 1640s. The vicissitudes of Grand Strategy appear most clearly in Spain's policy towards the Netherlands, since her commitment there lasted for so long, but a similar study could be carried out on any of Philip II's other provinces. (Professor Koenigsberger has already done one on Sicily – *The Government of Sicily under Philip II* – and Dr C. D. G. Riley has done another on Lombardy – 'The state of Milan in the reign of Philip II', Oxford University D. Phil., 1977.) In framing this 'list of imperial priorities' I received invaluable assistance from Professors J. H. Elliott and H. G. Koenigsberger, and from the members of the Anglo-Dutch Historical Seminar held at the Institute of Historical Research, to whom this paper was delivered in November 1969.

Spain, her Enemies and the Revolt of the Netherlands, 1559-1648

Some years ago, in his excellent review of the historiography of the Dutch Revolt, Professor J. W. Smit underlined the widespread reliance of twentieth-century historians of the Revolt upon the interpretations of their predecessors. To an extent which is fortunately uncommon in other fields, the geographical, chronological and ideological framework established by the great scientific historians of the last century – Groen van Prinsterer, Bakhuizen van den Brink, Fruin – still dominates sixteenth-century studies in the Netherlands.[1]

A great deal of exciting new work has been done since 1960. Above all, new historical techniques have been employed: precise statistical methods have been applied to establish the actual numbers of professing Calvinists and Catholics in the major cities and to pinpoint the exact composition of the urban patriciates at the time of the Revolt. There has also been considerable reinterpretation of the leading events in the light of previously unused documentary sources, especially the ecclesiastical archives and wage and price series. These advances in our knowledge are important and yet, one must admit, they are all concerned with the *traditional* issues. The Dutch continue to study their revolt from a standpoint which is basically domestic, introspective, at times even parochial. The native politics

18

and institutions of the Netherlands continue to monopolize the historical limelight.

Of course, a proper understanding of the internal dynamics and evolution of the Low Countries in the sixteenth century is indispensable to any consideration of the Revolt. It would indeed be foolish not to allow a central place in any account of the establishment of the Dutch Republic to the inner strengths which enabled a tiny group of provinces to resist the might of Spain for so long. However, this must not obscure the impact upon the Netherlands of the actions of other European states. A lofty contemplation of the ineptitude of foreign intervention in the Eighty Years' War – John Casimir, Anjou, Leicester – does not, as is often supposed, exhaust the subject. Today, even if the interdependence of events in France, England and the Netherlands has received adequate recognition, little attention is paid to the influence of events in neighbouring Germany or in Spain upon the course of Netherlands history.[2]

Habsburg Spain was, in the sixteenth century, unquestionably the most powerful state in western Europe. The revenues, dominions and armies of the king of Spain were by far the largest of any European potentate. Yet the very dimensions and daunting resources of the empire excited enmity. Spain's three imperial holdings in Europe – the Low Countries, much of Italy and finally Portugal – brought her sooner or later into open conflict with three other powers: England, France and the Ottoman Sultan. The Spanish kings were rich, but they did not control anything approaching the resources required to fight all three enemies at once, let alone to suppress simultaneously any domestic unrest, and therefore Spain was for ever balancing the needs of defence or action in one area against the needs of the others. There had to be a table of imperial priorities, a set of criteria which enabled the central government to decide how best to allocate its inadequate resources. Only if we take due account of Spain's general position can we hope to understand her reaction first to opposition and later to armed resistance in the Low Countries. As the perceptive Belgian historian Ernest Gossart wrote over sixty years ago: 'We have considered the religious side of the struggle too much; we have scarcely seen Philip II as anything but the champion of Catholicism; we have not taken sufficient account of the place occupied by the Low Countries in his general political system.' This sound advice has been rarely heeded.[3] The exact relationship of the Netherlands to Spain after 1559, despite the magisterial publications of Gachard, Cuvelier and Lefèvre, has remained a relatively neglected field.

Recently M. Pierre Chaunu, one of the foremost exponents of quantitative history, took up Gossart's challenge. He wrote a challenging article in 1960 which appeared to set the Netherlands, for the first time, squarely in the context of Habsburg imperialism.[4] M. Chaunu called for a new approach to the problems of the Revolt, seeing them through Spanish eyes, and he postulated a tentative schema which connected the vicissitudes of Spanish policy in the Netherlands with the cyclical fluctuations of Spain's trade with the New World. To Chaunu, a causal connection between the flow of money to the Spanish army in the Netherlands and the military fortunes of the war was axiomatic. From this basis he claimed that the health of the Spanish-American economy directly affected the remittances sent to the Netherlands: 'Broadly speaking, [he wrote] one can discern in the Eighty Years' War eleven more or less distinct phases, which coincide with the movements of the Seville trade. The correlation is perfect from 1559 to 1609.'[5]

M. Chaunu's article has not been seriously called into question, even though he freely admitted that he was familiar with only half the data necessary for such a study: he was unable to provide any quantitative information concerning the actual level of Spanish expenditure in the Low Countries, and he confessed that only when this was known could his assertions be verified.[6] In fact, when Spain's actual expenditure is considered, two basic flaws appear in the Chaunu hypothesis. First the fluctuations of the American trade which M. Chaunu discovered do *not* seem to bear any relationship to the level of the provisions sent to the Spanish Netherlands; second, it becomes clear that the level of those provisions did not always, as he assumed, govern the rate of the Spanish 'Reconquest'. To give two illustrations: the years 1572-5 and 1590-1600, when (according to M. Chaunu) the Seville trade was depressed, saw enormous remittances from Spain to the Netherlands but very little military success against the Dutch. Conversely, from 1580 to 1585, when the king's revenue from the Indies was double the figure of a decade before, the provisions to the Spanish Netherlands were about one-third as great, yet these were the years which saw the 'Reconquest' of all the southern provinces.

So we are back where we started. M. Chaunu was correct to postulate very considerable variations both in the volume of Spanish treasure sent to the Low Countries and in the military performance of the Spanish army there, but the first was by no means the sole influence on the second, and neither can be clearly correlated to the seductive rhythm of Spain's Atlantic trade. Yet the Eighty Years' War between Spain and the Dutch, and the years of conflict which preceded it, was not a casual affair. Spain did not spend her treasure in the north without plan or purpose. There were certain deep-seated policies and priorities which determined the level of Spanish commitment in the Low Countries, and it is the aim of this article to discover what they were.

Let us first examine in detail one of M. Chaunu's 'more or less distinct phases': the period between 1559 and 1566, called by Dutch historians the *Voorspel* (the Prelude) to the Eighty Years' War, which M. Chaunu saw primarily in terms of a 'difficulty of the economic conjuncture'.[7] It is now a commonplace that the salient feature of the Spanish empire in Europe after 1559 was the total dependence – political, military, financial – of all the component territories upon Castile. The wars of the 1550s had run the governments of Naples, Sicily, Milan and the Netherlands deep into debt. In the Low Countries, the state debt which in 1550 stood at a manageable 500,000 florins, rose steadily until in 1565 it reached a peak of 10,000,000 florins. The cost of paying interest on this debt and of financing the ordinary administration amounted to considerably more than the combined

21

state revenues: the peacetime deficit on the current account amounted to 500,000 florins annually.[8]

In fact the budget of the Netherlands government after 1559 could only be balanced if the king consented to send special additional funds for that purpose from Spain. In this way, between 1561 and 1567, 2,854,846 ducats (about 5·7 million florins) were sent from Spain to the Netherlands – a quarter of it in 1567 to prepare for the duke of Alva. This total, although far from negligible, was not enough to offset the deficit and provide the government in Brussels with the funds necessary to preserve law and order. Between 1551 and 1556, by contrast, Spain sent 22,000,000 florins to the Netherlands in order to finance the war against France. Why could it not repeat the effort in the 1560s to forestall the deepening civil crisis?[9]

Even before his return to Spain in September 1559, Philip II became absorbed in the defence of the Mediterranean against the Ottoman Sultan and his satellite in the west, the pirate king of Algiers. No sooner had peace been made with France at Cateau-Cambrésis than Philip II decided to mount an offensive in the Mediterranean, but the fateful decision was founded on a highly dubious premise: 'Peace has just been concluded with the king of France,' wrote Philip II, 'which leads one to suppose that the Turks, deprived of assistance and lacking any port [in the west Mediterranean] to accommodate their fleet, will not send it against Christendom.' Accordingly the king ordered his ministers to abandon the truce talks with the Sultan which were then in progress and prepare for war.[10]

Early in 1560, Philip II delivered the first stroke in his new duel with the Sultan. He sent an expedition against the town of Tripoli, lost to the Turks in 1551, and the neighbouring island of Djerba – two important strongholds in the central Mediterranean. The campaign was a fiasco. While the Christian forces were ashore on Djerba the Ottoman fleet surprised them. The troops panicked and tried to escape: twenty-seven galleys were captured or destroyed by the Turks; ten thousand of Philip II's subjects, marooned on the island, were made prisoner and taken to Constantinople. The

22

disaster of Djerba dangerously depleted Spain's galley fleet and gravely compromised her reputation.[11]

In 1561 and 1562 Philip II employed all his resources to construct a new fleet of galleys to replace those lost at Djerba. In October 1562, however, a freak tempest destroyed twenty-five more galleys on manoeuvres near Málaga. At one blow the Spanish Mediterranean fleet was reduced to the same unsatisfactory post-Djerba level. It was indeed fortunate for Spain that the Turkish fleet did not appear in great strength in the west Mediterranean in these years. In 1563, apart from rescuing Oran from siege, the programme for naval recon-struction was pressed forward and in 1564, partly in order to impress the Pope, Philip II was able to take the offensive again. Between ninety and a hundred galleys, scraped together with great difficulty, sailed to the stronghold of Peñón de Vélez near Tetuán and captured it – a considerable success, albeit somewhat blighted by the simultaneous uprising of Corsica against its Genoese masters (Spain's allies) while the combined war fleet of Spain and Genoa was taking the Peñón.[12]

Meanwhile, in the Netherlands, the years 1560-4 saw the establishment of a concerted opposition to the policies of Philip II's regency government. There was considerable pressure from certain groups first to remove the Spanish troops who, after 1559, acted as garrisons along the Nether-lands' southern border, then for the recall of the 'Spanish minister', Cardinal Granvelle. The decision to withdraw the former was taken late in 1560, when the catastrophe at Djerba – which made the Spanish veterans in the Low Countries very desirable in Spain – was known. Granvelle's recall was ordered on 23 January 1564, as the king prepared his fleet for the great expedition to the Peñón. Both resolu-tions were forced upon a reluctant king by the threat made by the Netherlands leaders – certain prominent members of the Council of State and the provincial Estates – to boycott all public business should the king not comply with their demands. It seems likely that Philip's pusillanimity over these two matters was prompted by his preoccupation with the campaign in the Mediterranean. He could not afford

23

trouble behind the lines.

The removal of Granvelle, which took effect in March 1564, left the control of affairs in the Netherlands in the hands of the Council of State, a body dominated by grandees, many of whom held the office of Stadholder in one or more of the provinces.[13] The Council wished to establish a permanent base for its new power. In particular it desired the appointment of four more grandees as councillors (Berghes, Montigny, Meghen and Noircarmes) and it called for the subordination of the Privy Council (the supreme judicial body) and the Council of Finance to the Council of State.[14] The grandees had no wish to centralize: they merely wanted to dominate the central government in order to secure their regional preponderance against the centralizing attempts of others. Their aim was a return to the early years of Charles V when the Stadholders had acted more or less independently in their own provinces.[15] In addition the Stadholders, in common with the town magistrates, the provincial Estates and the judicial tribunals, were anxious to abolish the 'New Bishoprics' and the diocesan inquisitors introduced at the king's command after 1559. The agents of both schemes were permitted to meddle in provincial affairs independent of the officers of the local government – hence their unpopularity among the established provincial élites.

During the course of 1564, the Council of State sought local support for these four aims, two political and two religious. By the end of the year they felt strong enough to send Count Egmont to Spain to seek the king's consent to their proposals. Egmont arrived at the royal court just as rumours turned to certainty that the Ottoman Sultan was preparing a major seaborne expedition against Christendom. Philip II was courteous with Egmont, he discussed at great length the Netherlands situation, but his mind was really on the defence of the Mediterranean. Spain must have forces prepared to parry the Turkish blow wherever it might fall.

Egmont left the court in March 1565. The king issued him with instructions concerning the measures to be taken in the Low Countries. One of the most significant royal proposals was that a committee of churchmen should be convened to discuss the possibility of finding a less severe yet reasonably efficient method of dealing with heretics. The king appeared to hint at the eventual mitigation of persecution. Egmont himself claimed that the king had promised a great deal more in conversation: that the king had tacitly endorsed the Council's whole programme. In the summer of 1565, encouraged by Egmont's description of affairs in Spain, the Council of State openly usurped the 'sovereign control of all public affairs'.[16] Even so, Egmont's confident assertions about the king's change of heart seemed to be contradicted by letters from Valladolid dated 13 May 1565 in which the king made no mention of relaxing the persecution. On 22 July a perplexed Regent asked the king to clarify his position: 'On several matters which Count Egmont had heard from the royal lips Your Majesty's letters [*sc.* of 13 May] appear, at certain points, to contradict the report he has made.' Despite the urgent, agitated tone of this and other letters from the Netherlands, Philip II did not state his views until 17 October.[17]

The king freely admitted the reason for his long silence: he had been too busy with other things: 'Madam my good sister: The great and varied matters of business which have come upon me for several months past have caused my long delay in replying to several letters which you have written me . . .'[18] The Turkish fleet lay off Malta in May 1565. The island's Christian defenders were blockaded for months: Spain strained every nerve to raise a relief force, but she only landed troops on Malta on 8 September.

The fate of the whole central Mediterranean hung in the balance during the months of the siege; it was only when the Turks withdrew defeated that Philip II had the leisure to consider the difficult issues which confronted him in the Netherlands. As it happened, part of the confusion over his real intentions during the summer of 1565 was accidental: it was the consequence of Philip's practice of handling matters in secret with a number of ministers. Some Spanish ministers, Ruy Gómez and Gonzalo Pérez, had drafted Egmont's Instructions in March, but two of the king's Netherlands advisers at the court, Tisnacq and Josse de Courtewille, wrote

25

the letter of 13 May which appeared to contradict it. Neither knew about the activities of the others.[19] Although unintentional, no doubt the uncertainty and committee-discussion which took up the summer months in Brussels were welcomed by the king as the best way to delay the despatch of what he knew would be an unpopular set of orders.

The first fears that Egmont had exaggerated the success of his mission provoked an important reaction. Discontented nobles began to discuss in secret the steps to be taken should the king not ratify the changes made by the Council of State – the 'Spa meetings' of July and August 1565. The situation became uncomfortably tense, and on 11 October Margaret of Parma's secretary Armenteros wrote that there would be trouble in the Netherlands if the letter of clarification which was expected daily from the king did not meet the nobles' demands. The relief of Malta, he pointed out to his cousin Gonzalo Pérez, would bring no relief to the Low Countries.[20]

With the Ottoman fleet defeated and back in Constantinople, Philip II supervised with infinite care the drafting of the 'Letters from the Segovia Woods' of 17 and 20 October 1565. He reaffirmed his support for the Inquisition and the 'New Bishoprics'; he appointed only one new member to the Council of State, and at that he named the duke of Aerschot, a man known to be the personal enemy of Orange and Egmont; and he claimed that further time was required before a decision could be reached about the subordination of the Collateral Councils to the Council of State. He thus rebuffed the opposition on every point.[21]

The king knew that his decisions would not be popular, but he can hardly have anticipated the amazing tempest which they provoked. He failed to realize that his long summer silence had been taken in the Netherlands to mean consent (*Quis tacet* . . .) and that the unexpected and brutally uncompromising restatement in October of the 'novelties' of 1559 amounted, in effect, to a declaration of war.

The reaction was immediate and dramatic. The informal association of the dissident Netherlands nobles moved into the open and found enormous support. They put forward

26

extreme programmes of grievances (the 'Compromise of the Nobility' and the somewhat diluted 'Request') and forced the regent to suspend the Inquisition and the placards against heresy, pending ultimate ratification from the king (April 1566). Margaret was not happy with this situation, but, as she pointed out to the king, there were only two possible courses of action left: either to put down the opposition by armed force, or to concede what they wanted. On 31 July 1566, declaring before a notary that he signed under compulsion, an anguished Philip II despatched a letter ordering his sister to moderate the heresy laws.[22] The reason for this acknowledgement of defeat is not hard to find. Close as rebellion seemed in the Netherlands, it was known to Philip II that the Ottoman fleet was bent on revenge for the defeat over Malta. The Sultan's offensive in 1566 began with the capture of the last Genoese island in the Aegean, Chios. The great fleet sailed west in triumph. July 1566 was the height of the crisis: Spain had all her troops and all her galleys standing to arms in the Mediterranean. Small wonder then that the king, in order to buy time, signed his letter of concession for the Netherlands.

As it happened, the royal retreat in the Low Countries came too late. The *Beeldenstorm* (or Iconoclastic Fury) began in August, the desecrated churches and urban riots making nonsense of the king's concessions. The arrival of the news at the Spanish court on 3 September is said to have sent Philip into raging fever. Yet it coincided with news of deliverance from another quarter: if the troubles of the Netherlands were at last out in the open, it began to seem as if the Ottoman fleet had been outmanoeuvred yet again. In August, instead of sailing against one of Spain's North African outposts as expected, the Turks entered the Adriatic. Even there they met with little success. The coastal defences organized by Venice and Spain to protect their territories limited the opportunities for booty. In September the Ottoman fleet returned to Constantinople. Shortly afterwards the Sultan, Suleiman the Magnificent, died and his successor faced immediate mutiny in the army and revolt in several outlying provinces.

27

Earlier in 1566, Philip II had been told that the Netherlands situation was so serious that only two policies were open to him: concession or repression. The first having manifestly failed, the alternative seemed clear. In the course of October and November 1566, long discussions between the king and his Spanish Council of State resulted in the decision to send to the Netherlands all the veteran Spanish troops who had served in the Mediterranean fleet and to augment their numbers with German and Netherlands troops until there were 60,000 soldiers in the Low Countries. Orders were issued early in November to assemble the Spanish veterans in Milan, and on 29 November the duke of Alva, a man known to be opposed to any compromise with the 'rebels', agreed to serve as Captain-General of the army to be formed in the Netherlands.

At first it was intended that the duke should arrive in Luxemburg, where the great army of 60,000 could be formed if necessary, by April 1567. Prudence prevailed. The king preferred to delay the departure of the veterans of the fleet until certain confirmation arrived that the Ottoman navy would not put to sea in 1567.[23] The necessary notification was at last received and the duke and his Spaniards left Lombardy for the Netherlands on 21 June. Order was quickly restored. At the duke's approach, the majority of the opposition fled the country; in 1568, under the prince of Orange and Count Louis of Nassau a full-scale invasion was mounted to challenge the duke. However the Sultan continued to favour Philip II's Netherlands policy. The Turkish fleet stayed at home in 1568 and so Philip II was free to send all the available funds to help Alva to crush the rebel incursions.[24]

Throughout the turbulent decade 1559-68, therefore, there was an intimate connection between Philip II's Mediterranean problems and his reaction to the political demands made upon him by the Netherlands opposition. It is important to realize that the Netherlands nobles were themselves fully aware of this relationship. They knew well from the letters exchanged between the ministers of Spain and their Netherlands colleagues (notably Erasso and Ruy Gómez to Egmont and Hornes, and Gonzalo Pérez to his cousin Armenteros) that Spain's principal preoccupation after 1559 was the Turkish maritime threat. They were not slow to draw the correct conclusion from this strategic dilemma of the Spanish Monarchy: as long as the Turks threatened, the king could do nothing in the Netherlands. In 1565 Brederode rubbed his hands gleefully when he heard that the Turks were off Malta, while Orange wrote to his brother: 'The Turks are very threatening which will mean, we believe, that the king will not come [to the Netherlands] this year.'[25] When the Sultan abandoned the Mediterranean in 1566, indirectly causing Orange's defeat and exile, the Prince took a remarkable – and hitherto unremarked – step. He sent his own ambassador to the Sultan, presumably with the object of securing a Turkish campaign in the Mediterranean which would remove Spanish pressure from the Netherlands. The French ambassador in Constantinople was concerned to sabotage this attempt: 'As for the prince of Orange's agent who is seeing the duke of Naxos [the Sultan's Favourite], whom I mentioned in my last letter, he has not achieved anything that I can discover; and I can reasonably assure Your Majesty that his enterprise will not have any effect, provided the situation does not change, so long as I have a hand in it . . .'[26]

All this is rather a long way from the engagingly simple 'economic difficulties' which M. Chaunu saw as the basis of Spain's attitude to the Netherlands problem during these years. The depression of the Seville trade after Cateau-Cambrésis did not prevent Philip II from deciding to provoke the Sultan into aggression by attacking Tripoli in 1560 and the Peñón in 1564. The question is not why Philip did nothing at all in the early 1560s, but why he preferred to spend his money in the Mediterranean rather than in the Netherlands. Certainly, until 1566, solving the Netherlands problem was basically a matter of finance: if the Regent had been sent the funds to raise loyal troops, most of the agitation would no doubt have been prevented. The king, however, stuck to his priorities: the defence of the Mediterranean came first. To a large extent, this remained the case in the 1570s.

Although the unspoken, unconscious *entente* between Orange and the Sultan broke down after 1566, the Turkish navy aided the Netherlands opposition once again. The Mediterranean was quiet in 1567, 1568 and 1569, which allowed Philip II to concentrate upon the despatch of Alva, the defeat of Orange's invasion and the initial moves to suppress the revolt of the Moriscos of Granada (which began at Christmas 1568). In 1570 the spectrum changed. It was the turn of the Turks to assume the offensive. In the west the king of Algiers captured Tunis from one of Spain's allies, while in the east the main Ottoman fleet took the Venetian island of Cyprus. These events were terrifying enough for the Pope, Venice and Spain to form an alliance, the 'Holy League', committed to organize the recovery of Cyprus. In 1571, although the last Christian stronghold on the island fell, the fleet of the League sought out its adversary and, at Lepanto, destroyed a considerable number of Turkish galleys. Such success led naturally to an expansion of Spain's commitment in the Mediterranean in the following year. This was crucial for the Netherlands, because it meant that less money was available for the duke of Alva when in April and May 1572 large areas of the Low Countries rebelled against his repressive policies.

The new revolt in the Netherlands was more serious than the outbreak of 1566-8 since the rebels quickly secured a strong provincial base (Holland and Zealand) while Alva's counter-measures were hampered by the heavy expenditure already undertaken in the Mediterranean. Time was particularly important because the longer the rebels were seen to survive, the more likely it became that they would receive aid from a foreign power hostile to Spain. The checking of the Spanish counter-attack before the walls of Haarlem in the winter of 1572-3 strengthened the rebels' diplomatic status as well as prolonging the cost of reconquest. Meanwhile in Constantinople the French ambassador laboured tirelessly to secure a truce between Venice and the Sultan. This was achieved and made public in February 1573: Spain was left to shoulder the entire burden of defending the west Mediterranean. It was remarkable that 1573, a year which started so badly for Spain, should have seen her score two notable successes: the eventual capture of Haarlem in July and Tunis in October.

But neither success won the war. Enormous sums were spent in 1574 to prepare for the inevitable Turkish expedition to avenge the capture of Tunis; while in the north Count Louis of Nassau's formidable invasion, although unsuccessful, led the Spaniards to spend heavily on counter-measures. And in the end most of this expenditure was fruitless: the Turks recaptured Tunis, and although Count Louis was defeated and killed at Mookerheide, the Spanish troops mutinied for their pay, abandoning most of their hard-won posts in Holland. The struggle in both theatres became an impossibly costly stalemate.

The five long years of war on two fronts between 1572 and 1576 were a financial nightmare for Spain. Philip II spent during these years roughly double his revenues (see Table 1) and the budgetary imbalance of the early 1570s resulted from Philip II's inability to disengage from either of his major wars. He knew that Spain was capable of victory in the Low Countries or in the Mediterranean in isolation, but could not succeed in both at once; yet he could not bring himself voluntarily to concede defeat. He had first to be brought to his knees by the financial consequences of maintaining an expenditure far in excess of the available resources.

There were many besides Philip II who realized that as long as Spain was fighting on two fronts she could not win on either. The French ambassador at Constantinople spoke on this theme for some time at an audience with the Sultan's advisers in May 1574:

I put to them the success of the affairs of the prince of Orange in the Low Countries, adding that it resulted only from the favour, men and money which the king [of France] had hitherto provided secretly . . . [and] that the Sultan should also start to contribute . . . And that for the benefit and advantage which it brought them, the king [of France] had agreed that he would continue to pay the said Prince one hundred thousand crowns each month, as

31

he has already done for eighteen months, provided the said Sultan would pay as much himself, *seeing that the matter affected him more than any other . . .*[27]

This demand for direct Turkish assistance to Orange's war-chest met with a cold response, but the daring idea was not entirely forgotten. Later in 1574 the Sultan did send two special agents armed with missives for the Moriscos of Granada and for the 'Lutherans' (*sc.* non-Catholics in a general sense) of 'Filandara' (*sc.* Flanders, the Netherlands), urging them to co-operate with each other to engineer the ruin of Philip II, and promising substantial aid from Constantinople and Algiers in this grand design. As it happened, this did not prove necessary. The strain of war on two fronts brought Spain down without any further co-ordination of the enemy forces.[28]

Table 1: The Budget of the Castilian Treasury, 1574

REVENUE	EXPENDITURE		DEFICIT
	Debt charges:	2,730,943	
	Defence and administration:	2,000,000	
	Netherlands:	3,688,085	
	Mediterranean:	2,052,634	
Total: 5,978,535		**10,471,662**	**4,493,127**

Sources: The figures of revenue, defence and debt-interest are based on the very detailed 'Relation' of the Spanish Treasury in 1574: IVdeDJ 24/16. The figures are in ducats of 375 *maravedis*. The figure in the 'Netherlands' column, in *escudos* of about 380 *maravedis*, comes from AGS CMC 2a/55, the Account of Paymaster Lixalde for 1567-77. The figure in the 'Mediterranean' column comes from AGS CMC 2a/814, the Account of Paymaster Juan Morales de Torre, for 1572-6. See also p. 210, n. 44 below.

The widening gap between revenue and expenditure from 1572 to 1575 was filled by government deficit borrowing on a wild scale. Merchant-bankers were induced by ever-greater interest rates to lend money to finance the penurious king's imperial designs, but by the summer of 1575 the bankers came to realize the scale of Philip II's deficit, and they began to fear that the government had no money to repay their loans. Accordingly they refused to lend at all. The crown was placed in the position of owing vast sums in old debts due for repayment – 36 million ducats: the equivalent of six or seven years' revenue – while unable to raise new loans to cover the cost of reimbursement. On 1 September 1575 Philip II, after almost two years of careful meditation and planning, broke out of this unfortunate situation by repudiating all his debts and reclaiming all the revenues alienated to repay his creditors. This solution may have been right for Spain, but it was disastrous for the wars in the Netherlands and in the Mediterranean. The king regained control of his revenues, but he simultaneously deprived himself of the machinery of credit and exchange by which alone revenues could be anticipated and the proceeds transferred from Spain to the armies fighting abroad. As the Governor-General in the Netherlands morosely observed: 'Even if the king found himself with ten millions in gold and wanted to send them all here, he has no way of doing so with this Bankruptcy . . . because if the money were sent by sea in specie it would be lost, and it is impossible to send it by letters of exchange as hitherto because there is no merchant there [in Spain] who can issue them nor anyone who can accept and pay them.'[29] The towns of Holland and Zealand had only to continue their dogged resistance until the financial shortage in the Spanish Netherlands, caused by the Bankruptcy, brought about the collapse of Spain's unpaid army in a wave of mutinies and desertion. By November 1576 the army which numbered 60,000 men on paper had sunk in fact to a mere 8000.[30] Spain admitted defeat and conceded all the rebels' demands in February 1577 (the Perpetual Edict). Victory may, according to the ancient Dutch proverb, have 'come from Alkmaar' – but it also came from Constantinople!

The collapse of Spanish financial power in 1575 had its effect on Philip II's Mediterranean policy too. Early in 1577 he sought an informal assurance that the Ottoman fleet would not operate in the west that year. To his immense relief the Sultan agreed. In 1578 the arrangement was consolidated into a formal 'suspension of arms' for one year, and this was in fact prolonged for over a decade. The final act in liquidating the tragic consequences of 1572-5 also occurred in 1577: after patient negotiations the king patched up an agreement with the bankers on whom he had defaulted at the Bankruptcy.

Spain was now free to set her house in order. Instead, however, in September 1577 the king decided to repudiate the Perpetual Edict and resume war in the Low Countries. Men and money were switched from the Mediterranean to the Netherlands in 1577 and 1578. It looked like a carbon-copy of the policies of 1566-7, but without any risk of distraction in the Mediterranean. The 'Reconquest' began.

All this was changed dramatically by the death of the childless king of Portugal, Dom Sebastian, in August 1578. Philip II was the ultimate heir to the Portuguese throne. This pushed the Netherlands into a subordinate position again on Spain's list of priorities. Although the war there went on, the Spanish veterans were withdrawn and sent straight to Portugal in 1580, while from 1579 until 1582 money only reached the skeleton army in the Netherlands in small quantities and after long delays. The position improved somewhat after 1582, when Portugal was finally annexed. The provisions were not great – under 4 million florins a year – but at least they were paid punctually. The total sum was specified in advance and it was despatched regularly in three equal instalments between 1582 and 1587. It was therefore possible, even though the money was not really enough, to plan operations rationally and conduct campaigns more efficiently. Yet despite the magnificent achievement of the Spanish army in the Low Countries in the 1580s, recapturing the southern provinces, the campaigns received nothing like the financial support accorded to the duke of Alva and Don Luis de Requesens (see Table 2). If the prince of Parma could reconquer half the Netherlands with two-thirds the resources placed at the disposal of his predecessors, it is interesting to speculate what he might have done with an equal sum. Above all, Parma might have been able to move more rapidly.

Spain, her Enemies and the Revolt

Table 2: Money Received from Spain by the Military Treasury of the Spanish Netherlands, 1572-85

1572-1577	22·24 million florins
1580-1585	14·95 million florins

Source: G. Parker, *The Army of Flanders and the Spanish Road* (Cambridge, 1972), p. 293.

As it was, the methodical lumberings of the Spanish army in its advance gave enough time for even Elizabeth of England to make up her mind that the 'rebels' of the Low Countries deserved her help. After endless negotiations, official English aid arrived in autumn 1585.

Philip II, unlike modern Dutch historians, rated the contribution of English men and money to Holland's resistance very highly. He and his field commanders were perplexed and annoyed to find that the States-General made virtually no move in the direction of compromise after the fall of Antwerp in August 1585. This was particularly surprising in view of the manifest treachery of political and military leaders fighting for the States between 1578 and 1585: a large number of Walloon nobles had succumbed to Spanish bribes; many garrison commanders had been persuaded to betray their posts; in 1585 itself the interprovincial jealousies of Holland, Zealand and Brabant had sabotaged the States' plan to relieve Antwerp until after the town surrendered. But after 1585, though there was no lack of discord among the States, there was no wavering in their determination to continue the war. Spain could only conclude that the English were to blame for the obduracy of the 'rebels'.[31] Philip knew that Elizabeth had bound herself by the Treaty of Nonsuch in August 1585 to maintain 6350 foot and 1000 horse in Holland, and to pay one-quarter of the total cost of the war against Spain.[32] This was a sharp break with the past. Several foreign powers had sent underhand assistance to the Dutch since 1572, but it had always been discreet. It was still possible, until 1585, to regard this struggle in the Netherlands as a purely domestic issue. The Treaty of Nonsuch changed everything. It was a formal

35

alliance between a foreign power and Philip II's rebels: it could not be overlooked; it had to be faced; it had to be stopped.

Philip II was perfectly prepared to mobilize all the money he could find against England. It was estimated that the 'Invincible Armada', planned in 1586, damaged by Drake in 1587 and destroyed in 1588, cost some 10 million ducats (30 million florins). Yet this was small beer compared to the cost to Spain of her intervention in the French wars of religion after 1589. The murder of Henry III in that year left a disputed succession: the obvious claimant, Henry of Navarre, was unacceptable to the Catholic party and also to Spain. Because he was a Protestant and because he was openly allied to the Dutch, Philip II decided to lend his weight to the cause of the French Catholics against Henry IV. The majority of his aid was sent through the Spanish army in the Netherlands.

Table 3: Money Received from Spain by the Military Treasury of the Spanish Netherlands, 1580-99

1580-5	14·9 million florins received (The Reconquest)
1585-90	44·7 million florins received (The Armada)
1590-5	37·8 million florins received (French aid)
1595-9	52·9 million florins received (*ibid.*)

Source: G. Parker, *The Army of Flanders and the Spanish Road* (Cambridge, 1972), p. 293.

The bulk of this enormous expenditure in the 1590s was channelled into France. For example, almost 4 million florins were received by the Military Treasury between August 1590 and May 1591; of this, three million were spent on the war with France, leaving less than one million for the defence of the Netherlands.[33] The perpetuation of this pattern of spending throughout the 1590s explains the failure of Spain, despite the massive overall outlay, to maintain her new conquests in the north in the teeth of Maurice of Nassau's resourceful and sustained offensive, underpinned by the bonanza in Holland's overseas trade and the considerable subsidies sent to the States by England and France.[34]

Spain's treatment of the Netherlands problem after 1598 at first differed little from the pattern established under Philip II. The surprising recovery of Spanish fortunes in the war between 1604 and 1607, with the capture of Ostend and the victorious campaigns of Spinola in Frisia, is largely explained by the peace Spain was able to conclude first with France (Vervins 1598) and then with England (London 1604). Philip III sent reasonably large provisions to the army in the Netherlands, and these were deployed solely against the Dutch. The Republic, frightened by its isolation and by Spinola's victories, concluded a truce with Spain in April 1607 which was eventually prolonged until 1621.

When hostilities were reopened in April 1621 the situation of 1604-7 was exactly repeated. France was torn by a recrudescence of her religious wars, while James I of England fervently hoped to marry his son and heir to a Spanish princess. Spain was thus able to devote all her energies to the war against the Dutch. Unlike Philip II in 1582-6, Philip IV sent all the money that he could find to the Netherlands. Under Spinola, the Spanish army scored some notable successes, culminating in the capture of Breda, the seat of the House of Orange, in 1625. At the same time, Spain waged a successful campaign of economic warfare against the Dutch, closing all Iberian ports to Dutch shipping, destroying Dutch herring fleets and harassing Dutch merchantmen. Between 1621 and 1627, the prosperity of the Republic's trade was seriously reduced. But before Spain's advantage could be exploited, her attention and her resources were diverted to another part of Europe.

The duke of Mantua died on 26 December 1627. His closest relative was the French duke of Nevers, but despite his clear claim Spain and the duke of Savoy demanded a slice of the Mantuan cake before they would recognize Nevers. They persuaded the Emperor, suzerain of Mantua, to withhold investiture and meanwhile their troops marched into the vacant duchy. By October 1628 only the fortress of Casale held out for Nevers. The king of France was deeply sympathetic to the cause of the Duke, but the war against the Huguenots was more important. Although only La Rochelle defied him, Louis XIII could not help Nevers until it fell. On 29 October 1628, just as victory in Lombardy seemed to be within Spain's grasp, La Rochelle surrendered. At once the French army left its encampments before the city and marched for the Alps. In March 1629, Louis XIII and a large army crossed into Piedmont to fight for Nevers. Spain resisted. The struggle escalated. Spain even procured an army from the Emperor to fight in Lombardy against France, but to no avail. In June 1631 Spain agreed to evacuate Mantua and recognize Nevers as the new Duke.[35]

The Mantuan succession crisis was as important for the independence of the Dutch Republic after the loss of Breda in 1625 as the Treaty of Nonsuch had been after the loss of Antwerp forty years before. Both developments were crucial for the Netherlands because they provoked Spain to abandon her 'Reconquest' in favour of another objective, considered to be more important. Until the Peace of Cherasco was signed in 1631, the provisions sent by Spain to the Netherlands were much reduced, as Table 4 shows, enabling the Dutch army to recapture Groenlo in 1627, the Indies Treasure Fleet in 1628, 's Hertogenbosch and Wesel in 1629 and the sugar-producing province of Pernambuco in Brazil in 1630. There was nothing Spain could do to recover these losses.

Table 4: Money Received from Spain by the Military Treasury of the Spanish Netherlands, 1621-35

1621-5	39·05 million florins received
1626-30	29·12 million florins received
1631-5	39·77 million florins received

Sources: Figures for 1621-32 and 1634-5 from G. Parker, *The Army of Flanders and the Spanish Road,1567-1659* (Cambridge, 1972), pp. 294-5; for 1633-4 from H. Pohl, 'Zur Bedeutung Antwerpens als Kreditplatz im beginnenden 17. Jahrhundert', in *Die Stadt in der europäischen Geschichte. Festschrift Edith Ennen* (Bonn, 1972), pp. 667-86.

Despite the recovery in the level of Spanish support for the Army of Flanders after 1631, it took some time before there were results to show. On the contrary, in 1632 the Dutch army captured the Maas strongholds of Venlo, Maastricht and Rheinberg, while in Germany the Swedish army inflicted one defeat after another on the Habsburg forces opposing them. In this situation, the ministers of Philip IV decided on a major offensive against the Dutch Republic in order to restore Spanish prestige in Europe and, hopefully, to encourage their enemies to make peace on terms favourable to Spain. In 1634 the king's brother, the Cardinal-Infante Don Fernando, was sent to the Low Countries with a large army. He marched through Germany, where he inflicted a major defeat on the Swedish-Protestant army at Nördlingen; and in 1635 he invaded Dutch occupied territory with 26,000 men and captured several strong-points on the Rhine and Maas. But these successes were largely cancelled out by the French declaration of war on Spain on 19 May 1635: thenceforward there was a split in Madrid between those ministers who favoured a defensive war against the Dutch and an offensive against France (which was attempted in 1636) and those who favoured the reverse (which was attempted in 1637 and 1638).[36] In 1639 Spain tried an entirely new strategy: victory at sea. One powerful fleet was despatched to Brazil with orders to reconquer Pernambuco from the Dutch, and a second was sent to the Channel with orders to destroy the Dutch navy in a great battle. Alas, in the event, the first was destroyed by bad weather and enemy action while the second was annihilated at the battle of the Downs by the Dutch under admiral Tromp. Once again, as in the 1590s, fighting on two fronts meant failure on two fronts.

More important than the failure of the Spanish forces to make headway in the north was the effect of the new war with France upon Spain. War imposed an impossible financial burden upon the empire, and at last the patience of Castile's partners gave way. Catalonia rebelled in May 1640 and was soon in receipt of substantial material aid from the French. Portugal followed with a rebellion in December 1640, supported again by the French and later by the English. As in 1572, the unforeseen revolt of a province of the empire found the central government unable to concentrate adequate resources until it was too late: by the time the crown had fully mobilized, the rebels were in receipt of foreign aid.

Table 5: Money Received from Spain by the Military Treasury of the Spanish Netherlands, 1636-50

1636-8	30·30 million florins received
1639-41	28·00 million florins received
1642-4	15·57 million florins received
1645-7	16·05 million florins received
1648-50	9·02 million florins received

Source: G. Parker, *The Army of Flanders*, p. 295.

For the Spanish Netherlands, the protracted resistance of Catalonia and Portugal heralded the *débâcle*. From a peak in 1637, the remittances despatched to the Military Treasury fell steadily as Philip IV concentrated an increasing proportion of his resources within the peninsula. This drastic and sustained reduction in the army's budget, the consequence of Castile's failure to end swiftly the Catalan and Portuguese revolts, explains the Spanish defeats at Rocroi and Lens (1643 and 1648) and finally the anxiety for peace in 1647-8 (see also pp. 56-63 below).

The figures for Spanish expenditure in the Low Countries between 1567 and 1650, printed above, form part of an almost complete series.[37] It is therefore possible to calculate with some precision the fluctuating level of Spanish expenditure in the Netherlands. But, interesting as that may be, figures alone can never tell the whole story. They do not relate what influences caused the variations nor on what principles the money sent was disbursed. Mere numbers do not tell us why money was pumped into the Spanish Netherlands in the 1590s and again in the 1630s – both decades of plague, famine and misery for Spain – yet not at other more prosperous times. We can grasp that the war of Mantua was partly responsible for the inaction of the Spanish army in the Low Countries between 1628 and 1631, but this does not explain why Spain considered it more important to go to war over Mantua than to continue unwaveringly with the struggle against the Dutch.

It would not seem that the level of expenditure was in any way determined, as M. Chaunu suggested, by the available revenues or the state of the economy. The scale of deficit finance revealed in Table 1 for 1574 was perhaps extreme, but there can have been very few years after 1540 when the government of Habsburg Spain managed to balance its budget. Instead, a mounting burden of consolidated debt was laid upon the Castilian revenues, absorbing an ever-larger slice of the tax-yield.[38] One should not be too surprised at this. Despite the seductive logic of M. Chaunu, it must be recognized that the sixteenth century saw far less in statistics, trends and cycles than historians of today, educated to recognize the importance of economic factors in history. Government policy in early modern Europe was seldom determined by economic desiderata.

This is not to say, however, that governments spent their money without *any* preconceived plan. What is interesting is not so much that they were prepared to incur enormous debts by going to war, but that wanton over-expenditure was considered justified in certain areas but not in others. It has been argued above that the very considerable variations in Spanish spending in the Low Countries were the result of the assessment made in Spanish court circles of the intrinsic importance of the Netherlands to Spain when measured against the importance of the other problems facing the empire. It emerges, moreover, that the priorities which affected the Netherlands were fairly simple, and changed little in the course of the Eighty Years' War.

It is clear that at the top of Spain's priorities came her fear of France.[39] Any war which involved France, even covertly, became of paramount importance. The war of Mantua and the revolts of 1640 became crucial to Spain largely by virtue of French involvement. The French succession struggle after 1589 and the open war from 1635 to 1659 were obviously problems which it was essential for Spain to solve in a manner favourable to her own interests. It was therefore inevitable that the Netherlands would suffer if Spain became involved in any war which also concerned France.

The other major question of imperial policy which clearly involved the Netherlands was the defence of Italy. There were always some councillors at the court of Spain who believed that the security of Italy and the war against the Turks at sea should be subordinated to the defence of the Netherlands and the war against the heretics; there were always councillors of the opposite persuasion. The problem of 'Lombardy or the Low Countries' divided the Spanish government as early as 1544. As we have seen, until the truce with the Sultan in 1578, the Mediterranean tended to receive pride of place, although there were many who protested – like the duke of Alva – that the Turks were far enough away to leave Spain alone while she dealt with the closer menace of the heretics.[40]

The temporary withdrawal of both Spain and the Sultan from the Mediterranean after 1578 did not decide the issue in favour of the Netherlands. In 1618-19 there was a major dispute in the court between those who placed intervention in the Emperor Ferdinand's struggle in Bohemia above all other considerations and those who felt that a renewal of war against the Turks in the Mediterranean was a more immediate problem. It was only after bitter debates that the entry of Spanish troops into Bohemia and the Palatinate was approved.[41] Later still, in 1632, after the war of Mantua and the withdrawal of the French, the government in Madrid kept in mind the relative importance of Lombardy and the Low Countries to Spain in case there should be another emergency. Official policy was clearly stated by an experienced member of the Council of State, the Marquis of Los Gelves: 'Putting into the balance the need to defend and maintain the provinces of Flanders or Lombardy, he held Lombardy to be more important.' This choice was based on sound strategic considerations: Lombardy, at the heart of the deepening European conflagration, was the nerve-centre of the Spanish Monarchy. 'Flanders' was simply an outlying province.[42]

It was simple political choices such as these which, more than anything else, determined the course of the war in the Netherlands because, far more than tax-yields, they governed the immediate level of Spanish expenditure there and elsewhere. Quantitative history or (as American historians have it) 'Cliometry' is invaluable in quantifying previously discerned trends and problems. However it is a highly dangerous

42

tool when used, as by M. Chaunu, to dig up fields which have not first been properly surveyed – such as the relations between Spain and the Netherlands, or the processes by which the Spanish government reached its decisions. Quantitative records can add precision and depth to qualitative material; they can never supplant it.

'Serial history', is, certainly, as M. Chaunu once wrote 'revolutionary . . . innovating and fertile',[43] but it does not dispense the historian from taking into account the principles of statecraft which guided the kings and ministers of Habsburg Spain in governing their great empire. We are driven back to the vintage advice of Ernest Gossart. We should try to see the Revolt of the Netherlands – at least sometimes – as Spain herself did: in the context of her overall imperial position.[44]

2

This paper was composed in the spring of 1972 for the seminar in Spanish studies run by the late Professor Edward M. Wilson at Cambridge. He wanted something of general interest to Hispanists who were studying the literature of the Golden Age (a subject on which he himself was so formidably learned) because of the large number of plays, poems and prose works which refer to the exploits of the Spaniards in the Low Countries. The structure of my argument, although the paper was subsequently delivered to about twenty different university audiences before I read it to the Royal Historical Society in June 1975, still bears the stamp of Edward Wilson's interest and encouragement.

The article examines three related problems concerning the Dutch Revolt: why Spain did not succeed in suppressing the revolt at the outset; why she nevertheless kept on trying for so many decades; and why a settlement was reached in 1648 rather than before or afterwards. These issues have been largely ignored by other historians, although to contemporaries they were matters of constant concern. The failure of Philip II, whose empire was global in scale, to crush the Dutch Revolt at once was the first sign to the world that Spain's status as a great power rested more on illusion than on reality; the second sign was Philip's failure to follow up Parma's reconquest of the South Netherlands in the 1580s with an attack on Holland and Zealand. After 1600, Spain's enemies joined the fray in the hope of securing a segment of the Habsburgs' far-flung dominions and, in the end, France gained parts of the South Netherlands and Catalonia; England conquered Jamaica and Dunkirk; and the Dutch secured an empire of their own in Asia, America and Africa. In Europe they also gained their independence, but only after a struggle which lasted over eighty years.

Why Did the Dutch Revolt Last So Long?

The Dutch Revolt lasted longer than any other uprising in modern European history – from the Iconoclastic Fury in August 1566 to the Peace of Münster in January 1648; and it involved more continuous fighting than any other war of modern times – from April 1572 to April 1607 (with only six months' cease-fire in 1577) and from April 1621 to June 1647. Its economic, social, and political costs were enormous.[1] The longevity of the revolt becomes even more remarkable when one remembers that the two combatants were far from equal. The areas in revolt against Spain were small in size, in natural resources, and in population – especially in the first few years. In 1574 only about twenty towns, with a combined population of 75,000, remained faithful to William of Orange; Amsterdam, the largest town in Holland, stayed loyal to the king until 1578.[2] Against the 'rebels' Philip II could draw on the resources of Spain, Spanish America, Spanish Italy and, of course, the Spanish Netherlands. Although by the seventeenth century the odds had narrowed somewhat – by then there were seven 'rebel' provinces with a combined population of over one million – Spain could still call on vastly superior resources of men and money. There were a number of occasions in the course of the war when Spain seemed to stand on the threshold of success. In 1575, for example, the conquest of the islands of Duiveland and Schouwen in South Holland divided the rebel heartland in two and appeared to presage the collapse of the revolt. A decade later, in 1585, Antwerp was recaptured against all predictions, leaving Holland and Zealand dispirited and prepared to discuss surrender. As late as 1625, with the reconquest of Breda in Brabant and Bahía in Brazil, Spain's final victory seemed near. But total success never came. Spain never regained the seven northern provinces of the Netherlands and by 1648 Philip IV counted himself lucky to have retained the ten southern ones.

It is not difficult to explain Spain's initial failure to suppress the Dutch Revolt. Rapid victory was ruled out, in effect, by a combination of logistical factors. In the first place the Dutch population may have been small, but it included some who were determined to resist the Spaniards by all means and at all costs. For the Sea Beggars, the Calvinists and the other exiles who returned to Holland and Zealand in 1572 there could be no surrender: they, like the Prince of Orange, had decided to make Holland and Zealand their tomb, either in victory or defeat.[3] The Anabaptists too, who had a powerful following in most of the northern provinces, had everything to gain by renouncing their obedience to Philip II: they had been the victims of ruthless persecution in the Habsburg Netherlands.[4] More surprisingly, perhaps, and more important, Orange had the support of the Catholic majority of Holland and Zealand. Although their first reaction was, understandably, to avoid a commitment to either side for as long as possible, the Catholics were soon forced into Orange's camp by the brutal behaviour of the government forces. In a conscious attempt to expedite the end of the Revolt, the duke of Alva pursued a policy of 'beastliness' towards certain rebellious towns. In October 1572 he allowed his troops to sack the city of Mechelen, which surrendered unconditionally, in the expectation that such an example would encourage the other Orangist towns in the south to make their peace with him. It did. In November the duke inflicted the same fate on Zutphen, which brought about the capitulation of all strongholds in the north-east. In December, the Spanish army proceeded to massacre the entire population of Naarden, a small Orangist town in Holland: 'Not a mother's son escaped' Alva reported smugly to the king, and he passed on to Amsterdam to await the surrender of the rest of the province.[5] But the massacre of Naarden did not have the desired effect. Catholics and Calvinists alike became terrified of admitting the brutal Spanish troops, and their fear was reinforced in July 1573 when the citizens of Haarlem surrendered on condition their lives would be spared. Alva nevertheless ordered the execution of a score or so of them, together with most of the garrison. Haarlem was the last town in Holland to negotiate a settlement. Leiden in 1574 preferred starvation to surrender; the burghers of Oudewater in 1575 set their town on fire rather than see it fall intact to the Spaniards.

There was, of course, more to the resistance of Holland and Zealand than desperate courage. The physical and military geography of the north-west Netherlands was also of crucial importance. The area was, in the words of an English traveller writing in 1652, 'The great Bog of *Europe*. There is not such another Marsh in the World, that's flat. They are an universall Quag-mire . . . Indeed, it is the buttock of the World, full of veines and bloud, but no bones in't'.[6]

It was certainly hard for the Spaniards to regain Zealand and South Holland, since the islands captured by the Sea Beggars in 1572 were separated from the mainland by deep channels (although with courage and resolution all things were possible, as the relief of Ter Goes in 1572 and the invasion of Schouwen in 1575-6 demonstrated). It was almost as hard for the Spanish army to operate in North Holland because of the great lakes, rivers and dikes which covered the country, much of which was below sea-level. In 1573 at the siege of Alkmaar and in 1574 at the siege of Leiden, dikes were broken in order to flood the fields around the town and thus prevent the formidable Spanish infantry from launching an attack on the walls. But Holland was not only a 'great Bog'; it was also almost an island and the Dutch took care never to lose control of the sea which surrounded them. Between 1572 and 1574, the war fleet of the Brussels government was destroyed in a series of violent engagements. Some of the actions were Spanish successes (like the battles on the Haarlemmermeer during the siege of the city); others were Spanish defeats (like the battle off Enkhuizen in October 1573 and the battle off Bergen-op-Zoom in February 1574). But whatever the result, the Spaniards lost ships which they were incapable of replacing since the principal shipyards (and the naval arsenal at Veere) were in rebel hands and it proved impossible to send new ships from Spain. The Dutch were thus able to keep their own ports open to receive reinforcements and supplies from

47

abroad (especially from the exiled Netherlandish communities in England),[7] and to continue their vital trade with the Baltic (in 1574, almost 1000 Dutch ships passed through the Danish Sound).[8] Surely, the royalist Owen Feltham speculated in 1652, the Dutch Revolt had succeeded because of:

> their strength in shipping, the open Sea, their many fortified Towns, and the Country by reason of its lowness and plentifull Irrigation becoming unpassable for an army when the winter but approaches. Otherwise it is hardly possible that so small a parcell of Mankind, should brave the most potent Monarch of Christendome who . . . hath now got a command so wide, that out of his Dominions the *Sunne* can neither rise nor set.[9]

Philip II's empire was indeed one on which the sun never set, and to most contemporaries the advantage in the Low Countries Wars, at least during the reign of the Prudent King, seemed to lie with Spain. After all, only a few Dutch towns, such as Alkmaar or Rammekens, were entirely protected by an effective system of defence, with bastions, in the 1570s, and even they might have been starved out in time.[10] Antwerp, Ghent and Brussels, three of the best-fortified towns in Europe, capitulated after a year's siege in 1584-5 and Antwerp (at least) possessed all the natural advantages of the Holland towns. It was near the sea, it was surrounded by low-lying land which could be (and was) flooded, and its population was predominantly Protestant.[11] Yet in spite of stout hearts, naval superiority and superb defences, Antwerp fell; and there is every reason to suppose that, given time, the towns of Holland and Zealand would have succumbed too. Time, however, was what the Spanish government lacked; time and money. The total cost of the Spanish army in the Netherlands between 1572 and 1576, a force of over 80,000 men at times (at least on paper), was estimated at 1.2 million florins every month. Spain simply could not provide such a sum. 'There would not be time or money enough in the world to reduce by force the twenty-four towns which have rebelled in Holland, if we are to spend as long in reducing each one of them as we have taken over similar ones so far,' wrote the Spanish commander-in-chief, Don Luis de Requesens, in October 1574. 'No treasury in the world would be equal to the cost of this war,' he repeated in November.[12] The siege of Mons in 1572 took six months; the siege of Haarlem in 1572-3 took eight months; the siege of Zierikzee in 1575-6 took nine months. Admittedly all three blockades were eventually successful, but while the Spanish field army was occupied in the sieges, the 'rebels' were free to attack and capture other strongholds in other areas. Moreover this siege warfare, with the winter months spent in frozen trenches three years running, was unpleasant for the troops; and the unpleasantness was exacerbated by the inability of the government to pay its soldiers for their heroic service. Inevitably it produced discontent in the Spanish army and both desertion and disobedience grew to alarming proportions. Whole companies broke away from the army and fled to France; whole regiments defied their officers and mutinied, and it might take weeks, even months, and millions of florins, before they could be brought back into service. The deliverance of Alkmaar (1573), Leiden (1574) and Zierikzee (1576) from the grip of the king's forces can be confidently ascribed to the Spanish mutinies.[13]

To some extent, however, the Spanish troops in the Low Countries were actors on a wider stage. The punctual payment of their wages lay at the mercy of political decisions taken elsewhere. Philip II had other problems to resolve besides the Netherlands. He had to maintain Spanish influence in the Caribbean in the face of English and French competition: the French Huguenots attempted to plant colonies in Florida in 1563, 1564-5, 1568 and 1577-80; the English tried their hands at colonization too after 1560, but then found piracy at Spain's expense more rewarding.[14] Within Europe Philip II was concerned to keep both France and England as weak as possible, sending military aid to the French Catholics in 1563, 1567 and 1569, promising military aid to the English Catholics in 1570-1. It all cost money. Above all, the King of Spain had to defend the western

Mediterranean against the Ottoman Sultan and for most of the 1570s this was a major concern which tied down men, money and material resources in large quantities. In order to defeat the Turkish fleet at Lepanto in 1571 and capture Tunis in 1573, and even more in order to defend Spain and Italy against the Sultan's counter-attacks, Philip II had to maintain and man a permanent fleet of 150 galleys in the Mediterranean. Several times between 1572 and 1576 the king's advisers had to decide whether to allocate resources to the Mediterranean or to the Netherlands; almost always they decided in favour of the former.[15] Although it is possible that Philip II's revenues in the 1570s were not equal to the cost of the Army of Flanders in any case, Spain's commitment to the defence of the Mediterranean certainly accelerated the State Bankruptcy of 1575 and the military collapse in the Netherlands which followed in 1576.

Taken together, these logistical factors – the determination of the defenders and their strength by sea; the defensibility of the north-western provinces; and the diversion of Spanish resources to other theatres – explain Spain's failure to win an early victory over the Dutch Revolt. The collapse of Spanish power in the autumn of 1576 permitted the rebellion to spread to most of the other provinces of the Netherlands. In the south and east strong Calvinist cells were established and new fortifications were built, complicating Spain's subsequent attempts to regain the areas in revolt. Virtually no progress was made by force of arms between 1577 and 1582, while Philip II disengaged his forces from the Mediterranean and absorbed the Portuguese empire; but from 1583 until 1587 Spain's entire energies were channelled into the Netherlands offensive, and superior resources soon began to tell. One town after another fell into Spanish hands; all the south and east was recaptured, leaving only Holland, Zealand and parts of Friesland, Utrecht and Gelderland to continue the struggle. Even William of Orange, a crucial figure in the Republic, was assassinated in 1584. The outlook for the 'rebels' seemed bleak indeed.

Orange, however, had always known that the Dutch alone could not hope to withstand the might of Spain for long.

Ever since 1566 he had endeavoured to involve foreign powers in the struggle, either as mediators to deflect the wrath of Philip II, or as allies to divert his resources. In 1566-8 Orange and his associates had pinned their hopes on the Emperor and the German princes.[16] In 1572, 'all our hopes lay with France' – only to be shattered by the Massacre of St Bartholomew.[17] Thereafter England, France, the German princes and any other power not allied with Spain was importuned: in 1574 Orange even exchanged envoys with the Ottoman Sultan in order to co-ordinate his attacks on Spain.[18] However, none of these overtures succeeded in creating an alliance which would permanently divert Spain's attentions from the Netherlands.

Only in 1585 did a sovereign prince enter into formal alliance with the Dutch and offer permanent and substantial military aid. The Treaty of Nonsuch, signed by Queen Elizabeth of England in August 1585, may not have prevented the Spanish army from recapturing Grave in 1586 and Sluis in 1587, but it did provoke Philip II to transfer his resources from the reconquest of the Netherlands to the invasion of England. The decision to send the 'Invincible Armada' against England in 1588, followed by the resolution to intervene on the Catholic side in the French religious wars after 1589, proved a godsend to the Dutch. The two unsuccessful enterprises siphoned off most of Philip II's resources, causing new mutinies and defeats for the 'Army of Flanders' and enabling the Dutch to regain the north-east provinces and establish their frontier along the Maas and Rhine in the 1590s. The principal towns were now fortified according to the latest designs with bastions, ramparts and ravelins, and a sort of 'Hadrian's Wall' of connected forts and blockhouses was built in 1605-6 along the River Ijssel from the Zuider Zee to Nijmegen and from there westwards along the Maas to Tiel. These 'limes' of the Dutch Republic, although for the sake of economy built of earth and wood rather than of stone, effectively held back the powerful Spanish offensives of 1605 and 1606.[19]

It had clearly become impossible for Spain to achieve the sort of victory in the Netherlands that would force the Dutch

51

to submit, and many members of the Spanish government came to the conclusion that failure was more or less a foregone conclusion. The pessimism of Don Luis de Requesens, Philip II's commander-in-chief in 1574, has already been noted. It was entirely shared by the king himself and by his principal advisers. On 31 May 1574 (after only two years of war) Philip II wrote to his secretary that he believed 'the loss of the Netherlands and the rest [of his Monarchy], to be as certain as, in this situation, anything can be . . . It is a terrible situation and it is getting worse every day.'[20] The same refrain was heard again several times in the course of that year and in the years to come. In 1589 the Council of State warned that to speak of 'conquering [the rebellious provinces] by force is to speak of a war without end', and in 1591 Philip's faithful secretary Mateo Vázquez pointed out that the king's expensive policies in France, the Netherlands and the Mediterranean had depopulated Castile so that 'We may fear that everything here will collapse at a stroke'. 'If God wished Your Majesty to attend to the remedy of all the troubles of the World,' he added, 'He would have given Your Majesty the money and the strength to do it.'[21] Yet despite the widely held and persistent belief at the Spanish court that the war could not be won, Spain kept on fighting continuously from 1577 to 1607 and from 1621 to 1647.

There were several reasons for this curious reluctance to accept failure. Most important was an unwillingness to accept the conditions put forward by the Dutch for ending their rebellion. As early as February 1573 William of Orange enunciated two demands which he regarded as the indispensable preconditions to peace: 'I see nothing else to propose,' he informed his brothers, who were trying to negotiate a settlement, 'but that the practice of the reformed religion according to the Word of God be permitted, and that this whole country and state return to its ancient privileges and liberty.' These twin demands for religious toleration and 'constitutional guarantees' were fundamental to the Dutch cause and they were repeated at every round of negotiations between Spain and the Dutch.[22] And every time they were rejected: these were precisely the points on which

Philip II would admit of no compromise. In 1574 an English agent in the Netherlands observed that: 'The pride of the Spanish government and the cause of religion' constituted 'the chief hindrance to a good accord'. It was perfectly true. In August 1574 Philip II gave his lieutenant in the Netherlands permission to open talks with the Dutch, but forbade him to make any concession which would affect the exclusive position of the Roman Catholic Church or prejudice his sovereign power: 'On these two points,' he ordered, 'on no account are you to give in or shift an inch.'[23] The same reluctance to concede toleration and constitutional guarantees sabotaged the peace arranged in 1577 (the Perpetual Edict) and prevented the conclusion of a settlement in 1594.[24] As late as 1628, the count-duke of Olivares was able to summarize Spain's reasons for fighting the Dutch in much the same way as Philip II: 'The matter may be reduced to two points,' Olivares informed the king: 'religion and reputation'.[25] This remarkable consistency of outlook, which lasted from the 1570s until at least the 1630s, is explained by the prevailing concepts of statecraft at the court of Spain. 'Reputation', or prestige, was recognized to have a tangible influence in politics and diplomacy, and Spain feared that acknowledgement of weakness in the Netherlands would decrease her stature (*reputación*) as a world power. The view was expressed that if the Dutch Revolt were allowed to succeed, heresy and rebellion would immediately prosper in other parts of the Spanish Monarchy.[26] Even the need to preserve the Catholic religion in the Netherlands could be justified in terms of honour and reputation. It was, admittedly, a course of action by which 'Your Majesty will have done his duty to God', but the ability to protect Catholicism was also a touchstone of Spanish power. 'We should consider the issue of religion not only as a matter of piety and spiritual obligation, but also as a temporal one involving reputation,' Olivares told the king in 1628. He went on to say that 'He did not consider it possible to conclude a truce with honour, even if the Dutch expressly conceded us sovereign power, unless there is some improvement in the religious position'.[27]

53

Spain and the Netherlands

By 1628, however, another reason had emerged to strengthen Spain's determination to carry on the struggle: she was also fighting to preserve her overseas commerce. In the 1580s, Dutch ships began to trade directly with the Spanish and Portuguese empires in America and Africa, both now controlled by Philip II. At first this trade was intended to supplement the goods freely available in the Iberian peninsula (for with only a few interruptions – 1585, 1596, 1599 and 1601-2 – Dutch ships came and went to all Iberian ports relatively easily for most of the Eighty Years' War).[28] In the 1590s, however, an element of economic warfare crept in: Dutch vessels, like the English, sought to injure Habsburg commercial interests as well as maximizing their own profits.[29] Between 1598 and 1605, on average twenty-five ships sailed to West Africa, twenty to Brazil, ten to the Far East and one hundred and fifty to the Caribbean every year. Sovereign colonies were founded at Amboina in 1605 and Ternate in 1607; factories and trading posts were established around the Indian Ocean, near the mouth of the Amazon and (in 1609) in Japan.[30] By the time of the truce talks in 1607-9 the Dutch investment in these overseas trades was already so great that they were not prepared to forego them. Spain had encountered exactly the same problem in settling the peace with England in 1603-4. The talks almost broke down over the freedom of navigation to the East and West Indies ('the point of most moment and difficulty' according to the chief Spanish negotiator), and the issue had to be resolved by an ambiguous silence – the final treaty made no specific mention of overseas trade. Oldenbarnevelt made full use of this precedent and, in the end, the same solution had to be adopted in the Netherlands.[31] In February 1608 the States-General 'roundly' informed the Spanish delegation to the peace talks 'that they intended to continue their trade with the East and the West Indies by means of a general peace, truce or war, each on its own merits'.[32] It was this attitude which determined that there would be a truce and not a peace in the Low Countries War in 1609: Spain was not prepared to abandon for ever her monopoly status in the New World, but neither was she prepared to continue fighting in the

54

Netherlands for the sake of the Portuguese Indies (the Dutch had been chased out of the Caribbean – albeit temporarily – by a Spanish fleet in 1605). The Twelve Years' Truce, therefore, made no mention of areas outside European waters, and warfare did indeed continue there intensively. In the Far East the Dutch conquered Jakarta (renamed Batavia) in 1619; in Guinea they established their first trading post (Fort Mouree) in 1612; in North America, they appeared to trade along the Hudson River in 1614 and founded 'Fort Orange' near the site of present-day Albany (New York). The Dutch also planted more colonies on the 'Wild Coast' near the mouths of the Amazon, opened political and commercial contacts with the Indians of Chile, and began to make war on Spanish shipping and settlements on the Pacific coast.[33] Side by side with this geographical extension of Dutch trade, there was also a quantitative increase. The number of East Indiamen rose from an average of ten in the 1600s to seventeen in 1619 and twenty-three in 1620; the number of ships going to Guinea doubled (to forty); and the Dutch gained over half of the carrying trade between Brazil and Europe (there were twenty-nine sugar refineries in the northern Netherlands by 1622 as against three in 1595).[34] In the discussions at the Spanish court in 1619-20 over the possibility of renewing the Truce (due to expire April 1621), the strongest and perhaps the decisive argument against prolonging the existing arrangement was the damage which the Dutch were doing to the Indies and American trade. In the end Philip III (at death's door but for once determined on a specific policy) insisted on the reopening of the Scheldt and Dutch withdrawal from the Indies as the two inflexible conditions for the conclusion of any new truce; the questions of religion and royal authority were shelved.[35] The Dutch, however, were not prepared to give up either of these economic advantages and in June 1621, three months after the expiration of the truce, a Dutch West India Company was formed to promote trade and war in Latin America. In 1624-5 the Dutch occupied Bahía, the capital of Brazil; in 1628 they seized a Spanish treasure fleet worth 20 million florins in Matanzas Bay, Cuba; and in 1630 the province of Pernambuco in northern Brazil, the centre of the colony's sugar production, was captured by a Dutch expeditionary force of sixty-seven sail and 7000 men. Before long, three hundred miles of the coast and hinterland of north-east Brazil was in Dutch hands and sugar production began to rise again – this time to the advantage of the United Provinces.[36]

The following years brought more Dutch victories abroad – the seizure of parts of Guinea and Ceylon in 1637-8; the defeat of one Spanish navy in the English Channel in 1639 and another off Brazil in 1640; the capture of Malacca in South-East Asia, the Maranhão in South America and Luanda in southern Africa in 1641 – but by far the most important success was the conquest of Brazil. It immediately transformed the issues at stake in the Low Countries Wars. Brazil and its sugar were the mainstay of the Portuguese economy and without them Portugal's union with Spain rapidly became less popular. There was discontent in Lisbon, there were riots in Evora; and the Spanish government became fearful of the consequences should they fail to drive out the invaders. A perceptive Venetian observer noted in October 1638 that Brazil in Dutch hands was 'more damaging than the continuance of the Low Countries Wars'.[37] Olivares offered 3, 4, even 5 million crowns to the Dutch if only they would restore Brazil.[38] By 1640, according to Olivares, 'The item which seems to be indispensable [in any settlement with the Dutch] is the restitution of Brazil'; 'The restoration of Brazil is inexcusable', Philip IV echoed in May and he declared his readiness to bargain away everything else in order to regain it.[39]

And yet in the end Spain made peace without regaining Brazil, without retaining the monopoly of the East Indies trade, without reopening the Scheldt, without securing any official toleration for the Dutch Catholics and without persuading the Republic to recognize Spanish suzerainty in any way. After struggling for so long, Spain eventually gave in on all points.

This collapse came about for a number of reasons. First there was the deteriorating condition of Spain. The run of poor harvests, the falling tax returns and the decline of the

American trade with its silver remittances in the 1620s and 1630s were serious.[40] Far worse, however, was the spate of rebellions in the 1640s: the revolts of Catalonia and Portugal in 1640, the 'Huelga de los grandes' of Castile in 1642-3, the 'Green Banner' revolts in the main towns of Andalusia and the contemporaneous risings in Sicily and Naples in 1647-8.[41] All these problems encouraged the Madrid government to seek peace on all external fronts in order to concentrate its resources on quelling the unrest within the empire. Gradually the flow of Spanish treasure to the Netherlands dried up: the Army of Flanders received from Castile almost 4 million crowns a year from 1635-41, 3.3 million in 1642, but only 1.5 million in 1643.[42] On 19 May 1643 the Spanish army was decisively defeated by the French at Rocroi. It was, according to Philip IV's chief minister Don Luis de Haro, 'Something which can never be called to mind without great sorrow'. It was 'a defeat which is giving rise in all parts to the consequences which we always feared'; the French took Thionville and Sierck in August and their navy defeated Spain's principal Mediterranean fleet off Cartagena in September.[43]

It would not be true to say that serious negotiations for a settlement to the Low Countries Wars only began after these disasters, for there had been so many other rounds of fruitless talks.[44] However after 1640 a new urgency and a new desperation entered Spain's overtures for peace. 'A truce or a peace is necessary and unavoidable whatever the cost and whatever the price,' wrote one minister in 1645. Spain's leaders were prepared to 'give in on every point which might lead to the conclusion of a settlement'. Philip IV, according to one (admittedly hostile) observer, was so desperate for peace that 'If necessary he would crucify Christ again in order to achieve it'.[45] The king's broken spirits sank even lower after the death of his son and heir, Don Balthasar Carlos, in October 1646. He lamented: 'I have lost my only son, whose presence alone comforted me in my sorrows . . . It has broken my heart.'[46]

Fortunately for the depressed Philip IV, by 1646 the Dutch had also come to appreciate the advantages of a settlement even if they could not obtain everything they wanted. There

57

were several reasons for this change of heart. First there was the unwillingness of the Holland oligarchs (who paid almost two-thirds of the Republic's budget) to finance the war indefinitely: they had long resented the heavy cost of the army (in 1628 and 1630, when the Spaniards did not campaign, Holland refused to pay for more than defensive operations) and in 1645 and 1646 the province reduced its military outlay to a bare minimum, directing its resources instead to intervene in the war between Sweden and Denmark which threatened its Baltic interests.[47]

The prince of Orange also had his reasons for desiring an end to the war. In the first place, his son and heir was married to the daughter of Charles I of England and he earnestly desired a peace with Spain which would leave him free to help his Stuart relatives in the civil war. However at the battle of Sherborne in October 1645 the Parliamentary army captured a number of highly compromising letters concerning the aid offered to Charles by the prince of Orange behind the backs of the States-General. Early in 1646 these papers were printed in English and Dutch and they totally discredited the ageing prince. After Naseby, in any case, Frederick Henry realized that further attempts to save the Stuarts were futile.[48] Nevertheless the House of Orange continued to favour peace on other grounds, the chief of which was financial. A settlement with Spain would bring the restoration of the extensive Nassau lands in the South Netherlands (confiscated from Frederick Henry's father, William of Orange, in 1568) and it would bring immediate cash rewards from the king of Spain. The total gain was estimated at £350,000 per annum. Peace would be, in the phrase of Frederick Henry's wife, *'nostre avantasche'*.[49]

In the end, however, it was not the prince and princess of Orange, but the delegates of the seven United Provinces, or rather of the 2000 or so oligarchs who elected them, whose decision in favour of peace proved critical. Bribery played its part here too – Spanish gold undoubtedly eased a few consciences towards accepting the peace – but the States-General had two sound reasons of state for desiring a settlement with Spain. In the first place there was the growing power of France. Until 1640, France had seemed unable to get the upper hand in the war against the Habsburgs – peasant revolts, court intrigues and military defeats seemed to dog every French effort. Although Catalonia and Artois were overrun in 1640-1, a considerable Spanish victory at Honnecourt in May 1642 kept the French at bay, followed by the death of Richelieu (4 December 1642) and Louis XIII (14 May 1643). But five days after the king's death, the French victory at Rocroi effaced the memory of all previous defeats and it became the springboard for further successes. In 1645 alone, ten major towns in Spanish Flanders fell to the French.

The Dutch were not concerned by these encroachments on the southern border of the Spanish Netherlands; on the contrary they made use of the French presence to extend their own territory by capturing Sas van Gent in 1644 and Hulst in 1645, and they cheerfully renewed their 1635 treaty with France to partition the Habsburg Low Countries should they be entirely overrun (1 March 1644). Unknown to the Dutch, however, France and Spain were negotiating for a settlement. In the winter of 1645-6 Spain proposed a marriage between Louis XIV and Maria Theresa, Philip IV's eldest daughter, giving her part of the Spanish Netherlands as a dowry. News of this projected arrangement reached the United Provinces in February 1646. Immediately there was a major political storm: there were anti-French riots in the Hague; moves were made to expel all the French residents from the Republic; and consternation broke out in the States-General. The States of Holland passed a formal resolution declaring: 'That France, enlarged by possession of the Spanish Netherlands, will be a dangerous neighbour for our country.'[50] Fear of a separate Franco-Spanish deal provoked the first spurt of negotiations between Spain and the Dutch at Münster in March and April 1646. Undismayed by the mistrust of her allies, the French advance continued: Kortrijk fell in June 1646; Dunkirk, the only serviceable port of the Spanish Netherlands, in October. This increased the concern of the Republic's leaders that, unless Spain's forces on the Dutch frontier were released, the South Netherlands would be totally overrun, especially when the peace concluding the Thirty Years' War in Germany was signed, releasing France's armies in Alsace for operations in the Netherlands. A cease-fire between Spain and the Dutch was therefore agreed at length in June 1647. There were further delays before this preliminary agreement could be made permanent. French entreaties and French gold, liberally applied, kept in being a small but devoted party dedicated to sabotaging the peace, while French diplomats created 'an artificial labyrinth, constructed in such a way that those who allow themselves to be led into it can never find the exit', in order to place further delays in the way of all decisions. The system of government in the United Provinces which required unanimity in all major policy resolutions, naturally favoured the *status quo* at all times: continuing war during wartime, avoiding war when at peace. However in the mid-1640s the province which had most resolutely and consistently opposed a settlement with Spain – Zealand – was forced to change its mind by some unforeseen and unfavourable developments in the Iberian world.

As early as January 1634, just after the failure of another round of peace talks, the French agent at the Hague, Charnacé, noted that if Dutch Brazil were reconquered the States-General would be driven to negotiate an immediate settlement with Spain.[51] A decade later, that is precisely what happened, even though on the eve of the disaster the Dutch position in South America appeared to be stronger than ever. In 1637 the Dutch West India Company sent out Count John Maurice of Nassau, great-nephew of William the Silent, to govern Brazil. Almost at once the new governor captured another province (Ceará) and sent an expedition to Africa which captured São Jorge da Minha in West Africa, gateway to the Ashanti goldfields. In 1641 one more province was added in Brazil (Maranhão) extending Dutch control over 1000 miles of the Brazilian coastal plain between the São Francisco and the Amazon rivers, and an expedition sent from Recife to West Africa captured Luanda in Angola, key to the supply of slave labour upon which Brazilian sugar production depended. In the midst of these successes, in December 1640, Portugal successfully threw off its allegiance to Spain and a local grandee, the Duke of Bragança, became King John IV. There was no longer any risk of Spanish forces being sent to win back Brazil and in 1641-2 a truce was concluded between the new Portuguese regime and the Dutch. The States-General even sent an expeditionary force to Lisbon in August 1641 to bolster Portuguese resistance to Spain.[52]

So healthy did the Dutch position appear in 1643-4 that the Directors of the West India Company decided to economize by reducing their military establishment (which cost some 1.4 million florins annually) and John Maurice, together with many of his soldiers, was recalled. It was a fatal mistake. The Portuguese planters of Pernambuco had never accepted their new Calvinist masters whole-heartedly and they resented the high interest charged by Dutch moneylenders on the loans provided to restock the sugar plantations after the fighting of the 1630s. In June 1645 there was a major uprising of the Portuguese settlers against the Dutch. In August a battle was fought at Tobocas, outside Recife, which the settlers won. This minor engagement, fought 6000 miles from the Netherlands and involving under 1000 men on each side, was one of the most important 'actions' of the Eighty Years' War. It destroyed Dutch power in Brazil (only four toeholds on the coast, Recife the chief among them, remained). The great profits from the sugar trade were gone. The West India Company based on Zealand was therefore desperate to recover its lost empire and looked urgently at the means available. The short-term remedy was to send immediate relief to the beleaguered defenders in Recife and other places, and this was done in spring 1646: twenty ships with 2000 men set sail. However the rebellious settlers were in receipt of aid both from Bahía, the capital of Portuguese Brazil, and from Portugal herself, and it was clear that a far larger expedition would be required to restore Dutch power fully.

There were thus two problems: the first was to mount a major expedition from the Netherlands to reconquer Brazil; the second was to end the assistance from Portugal. In former years, the West India Company had vehemently opposed any settlement with Philip IV on the grounds that it would free

Spanish resources to defend the Portuguese Indies. After the rebellion of Portugal in 1640, however, this was no longer the case. On the contrary, a settlement with Spain might now be of benefit to the West India Company since Philip IV would be free to use some of his resources on the reconquest of Portugal, which would in turn prevent Portugal from sending reinforcements to Brazil. By itself, of course, peace with Spain would not be enough to regain Brazil: for that, the great fleet was still required. Throughout 1646-7, therefore, hard bargaining took place between the States of Holland and Zealand on these two connected problems. In the end, Holland offered to pay for a major expedition to save Brazil if Zealand would sign the peace with Spain. In August 1647, despite the efforts of the Portuguese and the French to sabotage the settlement, Holland and Zealand reached agreement on the terms for the reconquest of Brazil: a force of forty-one ships and 6000 men would be assembled ready to sail in October 1647; then the peace with Spain would be signed. Inevitably there were more delays, and the fleet did not sail for Brazil until 26 December 1647, but this did not affect the other half of the bargain: Zealand instructed her representative at Münster to sign the peace with Spain in any case, which he did in a solemn ceremony on 30 January 1648, bringing the Eighty Years' War to its formal close.[53]

For Owen Feltham, writing four years later, the Dutch were supermen. 'They are,' he wrote, 'in some sorte Gods ... They are a *Gideons* Army upon the march again. They are the Indian *Rat*, knawing the Bowels of the *Spanish Crocodile* ... They are the little sword-fish pricking the bellies of the Whale. They are the wane of that Empire, which increas'd in [the time of] Isabella and in [the time of] Charles the fifth was at full.'[54] The Dutch Revolt, which began among a few thousand refugees in north-western Europe, had spread until it affected the lives of millions of people and brought about the collapse of the greatest world empire ever seen. In the 1640s there was fighting in Ceylon, Japan and Indonesia, in southern and western Africa, on the Indian, Pacific and Atlantic Oceans, and of course in Brazil and the Low Countries. It all stemmed from the revolt of the Netherlands. The struggle had become, so to say, the First World War, and it is only when one surveys the global scale of the conflict and the complexity of the alliances and coalitions of the participants that one can satisfactorily explain why the Dutch Revolt lasted eighty-two years.

3

In 1976 the Dutch periodical *Tijdschrift voor Geschiedenis*, one of the best historical journals now published anywhere in the world, decided to devote an entire issue to the Dutch Revolt. Some of the contributors were invited to assess the importance of the Pacification of Ghent (signed four hundred years before) which, together with the Union of Utrecht (1579) and the Act of Abjuration (1581), was to become one of the founding charters of the Republic; the rest were to examine the way in which the troubles in the Netherlands had polarized religious, political and intellectual life both inside and outside the Republic. The following article deals with the diplomatic and military efforts of the Dutch to defeat their Spanish enemies by creating diversions elsewhere in the world which would, they hoped, reduce the direct pressure of the Army of Flanders against their frontiers. This policy was relatively cheap, totally safe (for the Spaniards could not retaliate effectively) and highly effective. Perhaps the most spectacular success came in 1640, when Spain's failure to achieve the recovery of the rich Brazilian province of Pernambuco, conquered from Portugal by the Dutch in 1630, caused first economic distress, then political unrest, and finally revolution in Portugal. Increasingly, the resources of the Spanish crown were tied down in the peninsula, where 1640 also saw the rebellion of Catalonia, and the war in the Netherlands became a purely defensive action (except for foolish escapades like Don Francisco de Melo's invasion of France in 1643 which resulted in the crushing defeat of Rocroi). The story of the attempts of the Dutch Republic to find allies in the struggle against Spain, attempts which lasted as long as the war itself and covered almost the entire globe, offers further proof (if any were still needed) that the Dutch 'war of independence' was an event of international importance which only makes sense when it is set in an international context. It also shows, since the Dutch conquests supplied the Republic with sugar, spices and other valuable trading commodities as well as undermining Spain's imperial position, that a good foreign policy can allow a state to eat its cake and have it too.

The Dutch Revolt and the Polarization of International Politics

Introduction

'During the whole course of the seventeenth century,' wrote Sir George Clark in 1929, 'there were only seven complete calendar years in which there was no war between European states: the years 1610, 1669-71, 1680-2 . . . War, therefore, may be said to have been as much a normal state of European life as peace.'[1] There were, as far as the present writer can see, even fewer complete calendar years without war in Europe during the sixteenth century. However, an important difference separated the hostilities which took place in the two centuries. Until the 1580s, at least, most European wars involved only two powers fighting a simple duel; thereafter, wars that involved rival blocs of allies were more common. In the seventeenth century, hostilities were so widespread, and the allies so numerous, that making peace became extremely difficult. The despair of Germany during the seemingly interminable Thirty Years' War was given ironic but effective expression by the novelist Hans Jakob Christoffel von Grimmelshausen. In his famous novel about the war, *Simplicissimus*, he put his plan for peace into the mouth of a wandering madman, 'The great God Jupiter'.[2]

There are a number of developments that help to explain why the various states of Europe allowed themselves to be drawn into war more frequently after 1580 than before. There were the significant improvements in diplomatic organization, with more (and more skilful) resident ambassadors, closer co-operation between neighbours, and firmer commitments between allies. There was the emergence of a number of dogmatic but antipathetic Christian churches in Europe, with adherents in one country willing and ready to go to the aid of their co-religionists elsewhere. These developments were facilitated by improvements in communications – better roads, faster ships, more (and more regular) postal services – which made it easier to co-ordinate diplomatic and, when necessary, military contacts across continents. Equally important, but less obvious, there was the appearance of a semi-permanent pole of political and religious ferment in north-western Europe: the Low Countries. The wars in the Netherlands tended to exert an influence on all other conflicts in Europe. As Gustavus Adolphus observed to a Dutch ambassador in 1625: 'The Hague was the stage on which all the negotiations and actions of Europe took place.' It is the argument of this paper that the war between Spain and her Netherlands 'rebels' between the 1560s and the 1640s played a crucial role in the polarization of international politics, both inside and outside Europe, into two hostile camps.[3]

The Struggle for Survival, 1565-85

Our guarantees that we shall not become the conquered province of another kingdom are as follows: God, the water, Batavian heroism [*den Bataafschen heldenmoed*], the balance of power in Europe, the mutual jealousy of our neighbours, and the fact that our Republic has survived for several centuries.[4]

This verdict of Johannes Meerman, a Dutch statesman of the later eighteenth century, was largely true. But it did not apply to the early years of the Dutch struggle against Spain. In the sixteenth century there was no 'balance of power' in Europe, and the survival of an independent state in the North Netherlands owed more to God, the water and 'Batavian heroism' than to the jealousy of foreign powers. Nevertheless, from the earliest days, the leaders of the Netherlands opposition to Philip II had appreciated the need to take account of the attitudes and deeds of Spain's enemies elsewhere.

Many of the Netherlands nobles were related to the leading families of other countries. Montigny and Hornes were close relatives of the Constable of France, Anne de

Montmorency (indeed, Montigny had been brought up in the Constable's household); William of Orange, himself the son of the Count of Nassau, married Anna, niece of the Elector of Saxony and granddaughter of the Landgrave of Hesse; Egmont married the sister of the Elector Palatine; Brederode and Hornes married into the family of the Counts of Neuenar. With such strong family connections, the Netherlands nobles naturally took a keen interest in the affairs of France and the Empire. However, foreign affairs in the 1560s were dominated by the Ottoman Turks. The 'Grand Seigneur' was, after 1559, the only ruler capable of challenging the power of Spain in open combat, and for twenty years after the Peace of Cateau-Cambrésis Philip II's principal preoccupation was the defence of the Mediterranean against the power of the Ottoman Sultan. It seems clear that the Netherlands nobles exploited this preoccupation in their opposition to the King. The Turkish siege of Malta in 1565, in particular, was undoubtedly used by Orange, Egmont and Hornes to secure concessions from the King. Brederode was not the only Netherlander to wish that the Turks 'were in Valladolid already'; he well knew that a Turkish victory would have made royal concessions in the Low Countries inevitable.[5]

But Malta did not fall, and there were no royal concessions. In 1566, therefore, serious attempts were made by the Netherlands opposition to draw together these random contacts and 'polarize' opinion and policies in neighbouring states. Montigny and Hornes took steps to establish a common front between the French Huguenots and the 'Gueux'.[6] In Germany a major propaganda campaign was mounted to whip up support for the opposition's cause: letters were written to leading princes; pamphlets were composed and printed; envoys were sent to the emperor (Count Hoogstraten) and to friendly princes (Gillis le Clercq); the Reichstag was petitioned when it met at Augsburg.[7] But the response to these initiatives was disappointing: the German princes stood aloof and the Huguenots never managed to send an army. The Dutch cause was offered active support, paradoxically enough, only by the Ottoman Turks.

Since 1526 the Sultan had had an understanding with the kings of France that, whenever possible, both would attack the Habsburgs together. In 1543 the Turkish fleet had even wintered in the ports of southern France. At about the same time, the *entente* had been extended to include the German Protestant princes, the leader of whom was the Landgrave of Hesse, later to become the grandfather-in-law and close correspondent of William of Orange.[8] The Landgrave's letters throughout the 1560s gave Orange news of Turkish developments. In 1566, however, it seems that the Sultan took the initiative and established direct contact with the Netherlands opposition to Philip II. The Catholic historian, Famiano Strada, who based his work on documents from the (now destroyed) private archive of Margaret of Parma, asserted that in October 1566 a letter from one of the Sultan's principal advisers, Joseph Miques, Duke of Naxos, was read out to the Calvinist consistory of Antwerp, pledging that 'the forces of the Ottomans would soon hit King Philip's affairs so hard that he would not even have the time to think of Flanders'.[9] It proved an empty promise. The death of Sultan Suleiman the Magnificent in September 1566, and the provincial rebellions and military mutinies that followed, prevented the Ottomans from attacking Spanish power for some years. However in 1568 the Prince of Orange sent a special envoy to Constantinople to renew contact with the Duke of Naxos (who had resided in Antwerp in the 1540s), and to persuade the Turks to attack Spain.[10] The Sultan's advisers were unmoved: they had already decided upon an attack on Ivan the Terrible, and in 1569 the Sultan's armies rolled northwards and attempted to dig a canal between the Don and Volga Rivers. The Netherlands, like the Moriscos of Granada, were neglected.[11]

To a large extent, the first revolt of the Netherlands, in 1566-8, had failed for lack of foreign support, and the opposition leaders decided that any future attempt to overthrow Spanish power in the Low Countries could take place only with full foreign backing. William of Orange and his brother Louis therefore laboured ceaselessly and, on the whole, successfully to persuade France, England, Sweden, and certain German and Italian princes to support their project to invade the Netherlands during the spring of 1572. The Sultan and the King of Algiers were also involved.[12] The outcome of all these plans is well known: England and Sweden stood back, French support was destroyed by the Massacre of St Bartholomew; only the Count Palatine (ruler of a small state of 400,000 souls) and the Count of Nassau (ruler of an even smaller state of only 50,000 people) sent substantial support. Again, as in 1566-8, without foreign support the rebellion foundered. Only about twenty towns in Holland and Zealand carried on their resistance after 1572. The Prince of Orange and the other exiles perforce threw in their lot with them, but the outcome of their desperate stand against Spain still depended upon aid from abroad. In May 1574, the Prince of Orange informed his brother:

> I see very little chance of being able to finance any special undertaking unless we find someone to help us. And in this connection I remember something which I said to you some time ago: that one could defend this country against all the forces of the king of Spain for the space of two years, but that we would then stand in need of help . . . and as the two years will soon be up, it is high time that some princes and potentates lent us a hand.[13]

In fact, Orange did not have long to wait. Already in 1573, Charles IX of France began to supply the Prince with a subsidy to finance his struggle against Spain, and in 1574 both Orange and Charles IX endeavoured to interest the Ottoman Sultan, Selim II, in a co-ordinated attack on Spain. The Prince sent a special envoy to Constantinople; Theodore Beza, from Geneva, sent letters; and the French king worked through his ambassador, the pro-Huguenot Bishop of Dax.[14]

The result of these initiatives was the despatch of a special messenger to the 'Lutheran sect' of 'Filandara', bearing an expression of the Sultan's support. The messenger, 'who knows the military affairs and conditions of that area', was also to put the Dutch in contact with the still-discontented

Moriscos of Granada and with the pirates of Algiers. Meanwhile the Sultan himself sent a great fleet into the western Mediterranean which reconquered Tunis in October 1574.[15]

The fall of Tunis, as both the French and the Dutch were quick to realize, inevitably reduced Spanish pressure on the Dutch.[16] In 1575, Philip II even held formal talks with his 'rebels' about a possible settlement to the revolt (the conference of Breda). But the talks broke down after three months, and once more foreign aid dried up. The death of Charles IX of France in May 1574 removed the crucial intermediary between Orange and the Sultan; after 1574 there was little direct contact. Although the Sultan was said to have encouraged Dutch resistance in 1576-7, and although a Turkish consulate ('De Griekse Natie') was established in Calvinist Antwerp in 1582, the Ottoman Sultan was no longer interested in the Netherlands.[17] In April 1577, Spain and the Turks reached a provisional agreement to cease hostilities and a formal truce was signed in 1580. All the Sultan's efforts after that were directed against Persia, and even the frenzied pleas of England, France and the Dutch in the Armada year, 1588, failed to persuade the Turks to attack Philip II again.[18]

The Netherlands at Bay, 1585-1609

For a decade after the death of Charles IX, the Dutch were unable to win over any great power to their cause. The Palatinate sent an army to the Netherlands in 1578; the French Huguenots sent another. In 1581 a third French army arrived, under the Catholic Duke of Anjou, who agreed to become sovereign ruler of the Low Countries in place of the now-deposed Philip II.

All these interventions were ill-starred, however. In 1583 the French, led by the 'sovereign' Duke of Anjou, tried to wrest control of the country from the States-General by staging an armed attack on the major cities of Flanders and Brabant. It failed, and Anjou retired disconsolate to France, where he died in June 1584. Almost at once, the situation was transformed. Anjou may have proved a miserable failure as ruler of the Netherlands, but he had fulfilled a vital role in France: as the nearest male relative of the childless Henry III (his brother), he was the personal guarantee that the next king of France would be a Catholic. After his death, Henry III's nearest male relative was the Protestant leader, Henry of Navarre (later to be Henry IV). The prospect of a Protestant succession so alarmed Philip II that he entered into a formal alliance with the league of French Catholics created by the Guise family: the Sainte Union. The King of Spain promised to pay a regular subsidy to the Union, and between 1585 and 1588 the Guise family received over a million ducats (almost three million florins) from Spain.

There seems to be no doubt that this alliance, the Treaty of Joinville (signed on 31 December 1584), frightened England. Queen Elizabeth had already been alarmed by the rising tide of Spanish success: the conquest of Portugal in 1580, the annexation of the Azores in 1582-3 in the teeth of tough local opposition (supported by France and England), and the steady subjugation of the South Netherlands. In the autumn of 1584, Lord Burghley, Elizabeth's chief adviser, impressed upon his sovereign the need to make common cause with Spain's other enemies. 'Your strength abroad,' he told the Queen, 'it must be in joining in good confederacy, or at least intelligence with those that would willingly embrace the same.' Burghley proposed alliances with the Turks, Morocco, Florence, Ferrara and Venice; but above all he counselled the despatch of immediate aid to the Low Countries, to make sure that Spain would not reconquer the provinces still in revolt. 'If he [Philip II] once reduce the Low Countries to absolute subjection, I know not what limits any man of judgment can set unto his greatness.'[19] After deep thought and protracted negotiations, Queen Elizabeth became the first sovereign ruler to make a formal alliance with the Dutch. The Treaty of Nonsuch, which guaranteed substantial English aid to the Dutch 'rebels', was signed on 17 August 1585. The situation of the two allies did not improve overnight. In August 1587, a correspondent of the Earl of

Leicester, English governor-general in the North Netherlands, lamented: 'The alliance and understanding of the duke of Parma with the Catholic League and the House of Guise; and we, on the contrary, have no league or alliance with the princes of our religion but, what is worse, we antagonize them from day to day'.[20] As the Spanish Armada sailed up the Channel in the summer of 1588, England and Holland found themselves alone: no foreign power would lend them money or material support. The Catholic-Habsburg domination of Europe was complete.

The diplomatic isolation of Queen Elizabeth and the States-General only ended when the assassination of Henry III, the last of the Valois (1 August 1589), intensified the struggle between the Protestants, led by Henry of Navarre, and the Catholic League for control of France. The Catholic states of western Europe sent massive aid to the Sainte Union. Spain provided 15,000,000 florins in cash subsidies between 1588 and 1595; she invaded Languedoc and sent a permanent military force to Catholic Brittany; and she mounted four major campaigns in northern France, using the Army of Flanders (1590, 1592, 1594, 1596). The Catholic Duke of Savoy, aided by a Spanish subsidy, invaded and occupied part of Provence. The Pope sent an army of 10,000 men to fight in France in 1591-2, at a cost of 1,500,000 florins.[21]

This grand alliance of the Catholic powers was soon matched by a similar association of Protestant states. Henry of Navarre received important military and financial support from several German princes, particularly the Elector Palatine, and from Queen Elizabeth.[22] The Dutch sent him 90,000 florins in 1588, 90,000 more in 1589, and 120,000 in 1591; they also despatched arms and munitions in 1591 and an expeditionary force in 1592, 1594, 1596 and 1597. The Dutch also collaborated closely with England: a Dutch contingent assisted in the capture of Cadiz in 1596, and Queen Elizabeth continued to provide a share of the Dutch war-budget. In Germany, the Dutch took advantage of a rising, engineered by Calvinist refugees in the city, to place a garrison in Emden 'to prevent anything untoward . . .' (April 1595);[23] in 1597 they attacked and captured several

Spanish-held strongholds in the archbishopric of Cologne. Most of these gains could not be held however. Diplomatic efforts were more fruitful. In 1594, Oldenbarnevelt sent Dr L. Myller to 'Duytslandt' to enlist the support of the princes of the Empire 'against the Spanish claims to universal monarchy or overlordship'. He failed.[24] An attempt by Maurice of Nassau in 1599 to enlist the aid of the princes of the West-phalian Circle of the Empire, whose lands had been plundered by Spanish troops the previous winter, also failed.[25] A new diplomatic offensive in 1602 produced better results: the Dutch occupation of Emden was made permanent and negotiations were begun with the Elector of Brandenburg. In April 1605, the Elector signed a treaty with the Dutch which promised a subsidy and an expeditionary force; much to Oldenbarnevelt's surprise, the Brandenburg 'hulptroepen' arrived in May and took part in the campaign.[26]

Despite this diplomatic success, however, the Dutch were again becoming isolated. In May 1598 Henry of Navarre made peace with Spain, achieving universal recognition as lawful King of France (albeit, since 1593, a Catholic one). Although Henry continued to provide the Dutch with a large annual subsidy (in all, almost 11 million florins were sent 1598-1610), this scarcely equalled the value to the Republic of the war in France, which had distracted Spain for almost a decade.[27] In August 1604 England, now ruled by James VI of Scotland (no friend of Calvinists), also made peace with Spain. Left on their own to oppose the might of Spain single-handed, the Dutch concluded first a cease-fire (April 1607) and then a twelve-year truce (April 1609).

The Dutch Take the Offensive

Although concluded largely through isolation and exhaustion, the Twelve Years' Truce was a major success for the Dutch. Apart from the economic benefits brought by peace, the truce conferred complete political respectability on the Republic. The truce talks at the Hague in 1608-9 were attended

73

by representatives from France, England, Denmark, Hesse, the Palatinate and Brandenburg; and in the end the Republic was recognized by Spain 'as if it were a sovereign power'. Almost immediately, other states followed suit: in July 1609 the Dutch envoy in London was recognized as a full ambassador representing a sovereign power, and in September James VI and I accorded his agent in the Hague similar promotion. Later in the year the same thing happened in the Republic's diplomatic contacts with France and Venice.[28] Before long, 'We can see all Christian nations, large and small, and even the Turks and Muscovites, becoming concerned about the fate of our Netherlands.'[29] The Republic was in the process of forming alliances 'with all the princes and potentates who ... opposed the tyranny and the claims to universal monarchy of Spain, such as the kings of France, England, Denmark and Sweden, with the Republic of Venice, the Hanseatic League and others'.[30] The 'others' included Brandenburg (after 1605), Muscovy (after 1631), Transylvania (after 1626), the Turks (after 1611), Morocco (after 1608), and Algiers and Tunis (after 1622). These allies were not idly chosen. The motive for the treaties was often explicitly admitted to be 'because the same towns or kingdoms had ... a powerful hostility towards Spain'.[31]

Spain was still a menace. She emerged during the decade following the signing of the Truce, as she had in the 1590s, as the backbone of a militant Catholic alliance. The Protestant states of Europe again began to fear that Spain headed a 'Catholic international' which sought to 'plant the Popes Law by Armes, as the Ottomans doe the Law of Mahomet'.[32] In August 1610 the King of Spain agreed to become the 'Protector' of the League of German Catholic princes, and he engaged himself to provide 30,000 *escudos* (about 75,000 florins) every month for two years, to enable the League to raise and maintain an army. In 1611 this army, financed by Spain, invaded Bohemia; in 1614, aided by troops from the Spanish Netherlands, it invaded and occupied parts of the disputed duchies of Cleve and Julich. In 1616-17 Spain paid for a part of the Habsburg army fighting against Venice in Dalmatia.[33] In 1618, following the outbreak of rebellion in

74

Bohemia, Spain promised the immediate despatch of men and money to the Emperor: in the course of 1619 some 10,000 Spanish troops and about 500,000 florins were sent to Vienna and in 1620 another Spanish army was sent from the South Netherlands to occupy the lands of the Elector Palatine, who had rashly agreed to become the king of the Bohemian rebels.[34] Other Catholic potentates soon intervened in the struggle to help the Emperor and Spain: Louis XIII of France persuaded the German Protestant princes to remain neutral while Maximilian of Bavaria, the greatest Catholic prince in the empire, loaned his army to the Habsburgs. Above all, the Pope sent large sums of money: between 1619 and 1623, the Curia sent 400,000 *escudos* (1,000,000 florins) to the Emperor, almost 350,000 *escudos* to the Duke of Bavaria, and a further 16,000 *escudos* to another ally of the Habsburgs, the King of Poland.[35] Of course this Catholic aid to the Emperor did not end in 1623. The Papacy continued to send regular subsidies to the Emperor and the League until at least 1635.[36] Spanish forces continued to occupy the Rhine Palatinate until the 1640s while in 1634 a major army, commanded by the King of Spain's brother Ferdinand (the Cardinal-Infante) invaded Germany and routed the Protestants at the battle of Nördlingen. Following this victory, Spain sent enormous sums of money to the German Catholics: 5,339,985 Rhine *gulden* (about 8,500,000 Dutch florins) were spent by the Spanish Treasury in Germany between April 1635 and March 1643.[37] In return for such substantial assistance, in 1629-31 the Emperor sent troops to fight in Italy for Philip IV, and in the 1620s, 1630s and 1640s, imperial troops fought periodically in the Netherlands against the Dutch.

In the face of this militant Catholic axis, linking Madrid, Brussels, Vienna, Munich and Rome, the rest of Europe felt threatened. Several opposition groups were formed. In the west, there stood the ancient 'triple alliance' of England, the Dutch, and the French Protestants; in the east, a looser association of Calvinists existed, led by the Elector Palatine Frederick V, his ministers Christian of Anhalt and Ludwig Camerarius, the Prince of Transylvania Bethlen Gabor, and the leaders of the Protestant minorities in the Habsburg hereditary lands.[38] To the south of this Calvinist network lay the traditionally anti-Habsburg Republic of Venice and the Islamic states of the Mediterranean; to the north were the Lutheran kingdoms of Denmark and Sweden and the Orthodox Tsardom of Muscovy. The overriding problem facing those who wished to oppose the might of the Catholic axis after 1609 was, therefore, not where to find support, but how to weld the numerous enemies of Spain into a coherent rival 'international' or axis.

In 1615, the Dutch attempted to mediate a peace between Sweden and Russia; in 1616 they promised military aid to Savoy; and in 1617 they sent 3000 troops and 12 warships to fight for Venice against the Habsburgs.[39] But none of these efforts were successful. Aid sent to the Bohemian rebels after 1618 achieved little more, although both the Bohemians and the Elector Palatine had a long tradition of association with England and the Dutch Republic.[40] In the end, only 5000 men and 550,000 florins actually reached Bohemia, and in 1620 Catholic armies overran the Palatinate and all the rebellious Habsburg lands.[41] The Protestants fled into exile, many of them joining their ex-king, Frederick, in the Hague, and his efforts to create a new 'international' which included England, France, Denmark, Sweden and a host of lesser potentates (Treaty of the Hague, December 1624).[42]

Although, however, the new network was centred in the North Netherlands, the Dutch had done little to create it. The list of treaties made by the Republic included several that were not the work of Dutch diplomats. In many cases the groundwork was done by the Palatine and Bohemian exiles. Just as the exiles from Flanders and Brabant strengthened the militant foreign policy of the Republic in the 1590s, so the exiles from central Europe acted as a 'general staff' for the anti-Habsburg alliance in the 1620s and 1630s.[43] The Dutch provided a headquarters, funds and respectability, but they lacked the single-minded determination to organize and coordinate a European struggle. They also lacked the means. On the one hand they found it difficult to recruit a sufficient number of suitable diplomats; on the other they were reluctant to spend money without evident cause.[44] In 1628 and

1631, because the Brussels government was known to have no money to mount a campaign, the States-General economized and in the 'War estimates' we read, 'There was no campaign this year.' In 1640-1, although a fleet and an expeditionary force were sent to aid the Portuguese rebellion against Philip IV, the Dutch sent none to the Catalans, even though they recognized their 'common interest' with any other rebels against the King of Spain.[45]

The Republic thus tended to fight shy of all foreign commitments that might cost money, although they fully realized the advantages that accrued from the diplomatic efforts of others to polarize European politics into a mutually hostile balance of power. 'The preservation of this state depended on the jealousy of its neighbours,' wrote Lieuwe van Aitzema in the 1660s: 'Everything has been due to the jealousy of Spain, France and England.'[46] But that 'jealousy' was not entirely of Dutch making. They also reaped a harvest sowed by others.

The distinctive contribution of the Dutch to the polarization of international politics in the seventeenth century was not, in fact, made in Europe at all, but in Africa, Asia and America. Overseas, the Dutch were far more 'positive' in their foreign policy, creating enemies for the Iberian world empires where none had existed before. In this they followed the policy of Queen Elizabeth of England, who had ever believed that:

> If you touche him [the King of Spain] in the Indies, you touche the apple of his eye, for take away the treasure which is *nervus belli*, and which he hath almoste [all] out of his West Indies, his old bandes of souldiers will soone be dissolved, his purposes defeated, his power and strengthe diminished, his pride abated, and his tyranie utterly suppressed.[47]

However, where the English had been content to sink Spanish shipping and plunder isolated colonies, the Dutch set out more systematically to create a rival colonial and commercial empire and to discover 'in what ways we could

77

injure this powerful enemy with his own resources'.[48]

Inspired by Willem Usselincx, one of the Flemish exiles, attempts were made to foment discontent among Spain's Indian vassals, while in the Netherlands public opinion was stirred up by a 'Black Legend' propaganda campaign against Spanish 'atrocities' in America. A Dutch edition of Bartolomé de las Casas's *Brevíssima relación de la destrucción de las Indias*, published at Amsterdam in 1620, asserted that the Dutch (in view of Spanish brutality) had a manifest destiny to liberate the Indians from their Iberian oppressors.[49] Already steps had been taken to achieve this. In 1614 a fleet under Joris van Spilsbergen left the Netherlands with orders to make contact with the Indians of America, especially with those of Chile who were known to be hostile to the Spaniards. This initiative failed (the Indians were as suspicious of the Dutch as they were of the Spaniards), but more substantial efforts followed the foundation of the West India Company in 1621 (inspired by Usselincx). Since 1619 a purpose-built fleet had been under construction ready to sail to South America and capture a major port, provoke a native rising against the Iberian settlers and create a Dutch colony in its place.[50] In this they could count on the assistance of a 'fifth column' of Jewish residents, most of them Portuguese Marranos, some of whom had reached America only after a period of exile in Holland, who 'would rather see a couple of Dutch pennants than an inquisitor'.[51] Some of these Marranos appear to have acted as secret agents.[52]

Despite the long preparations and the advantage of surprise the Dutch attack on Callao (capital of Spanish Peru) failed totally, and the occupation of Bahía (capital of Portuguese Brazil) lasted only a year (May 1624-May 1625).[53] The Dutch did not give up, however. In 1630 they again made use of Jewish and other anti-Portuguese elements in Brazil to seize the province of Pernambuco, the most populous area of the viceroyalty and the centre of its sugar production. By 1644 the invaders controlled over 1000 miles of the coastal plain of Brazil, and an expedition from the province gained control of most of Angola, the region that provided the slaves needed to farm the sugar plantations.[54] Dutch Brazil became a thriving concern until the revolt of the settlers in 1645. Even before this, however, the Dutch had lost much of their credibility in South America. Once she had herself become a colonial power, the Republic could not pose convincingly as the liberator of the oppressed Indian. A new effort under Admiral Hendrik Brouwer to interest the Araucanian Indians in concerted action against the Spaniards (1642-3) proved a failure, even though Brouwer's men founded a small post in Chile in the hope of establishing permanent contact.[55]

More sustained and more successful efforts were made by the Dutch to sap the King of Spain and Portugal's power in Asia. Although the admirals of the *voorcompagnieën* were instructed to avoid armed conflict with other Europeans in the Far East, after 1602 and the merger of the companies into the Vereenigde Oostindische Compagnie, aggression against the Portuguese and the Spaniards became an established feature of Dutch operations in Asia.[56] In 1602 a Dutch expedition under Joris van Spilsbergen arrived in Ceylon, the centre of cinnamon production, bearing an offer from Prince Maurice of Nassau to aid the King of Kandy against the Portuguese. The offer was renewed in 1612 and it was eventually taken up in 1636: for twenty years the Dutch and the King of Kandy co-operated to expel the Portuguese from the island.[57] Much the same pattern of anti-Iberian activity was repeated elsewhere: on the Coromandel coast of India (where the Dutch established trading contacts in 1605, thanks to the intervention of a local Jewish resident), in Indonesia, in China and above all in Japan.[58]

The first Dutch trading mission to Japan arrived in 1609 and at once the 'merchants' set about discrediting the Iberian powers, which had conducted trade with the Japanese for sixty years. They played upon the fears of the Japanese court that Portuguese missionaries were trying to 'Christianize' the country. (The Dutch themselves never flouted their religion and the Japanese, like the Turks, were said to prefer the Dutch to their competitors because they were 'less Christian'.) Partly due to Dutch insinuations, the Spaniards were expelled from Japan in 1624, the Portuguese in 1636.

79

This was a major success for the Dutch, for they became the sole middlemen in Japan's lucrative trade with the outside world; but there was a price to be paid for continued Japanese favour. In 1637 a civil rebellion broke out among the largely Christian population of Kyushu island. The Japanese government decided, partly at the suggestion of the Dutch, that the revolt was the work of the Portuguese (whose factory was at Nagasaki, on Kyushu). The authorities therefore resolved to end all contact with the Portuguese and to extirpate all Christian worship in Japan. By 1638 the rebels, most of them Christians, were driven back and forced to take refuge in Hara castle on the coast. The imperial government ordered the Dutch factor in Japan to send his warships to attack Hara. He obeyed, and from 24 February until 12 March 1638 the Dutch ships aided the blockade of the castle. Shortly afterwards Hara surrendered and the defenders, including thousands of Christians, were massacred. The Dutch thus proved that they were 'safe', and so retained their control over Japanese foreign trade (worth four million florins a year). For two hundred years, thanks to the massacre of Hara, the Dutch provided the only contact between Japan and Europe.[59]

The motives of the Dutch in Japan, and in many other situations overseas, were obviously political and economic rather than religious. A measure of 'polarization' was advantageous to the interests of the Dutch economy and was bound to follow in the wake of Dutch trade. And yet there was undoubtedly an element of crusading zeal, of 'godliness' in many seemingly spiteful attacks made by the Dutch or their fellow-Europeans. Many Dutchmen clearly regarded any blow struck against Spain, whether or not it aided their struggle for 'liberation', as a blow against Roman Catholicism and therefore as something good in itself. Piet Heyn, who captured the New World silver fleet off Cuba in 1628, seems to have been seen by some as God's instrument to scourge the Catholics.[60] The efforts of the Spaniards – *maraens* as the Dutch normally called them – to defeat or subjugate the Calvinist Republic were viewed as some sort of *crimen lesae majestatis divina*, treason to God. In the words of one of the

80

Geuzenliederen ('Sea Beggar Songs'): '*Maraen*, how dare you raise your sword and musket against God!'[61] This, however, was a song composed in the Netherlands. It did not reflect the sentiments of the Dutchmen actually fighting in the colonies where, as Oliver Cromwell observed, gain was preferred to godliness, politics to religion.

Yet was there any alternative? Throughout their struggle with Spain, the Dutch were at a disadvantage in terms of population, size and resources. As Cornelis Pieterszoon Hooft wrote in 1617, 'Our origins were very small and modest. In comparison with the king of Spain we were like a mouse against an elephant.'[62] And although the mouse grew to formidable size, it was never really the equal of Spain or any of the other 'great powers' of Europe. The basic problem of the Republic was 'The ambiguity of the Dutch position as a first-rate commercial power without a corresponding territorial and demographical basis. It was the problem of a nation seeking security in peace, in a world which granted no profit without power, no safety without war.'[63]

I have tried to show in this paper that the preferred solution of the leaders of the Republic to this problem was to 'polarize' the vague diplomatic forces both inside and outside Europe for their own ends. In that, perhaps, lay the most significant achievement of the Dutch Revolt.

II

The Military Context
of the Revolt

4

Arguably the most important general article on the military history of early modern Europe written since World War II is 'The Military Revolution' by Michael Roberts. It certainly influenced the direction taken by my research into the Spanish Army of Flanders, and I expected my findings to support his conclusions. However, when I came to write my doctoral thesis in the spring of 1968 I could not disguise my doubts concerning Roberts's contrast between a conservative, backward Spanish army practising outmoded tactics, and the dynamic, efficient Swedish army pioneering new ones. In particular, this model did not explain why, on 6 September 1634, the 'new model' Swedish forces, under experienced commanders, were annihilated by the traditionalist Spaniards at the battle of Nördlingen. And it was indeed annihilation: out of 25,000 Swedish and German Protestant troops, at least 15,000 were killed and a further 4000 (including the Swedish Commander, Gustav Horn) were captured.

These doubts were presented in the last chapter of my thesis, and it was therefore with some trepidation that I learned that Professor Roberts himself had been chosen to be my external examiner. But I need not have worried. He accepted most of my criticisms, and even suggested where I might look for further supporting evidence. He also recommended that the last chapter of the thesis should be published separately as an article, and not as part of *The Army of Flanders and the Spanish Road*. I accepted the second part of his advice at once, but did nothing to reinforce my critique of the 'military revolution' until, six years later, I was invited to give one of a series of lectures on 'War and Society' which was being organized at King's College, London. The following article is almost exactly the same as the text which I gave in the lecture theatre at King's in November 1974.

The 'Military Revolution, 1560-1660' – a Myth?

'The sixteenth century constitutes a most uninteresting period in European military history,' wrote Sir Charles Oman in 1937, and no one then dared to disagree with him. Today, however, few historians would endorse his verdict. The early modern period has come to be seen as a time of major change in warfare and military organization, as an era of 'military revolution'. This shift in historical perspective is mainly the work of one man: Michael Roberts, until recently Professor of History at the Queen's University of Belfast. His inaugural lecture, entitled 'The Military Revolution, 1560-1660' and delivered at Belfast in January 1955, was an undisguised manifesto proclaiming the originality, the importance, and the historical singularity of certain developments in the art of war in post-Renaissance Europe. Now most inaugural lectures, for better or worse, seem to fade into the seamless web of history, leaving little trace; yet Professor Roberts's inaugural is still quoted time after time in textbooks, monographs, and articles. His conclusions, as far as I know, have never been questioned or measured against the new evidence which has come to light in the twenty years or so which have elapsed since he wrote. Such an examination is the aim of this paper.[1]

Roberts's 'military revolution' took place between 1560 and 1660 in four distinct areas. First and foremost came a 'revolution in tactics': certain tactical innovations, although apparently minor, were 'the efficient cause of changes which were really revolutionary'.[2] The principal innovation in the infantry was (he claimed) the eclipse of the prevailing technique of hurling enormous squares of pikemen at each other in favour of linear formations composed of smaller, uniform units firing salvos at each other; likewise the cavalry, instead of trotting up to the enemy, firing, and trotting back again (the *caracole*), was required to charge, sabres in hand, ready for the kill. According to Roberts, these new battle procedures had far-reaching logistical consequences. They required troops who were highly trained and disciplined, men who would act as cogs in a machine; and the cogs had to learn how to march in step and how to perform their movements in perfect unison – they even had to dress the same.[3] Individual prodigies of valour and skill were no longer required. Of course all this training cost money; and, because the troops had acquired their expertise at the government's expense, Roberts claimed that it was no longer economical for armies to be demobilized when the campaigning ended: the trained men had to be retained on a permanent footing. The new tactics, he argued, thus gave rise inexorably to the emergence of the standing army, and the first to pioneer these tactical reforms – and therefore one of the first to create a standing army in Europe – was Maurice of Nassau, captain-general of the army of the Dutch Republic.[4]

A 'revolution in strategy' formed the second major strand of Roberts's thesis. With the new soldiers, it proved possible to attempt more ambitious strategies: to campaign with several armies simultaneously and to seek decisive battles without fear that the inexperienced troops would run away in terror. Gustavus Adolphus of Sweden, victor of the Breitenfeld and conqueror of Germany, certainly put these new strategic concepts into effect; according to Roberts, he was the first.

A third component of the military revolution theory was a 'prodigious increase in the scale of warfare in Europe' between 1560 and 1660. The new strategy, Roberts pointed out, required far more troops for its successful execution: an articulated force of five armies operating simultaneously according to a complex plan would need to be vastly more numerous than a single army under the old order. Fourth and finally, this prodigious numerical increase dramatically accentuated the impact of war on society. The greater destructiveness, the greater economic costs, and the greater administrative challenge of the augmented armies made war more of a burden and more of a problem for the civilian population and their rulers than ever before.

These four assertions form the kernel of the military revolution theory. There was, of course, a great deal more –

87

the development of military education and military academies,[5] the articulation of positive 'laws of war',[6] the emergence of an enormous literature on war and war studies,[7] and so on – but the four essential ingredients of the theory were tactics, strategy, army size, and overall impact. Have these assertions been modified in any way by recent research?

In the first place, it has become clear that the choice of the year 1560 as the starting point of the military revolution was unfortunate. Many of the developments described by Roberts also characterized warfare in Renaissance Italy: professional standing armies, regularly mustered, organized into small units of standard size with uniform armament and sometimes uniform dress, quartered sometimes in specially constructed barracks, were maintained by many Italian states in the fifteenth century. Machiavelli's oft-quoted jibe about the campaigns of the *condottieri* – that they were 'commenced without fear, continued without danger, and concluded without loss' – was unfair and untrue. The armies of Renaissance Italy were efficient and effective; and the French, German, Swiss, and Spanish invaders had to adopt the methods of the *condottieri*, both in attack and defence, before they could make real headway against them. To a remarkable degree, as we shall see, the character of early modern European warfare, even down to its vocabulary, came direct from Renaissance Italy.[8]

There is no doubt, however, that Maurice of Nassau and his cousin William-Louis made some important tactical innovations in the army of the Dutch Republic. They reduced the size of their tactical units and increased significantly the number of officers and under-officers; they increased the number of musketeers and arquebusiers (the 'shot') in each unit; and they introduced the classical technique of the 'countermarch', whereby successive ranks of musketeers advanced, fired, and retired to reload in sequence. The latter was certainly new, but, until the introduction of a more accurate musket which could also be swiftly reloaded, the countermarch was of limited practical value.[9] Moreover, Maurice's other tactical innovations, described by Roberts, derived at least some of their 'revolutionary' character from a rather unfair portrayal of the 'prerevolutionary' warfare of the earlier sixteenth century. The Spanish army in particular, which Roberts used as a foil to the tactical reforms of Maurice of Nassau, was a force of impressive military efficiency. By the 1560s Spanish infantry on active service was normally made up of small, uniform companies of between 120 and 150 men, grouped into *tercios* (or regiments) of between 1200 and 1500 men.[10] The Spanish infantry normally contained a heavy concentration of shot – it was the Duke of Alva who pioneered the introduction of musketeers into every company in the 1550s – and in the 1570s there were at least two companies which consisted solely of shot in every *tercio* on active service.[11] Throughout the Spanish army, as elsewhere, the basic tactical and administrative unit was the company: men were raised, trained, and paid in companies, not in regiments and not as individuals. Although the Spanish army had no larger formal tactical units like the brigades or battalions of the Swedish army, it was Spanish practice to group a number of experienced companies together for special assignments to form a task force, known as an *escuadrón*, which might number anywhere between 600 and 3000 men, depending on the task to be performed.[12] This flexible, informal arrangement for the infantry proved highly satisfactory. The Spanish cavalry, too, was impressive in action. It comprised mainly companies of light horse, each numbering between 60 and 100 troopers, some of them lancers and some of them mounted gunmen (*arcabuceros a caballo*). In battle, as at Gembloux in 1578, their intervention was decisive; at other times they policed the countryside with ruthless efficiency. Dressed in turbans like the Turkish light horse, whose tactics were successfully emulated, the Spanish cavalry was as feared and as formidable as the *tercios*.

Spain's more permanent armies were also distinguished by a sophisticated panoply of military institutions and ancillary services. In the Netherlands and Lombardy, at least after 1570, there was a special military treasury, an elaborate and autonomous hierarchy of judicial courts, a well-developed system of medical care – with a permanent military teaching hospital, mobile field-surgery units, and resident doctors in every regiment – and a network of chaplains under a chaplain-general covering the entire army.[13] Some, if not all, of this administrative superstructure was also to be found attached to the permanent Spanish forces in Naples and Sicily. Sixteenth-century Spain also had a complex training scheme for its men. In the words of an envious English observer of 1590, 'Their order is, where the Warres are present, to supplie their Regiments being in Action with the Garrisons out of his dominions and provinces; before they dislodge, *besonios* supply their place; raw men as we tearme them. By these means he traines his *besonios* and furniseth his Armies with trained Souldiers.'[14] From at least the 1530s Spanish recruits were sent initially not to the front line but to the garrisons of Italy or North Africa, where they learned the rudiments of arms drill and combat discipline for a year or two before leaving for active service. Their places were then taken by another generation of recruits.[15] It was an extremely efficient system, and it helps to explain the remarkable military calibre, reputation, and track record of the *tercios*. It was they, after all, who routed the 'new model' Swedish army at Nördlingen in 1634.

Lest this should seem like special pleading from a starry-eyed student of Spanish history, one could point equally effectively to the Austrian Habsburgs, who introduced much the same system for their permanent armies on the Croatian and Hungarian borders with the Ottoman empire during the 1570s.[16] And, if even that were not enough, there are the military organizations of France, England, and the Italian states during the fifteenth century: all developed permanent standing armies which were highly trained; seasoned in garrisons before they went to the front; capable of fighting in linear formations as well as in columns or squares; organized into small, self-contained tactical units; and controlled by a special military administration.[17] The simple fact is that, wherever a situation of permanent or semi-permanent war existed, whether the Hundred Years' War of the later Middle Ages or the Thirty Years' War of the seventeenth century, one finds, not surprisingly, standing

90

armies, greater professionalism among the troops, improvements in military organization, and certain tactical innovations. Gustavus Adolphus in the 1620s and Maurice of Nassau in the 1590s were forced to overhaul their armies dramatically because of the disastrous defeats which their predecessors had suffered in the preceding years. For inspiration, it is true, they turned in part to classical writers like Frontinus, Vegetius, and Aelian; but, like other rulers, they also turned to other more successful military practitioners, especially to the generals of Spain. Three of the best English military writers of the reign of Elizabeth – William Garrard, Humphrey Barwick, and Sir Roger Williams – had all served in the Spanish Army of Flanders for several years and held up its practices as examples to others.[18] The war in the Low Countries was a seminary in which many of the great commanders of the German Thirty Years' War and the English Civil War were formed.[19] It is no accident that a large part of the military vocabulary of northern Europe should have come from Spanish.[20]

The Dutch, however, did make a distinctive contribution of their own. Maurice of Nassau and his cousin were convinced of the need for standardization and uniformity in their forces. In 1599 they secured funds from the States-General to equip the entire field army of the Republic with weapons of the same size and calibre. At about the same time, Count John II of Nassau began work on a new method of military training: the illustrated manual. He analysed each of the different movements required to manipulate the principal infantry weapons, gave each of them a number, and prepared a series of corresponding drawings to show what was required. There were fifteen drawings for the pike, twenty-five for the arquebus, and thirty-two for the musket. In 1606-7 the whole scheme was recast – now there were thirty-two positions for the pike and forty-two for each of the firearms – and a sequence of numbered pictures was engraved and published under Count John's supervision: Jacob de Gheyn's *Wapenhandelingen van roers, musquetten ende spiessen* [Arms drill with arquebus, musket and pike] (Amsterdam, 1607). The book went rapidly through numerous

91

editions in Dutch, French, German, English, even Danish; there were pirated and plagiarized versions; there were many subsequent attempts to produce rival manuals (of which the best were Johan Jakob von Wallhausen's *Kriegskunst zu Fusz* of 1615, Henry Hexham's *Principles of the Art Militarie* of 1637, and Jean de Lostelneau's *Mareschal de bataille* of 1647). The sudden popularity of the new genre of military textbook is explained by the tactical changes of the sixteenth century. The evolution from monolithic, massed pike formations to articulated combinations of pike and shot, which made a more elaborate hierarchy of ranks necessary, placed an increasing burden on the junior officers and under-officers. They became the crucial links between the army commanders and the small tactical units; they had to control, discipline and drill their men. It was to answer their needs that de Gheyn and the rest produced their drill books. The situation depicted in a picture of a company of the Amsterdam militia in 1625, painted by W. van den Valckert, must have been fairly typical: the captain is shown standing with de Gheyn's *Wapenhandelinghe* actually open in front of him, trying to work out what to do next! The Dutch may not have invented the 'revolution' in tactics, but they certainly invented the best way of coping with some of its effects.[21]

There is thus room for doubt concerning the novelty of the tactics and the standing armies introduced by Prince Maurice and King Gustavus. There is also some question about the originality of Gustavus's strategy. Again, Roberts starts with a damaging critique of the practice of sixteenth-century generals: 'The sterility of warfare in Europe, in the time of Prince Maurice, is the accurate measure of the strategic thinking of the age.' And in another passage, 'Strategic thinking withered away; war eternalized itself.'[22] Now the crucial influence on the evolution of strategic thinking in the sixteenth century was the appearance of an entirely new type of defensive fortification: the *trace italienne*, a circuit of low, thick walls punctuated by quadrilateral bastions. In the course of the fifteenth century it became obvious that the improvements in gun founding and artillery had rendered the high, thin walls of the Middle Ages quite indefensible. A

92

brief cannonade from the 'bombards' brought them crashing down. The reason why the kingdom of Granada fell to the Christians so easily in the 1480s, when it had resisted successfully for seven centuries, lay in the fact that Ferdinand and Isabella were able to bring a train of almost one hundred and eighty siege guns against the Moorish strongholds.[23] The English possessions in France were likewise reconquered in the 1430s and 1440s largely by Charles VII's artillery; at Castillon in 1453, the big guns even won a battle. The initiative in warfare now lay with the aggressor, and, not surprisingly, by 1500 every major European state possessed a powerful artillery park for use against its neighbours or against its dissident subjects. Military architects in Italy, where siege warfare was most common, were the first to experiment with new techniques of fortification which might withstand shelling; and Professor John Hale has traced the evolution of the bastion defence in Italy from about 1450, when it made its first appearance, until the 1520s, when it was fully fledged. It was a development which 'revolutionized the defensive-offensive pattern of warfare', because it soon became clear that a town protected by the *trace italienne* could not be captured by the traditional methods of battery and assault. It had to be encircled and starved into surrender.[24] The French military writer Fourquevaux declared in 1548 that towns whose fortifications were more than thirty years old, that is, which were built before the age of bastions, hardly deserved to be called fortifications at all. 'We must confesse,' echoed Sir Roger Williams, 'Alexander, Caeser, Scipio, and Haniball, to be the worthiest and famoust warriors that euer were; notwithstanding, assure your selfe, . . . they would neuer haue . . . conquered Countries so easilie, had they been fortified as Germanie, France, and the Low Countries, with others, haue been since their daies.'[25] There was therefore a scramble among the great powers to build the new 'miracle' defences wherever there existed a risk of attack: in Lombardy, in Hungary, in the Low Countries, along the south coast of England, and elsewhere.

As it happened, these areas were all large plains – 'continental islands', to use the language of Fernand Braudel –

where a few great towns dominated the countryside. Whoever controlled the towns controlled the countryside; and therefore in all these areas war became a struggle for strongholds, a series of protracted sieges. Battles were often irrelevant in these areas unless they helped to determine the outcome of a siege. Even total victory in the field did not necessarily compel the well-defended towns to surrender: they could continue to resist, as did St Quentin after the famous battle in 1557, or as the towns of Holland and Zealand were to do after 1572, either until they were starved into submission or until the enemy gave up through exhaustion.[26] Naturally, since the *trace italienne* was introduced in those areas most likely to be fought over, and since most of the fighting of the sixteenth century did in fact take place there, it is true to say with Roberts that most generals, like Maurice of Nassau, 'had no ambition whatever to fight battles'. This proves only that they had a sound grasp of strategic realities. But whenever wars happened to occur in areas where the *trace italienne* was absent – in Italy before 1529, in central France during the religious wars, in the British Isles, or in Germany – then battles were both frequent and important: Pavia in 1525, Mühlberg in 1547, Ivry in 1590, and so on. It was even possible in such areas to operate a conscious *Vernichtungsstrategie*.[27] It was also true that, where bastions were absent and battles more frequent, cavalry was more prominent: on Europe's steppe frontier, for example, with the cossacks and stradiots, or during the civil wars in Germany and England, with the furious charges of Pappenheim, Prince Rupert, and Cromwell's Ironsides. But even in these theatres of conflict, battles were seldom 'decisive', in the sense that they brought the wars to an immediate end. Neither the Breitenfeld, nor Lützen, nor Wittstock, nor Jankow – four resounding victories for the 'new-model' Swedish army – terminated the Thirty Years' War. The two battles of the war which came nearest to achieving 'total' victory were, as it happened, won by Spanish 'old-style' forces: the White Mountain in 1620 and Nördlingen in 1634.

The generals of the seventeenth century, like their predecessors, were compelled to respect the dictates of military geography. When in 1632 the imperial army under Wallenstein retreated into the Alte Veste, a specially prepared stronghold near Nuremburg, Gustavus Adolphus was compelled to expend a great deal of time, men, and money in trying to starve them out. And in the end he failed. In France, Vauban diligently erected a chain of modern defences all around the sensitive and exposed frontiers of the country. Coehoorn did the same in the United Provinces. These fortifications of the later seventeenth century, vast star-shaped complexes which kept the besieging artillery out of range of its prey, continued to be of strategic importance until the 1860s. Wherever they existed, they made battles irrelevant – and therefore unusual. Throughout modern times, as in the Middle Ages, military geography shaped strategy.[28]

There is thus some doubt about the significance of both the tactical and the strategic aspects of Roberts's military evolution. But there is absolutely no doubt about its third constituent: the growth in army size. Between 1530 and 1710 there was a ten-fold increase both in the total numbers of armed forces paid by the major European states and in the total numbers involved in the major European battles. Table I demonstrates the inflation in armies – which was paralleled in navies – and the rise in combatants is obvious when one compares battles like Pavia (1525) and Nieuwpoort (1600), with 10,000 combatants on either side, and a battle like Malplaquet (1709), with 200,000 men involved.

If, however, we can accept Roberts's assertion about military manpower growth, we cannot *a priori* accept his explanation of it. It cannot stem, as he thought, from the tactical and strategic innovations of Maurice of Nassau and Gustavus Adolphus: first, because these modifications were not so new; second, and more important, because the rapid and sustained growth in army size predated them. The Emperor Charles V had 55,000 men at the siege of Metz in 1552, long before Maurice was born, and the Spanish Army of Flanders already numbered 86,000 men in 1574, when the prince was only six years old. There were, in fact, certain

95

Spain and the Netherlands

Table 1: Increase in Military Manpower, 1470-1710

Date	Spanish Monarchy	Dutch Republic	France	England	Sweden	Russia
1470s	20,000		40,000	25,000		
1550s	150,000		50,000	20,000		
1590s	200,000	20,000	80,000	30,000	15,000	
1630s	300,000	50,000	150,000		45,000	35,000
1650s	100,000		100,000	70,000	70,000	
1670s	70,000	110,000	120,000		63,000	130,000
1700s	50,000	100,000	400,000	87,000	100,000	170,000

Sources: For figures on Spain, *Castilla y la conquista del reino de Granada* (Valladolid, 1967), p. 159; G. Parker, *The Army of Flanders*, p. 6; and H. Kamen, *The War of Succession in Spain 1700-1715* (London, 1969), pp. 59-60 (for metropolitan Spain only). For the Dutch Republic, F. J. G. Ten Raa and F. de Bas, *Het Staatsche leger, 1568-1795*, 6 vols. (Breda 1911-18), vol. I, passim. For France, Contamine, *Guerre, état et société* pp. 313-18; F. Lot, *Recherches sur les effectifs des armées françaises de. guerres d'Italie aux guerres de religion (1494-1562)* (Paris, 1962), pp. 135-88; L. André, *Michel le Tellier* (Paris, 1906), pp. 271-328; and H. Méthivier, *Le Siècle de Louis XIV* (Paris, 1962), p. 68. For England C. G. Cruikshank, *Elizabeth's Army* (Oxford, 1966). passim; C. Firth, *Cromwell's Army* (London, 1962), pp. 34-5; and R. E. Scouller *The Armies of Queen Anne* (Oxford, 1966), Ch. 3. For Sweden, M. Roberts, *The Early Vasas: A History of Sweden, 1523-1611* (Cambridge 1968), pp. 399-404; and C. Nordmann, 'L'armée suédoise au XVII⁰ siècle', *Revue du Nord*, LIV (1972), pp. 133-47. For Russia, *New Cambridge Modern History*, V (Cambridge, 1964), p. 577.

other tactical changes which cleared the way for the 'prodigious increase' in army size.

For most of the Middle Ages, the principal arm in any military force was the heavy cavalry, made up of fully armed knights on horseback, three hundredweight of mounted metal apiece, moving at speed. The knights were clumsy expensive, and scarce; but they were capable of winning great victories: Antioch (1098), Bouvines (1214), and Roos beke (1382), for example. There were also, however, disastrous defeats, especially in the fourteenth and fifteenth centuries when it was discovered that a heavy cavalry charge could regularly be stopped either by volleys of arrows or by a forest of pikes. Later it was found that pikemen could be used offensively to charge other groups of pikemen, once the mounted knights had been impaled and disposed of. The

96

victories of the Swiss infantry against Charles the Rash of Burgundy in the 1470s wrote the lesson large, and in the Italian wars the infantry component in every army became steadily more numerous and more decisive. Charles VIII's army in 1494 comprised about 18,000 men, half of them cavalry; Francis I's army in 1525 comprised some 30,000 men, one-fifth of them cavalry. The number of horsemen had decreased both absolutely and relatively.[29] This shift in emphasis from horse to foot was crucial for army size. Whereas there was a limit to the number of knights who could manage to equip themselves and their horses ready for a charge, there was none to the number of ordinary men who could be enlisted and issued a pike, sword, and helmet. A pikeman's basic equipment cost little more than his wages for a week, and in some cases even this paltry sum could be deducted from the soldier's pay.

Thanks to the triumph of the pikemen, therefore, it became possible for governments to recruit, arm, and train an unlimited number of men. The road to unrestrained military increase lay wide open. But it only lay open. There was nothing in all this which actively *compelled* an army to augment its numbers. Indeed, over fifty years were to pass between the final defeat of Charles the Rash in 1477 and the first major increase in army size in the 1530s, an increase necessitated by the vast number of men required to starve out a town defended by the *trace italienne*. After this period of growth came four decades of stagnation: there was no further increase in army size until the 1580s. No government could dream of bringing larger concentrations of troops into action, for the simple reason that none possessed the organization necessary to mobilize, pay, and supply such a force. By the middle of the sixteenth century, there were only ten cities in all of Europe with a population in excess of 60,000. Before the promise of the Swiss achievement could be fully realized, before the threshold of medieval army size could be crossed, there had to be important changes in the financial and administrative resources of the European states.[30]

The growth of military manpower depended not only on internal factors like tactics but also on a number of extrinsic factors, totally unrelated to the art of war itself. Perhaps four can be identified as critical. In the first place, there clearly had to be governments capable of organizing and controlling large forces. It is interesting to note that the major waves of administrative reform in western Europe in the 1530s and 1580s and at the end of the seventeenth century coincided with major phases of increase in army size.[31] On the one hand, the growth of a bureaucracy was necessary to create larger armies; on the other, it was necessary to control them. The rapid numerical expansion of the early seventeenth century forced some decentralization: governments used entrepreneurs to raise their soldiers, sailors, and (in the case of the Mediterranean states) their galley fleets. It has been estimated that between 1631 and 1634 there were some 300 military enterprisers raising troops in Germany alone, ranging from Albrecht von Wallenstein, Duke of Friedland and imperial commander-in-chief (who raised entire armies under contract) to minor gentry from Switzerland and the Tyrol (who raised single companies or even single squadrons). It was the same story in most areas of Europe, even in countries like Spain, where troop raising had been a jealously guarded royal monopoly in the sixteenth century.[32] However, it is important to note that, in all Europe, only Oliver Cromwell managed to emulate the generals of Rome or the *condottieri* of Italy and wrest political power from his civilian employers. Elsewhere, if we except the Ottoman empire with its janissaries, governments always maintained a close rein on their commanders and kept their armies under constant surveillance. War departments proliferated in every country, squeezing out military entrepreneurs and other middlemen and establishing a direct link with every soldier in the army. Detailed records of the troops began to be kept, so that the only surviving historical trace for hundreds of thousands of men in early modern times is their army pay-sheets.[33]

The numerical expansion of armies was also dependent on certain elementary technological improvements. In order to supply 50,000 men (and camp followers) on the march, it had to be possible to concentrate enough ovens to produce

50,000 loaves of bread a day; enough water, wine, and beer had to be concentrated for them all to drink; and there had to be enough carts and horses to carry their baggage (which might amount to half a ton per man!) and enough tents, beds, or shelters to accommodate at least the officers.[34] Only in the later sixteenth century did it become possible to meet these basic human needs on a grand scale. Another elementary technological frontier to be crossed concerned roads. It was not possible to move large concentrations of troops at speed before the seventeenth century because there were no roads outside Italy which were capable of carrying a large army, its supply train, and its artillery. In the sixteenth century, even on a route used regularly by troops, like the 'Spanish Road' from Lombardy to Luxemburg, it was necessary to build new causeways in the mountains and across marshes and to construct special bridges over rivers and streams for every military expedition – once every two years on average – because, after the troops had passed, everything was allowed to revert to its former state.[35] Only in the later seventeenth century did governments see the need, and possess the means, to construct and maintain permanent military highways: Charles XI of Sweden and Louis XIV of France led the way during the 1680s. In the eighteenth century roads even began to be used as an instrument of imperialism, as they had once been by the Roman, Chinese and Inca empires, with General Wade's network of military roads, laid out mainly between 1726 and 1767, to tame the Scottish highlands.

However, for all this one needed money, and here we come to two other, and perhaps more important, extrinsic limits to military growth. First, there had to be a certain level of wealth in society before heavy and prolonged military expenditure could be supported; second, there had to be ways of mobilizing that wealth. It would seem that between 1450 and 1600 the population of Europe almost doubled, and in some areas it more than doubled; and there is little doubt that, over the same period, there was a notable increase in the total wealth of Europe. After about 1660 both population and wealth began to increase again. This new prosperity was tapped everywhere by taxation, either indirectly through

99

excise duties upon consumer goods or directly by a variety of levies on land, capital, and (very rarely) income. Government revenues increased everywhere in the sixteenth century, delving ever deeper into the pockets and purses of the taxpayers. However, no government could pay for a prolonged war out of current taxation: the income which sufficed for a peacetime establishment could in no way prove equal to the unpredictable but inevitably heavy expenses of a major campaign. The state therefore had to spread the costs of each war over a number of peaceful years, either by saving up in anticipation (as Queen Elizabeth did before she decided to make war on Spain in 1585) or by spending in advance the income of future years with the aid of loans from bankers and merchants. With a small army this might not be such a great problem – France appears to have financed her Italian wars from 1494 until 1529 with few ill effects[36] – but in the sixteenth century the problem was very different because, apart from the growth in numbers and the greater duration of wars (which of course increased the overall cost), there was also the 'price revolution', which meant that it cost far more to put a soldier into the field in 1600 than it had in 1500. This fact naturally did not escape the notice of contemporaries: 'If comparison were made between the present cost to His Majesty [Philip II] of the troops who serve in his armies and navies and the cost of those of the Emperor Charles V [his father], it will be found that, for an equal number of men, three times as much money is necessary today as used to be spent then.'[37] Written in 1596, this was, if anything, an underestimate; but it was indisputable that each war cost more than the preceding one and that for Spain, involved in so many long-enduring conflicts, the progression was particularly alarming (see Figure 1). Fortunately for Habsburg imperialism, the Spanish crown was able to draw on a relatively efficient financial system which enabled it to borrow (or 'anticipate') the revenues of up to ten years in advance and, by brutal treatment of its lenders, to keep the interest rate down to 7 per cent or less. But even this did not produce all the money required for wars and many of the troops were left unpaid, sometimes for months and sometimes even for years. As a result, Spain's soldiers regularly mutinied for their pay; and mutiny became almost an institution of military life. However, it was an institution shared with other armies. The Dutch army was periodically paralysed by mutinies in the 1580s, as was the Parliamentary army during the English Civil War (especially in 1644 and 1647). Many units of the

Figure 1: Average annual cost of Spain's foreign wars.

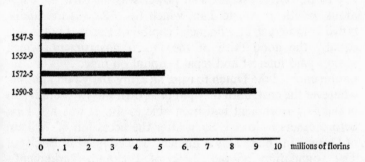

Source: G. Parker, *The Army of Flanders*, pp. 134, n. 2, 287.

Swedish army in Germany mutinied in 1633, dissipating the prestige won by the victories of the Breitenfeld and Lützen, and again in 1635, encouraging many German Protestants to make peace with the Habsburgs. The fact that the second mutiny was called an 'alteration', the term invariably used by the Spanish mutineers to describe their activities, betrayed the parentage of the practice (see p. 242, n. 23 below). The perennial problem for the Swedish, the Spanish, and indeed every government in wartime was money. In the words of an English adviser to the Dutch Republic during their war with Spain: 'The matter of greatest difficulty [in war] . . . is in proportioning the charge of the warres and the nombers of the souldiers to be maynteyned with the contribucions and meanes of the countreys.'[38] It was, above all else, the financial resources of a state which held down the size of its armed forces. If too many troops were engaged, or if they were engaged for too long, mutiny and bankruptcy resulted.

101

It was the Dutch who first perfected techniques of war finance capable of sustaining an enormous army almost indefinitely. The cost of the war with Spain from 1621 until 1648 steadily increased (from an average of 13 million florins in the 1620s to an average of 19 million in the 1640s), but there was not a single mutiny or financial crisis. On the contrary, in an emergency, the Dutch Republic could raise a loan of 1 million florins at only 3 per cent in two days. The key to this effortless financial power was, in part, the enormous wealth of Amsterdam, which by 1650 was the undisputed commercial and financial capital of Europe; but it was equally the good faith of the Dutch government, which always paid interest and repaid capital on time. This combination enabled the Dutch to raise an army and go on fighting, whatever the cost, until they got their own way: something no previous government had been able to do. It was not long before others followed. Soon after the accession of William of Orange in 1689, 'Dutch finance' was adopted in England. The foundation of the Bank of England, Parliament's guarantee of all government loans, and the organization of a sophisticated money market in London made it possible for a British army of unprecedented size – 90,000 men – to fight overseas for years; while in France the credit network of Samual Bernard and other Swiss bankers financed Louis XIV's later wars.[39]

Thanks to all these improvements, by the first decade of the eighteenth century the major wars of Europe involved some 400,000 men on each side, and major battles involved up to 100,000.[40] It therefore comes as something of a surprise to find that the major conflicts of the 1760s and 1780s involved no more – that there was no further growth in army size until the French Revolutionary wars. In the eighteenth century, as in the fifteenth, it seems that the military power of the various European states had reached a threshold. Further economic, political, technological, and financial advances would be required before this new threshold could be crossed in the 1790s.

However, the revolution in military manpower between 1530 and 1710 was extremely important. It certainly had all the significant consequences which Roberts attributed to it: it made war impinge more upon society; it increased the authority of the state (partly at the expense of the citizen); it accentuated social mobility; and it undoubtedly retarded the economic development of most participants (although it stimulated that of many neutrals).[41] In addition, it certainly helped to precipitate the numerous confrontations between governments and the governed which are commonly referred to as the 'general crisis' of the seventeenth century. The 'prodigious increase in the scale of warfare' alone merits the title of 'military revolution' which Roberts bestowed upon it twenty years ago.

It has been suggested that the half-life of major historical theories is roughly ten years; and the fates of Trevor-Roper's 'general crisis', Elton's 'Tudor revolution', and Porshnev's 'popular uprisings' seem to bear this out. By this standard, Roberts's 'military revolution' has lasted well. Hitherto unchallenged, even this extended examination has failed to dent the basic thesis: the scale of warfare in early modern Europe was revolutionized, and this had important and wide-ranging consequences. One can only conclude by wishing the theory and its author many more years of undiminished historical life.

5

Seated one wet day in 1967 in the Archives générales du royaume of Belgium, then uncomfortably housed in an office block in the Galerie Ravenstein while its palatial new premises (more like a temple than an archive) were constructed, I ordered a volume of papers listed in the inventory as 'Military Papers'. It contained letters addressed to the government of the Spanish Netherlands in the 1590s, but I could not at first ascertain who had sent them: the letters were written on good-quality paper, in a smooth italic hand, and were authenticated with a number of different yet intricate seals (see below). They were signed 'Your most attentive servant, I the Electo', and were countersigned, in the best traditions of the Spanish chancery, by a secretary.

Seal of the mutineers   Seal of the mutineers
of Pont-sur-Sambre (1593-5)   of Zichem (1594-6)

Source: AGRB *Audience* 1841/1 (1½ times actual size.)

Suddenly I realized that this bundle of documents, and some others which I later discovered, contained the government's negotiations with the various detachments of the Army of Flanders which had mutinied in protest against their unpaid arrears of wages. I longed to find some further information about these intriguingly sophisticated rebels, but nothing came my way until, some three years later, working in the splendid 'Students' room' in Simancas Castle (the Public Record Office of Spain), I found the rest of the mutineers' papers. I had decided to look at a series of about one hundred fat bundles of financial papers enigmatically labelled 'accounts' in the archive's inventory. I knew that two volumes in the series concerned the Army of Flanders, and I wondered whether some of the others might be related: in fact they contained the complete papers of the Military Audit Office (the *contaduría del sueldo*) of the Spanish Netherlands between 1567 and 1602. The pay-sheets of every individual mutineer, the detailed negotiations for settling each dispute, the ordinary wage records of every unit paid by the Military Treasury over a period of thirty-five years – all of them were there: jumbled, often decaying, but complete.

I suppose that every historian experiences, at least once in his professional career, the sort of tingling excitement in his spine and neck which I felt as I identified one name after another in the documents as soldiers of the Army of Flanders. The feeling is unforgettable, but alas it cannot be communicated to others. By the time the 'finds' are written up in books and articles, they have lost their sparkle and uniqueness. To me, the chapter of *The Army of Flanders and the Spanish Road* which deals with the mutinies is the most satisfying; but it is unlikely that this feeling is shared by others, for no one else shared the lonely yet exciting hours piecing together a part of the past of which no other historian was aware. It was partly to rectify this situation that I wrote the following article, which is really a sustained plea that military revolts should be set in the general context of other popular revolts in early modern times. It was prepared in response to an invitation from Dr Norman Ball, another Simancas veteran, to lecture at the University of Southampton, and it was delivered there in January 1972, and again to the Cambridge Historical Society the following month. It was much improved by comments made by both audiences.

Mutiny and Discontent in the Spanish Army of Flanders, 1572-1607

Anyone who considers European history on a broad front between the 1350s and the 1840s must surely be struck by the large number of revolts and riots, armed seditions and tumults, which at measured intervals paralysed the life of towns and villages all over the continent. At least 130 popular revolts occurred in Provence between 1596 and 1635; almost 500 broke out in Aquitaine between 1590 and 1715; and it was the same in many other areas. In an age which tolerated a high level of interpersonal violence as an everyday occurrence, as a legitimate weapon in a feud or a quarrel, a considerable amount of collective violence was also accepted. Popular revolts, it has been justly observed, were as much a part of pre-industrial European society as strikes are a part of the western world today.[1] They formed, as it were, an institution of European life; and it is an institution which has suffered no shortage of historians to study it. Some areas have been particularly well covered (sixteenth-century Germany by Günther Franz and, more recently, by a team of scholars from the DDR; seventeenth-century France by B. F. Porshnev, R. Mousnier and a host of others; eighteenth-century England by E. P. Thompson and his students from the University of Warwick Centre for Social Studies). Other areas have been relatively neglected until recently (for example Castile and the Netherlands).[2] But all students of early modern collective disorder seem to have overlooked one very common type of popular revolt: the military mutiny.

In the age before permanent, professional standing armies, the difference between soldiers and civilians was often slight: until at least 1630, few soldiers wore uniforms, lived in barracks or underwent prolonged specialist training. Instead they lived, ate and slept in billets in the bosom of the civilian society from which they came and to which, at the end of the war for which they had been recruited, they would return.

Some did not even wait for demobilization: between one-tenth and one-half of the soldiers in every unit in every army deserted in the course of every year.[3] There were therefore a considerable number of ex-soldiers in civilian society, and not a few peasant revolts were made more efficient (and therefore more dangerous) by the presence of deserters and veterans from the army in the ranks of the rebels.[4] So it should come as no surprise to discover that the prevailing patterns of behaviour among those who opposed the military authorities resembled those found in civilian revolts. These similarities are best exemplified in the collective disobedience of the troops maintained by Spain in the Netherlands after 1572. Few fighting forces could boast of as many mutinies or of mutinies better organized than the Army of Flanders, a heterogeneous body of some 70,000 men drawn largely from the Habsburg states in Germany, the Netherlands, Italy and Spain. This army was permanently at war between 1572 and 1607 and during this period it was shaken by no less than forty-six mutinies, mainly concentrated in two cycles: five between 1572 and 1576 and thirty-seven between 1589 and 1607 – an average of over two a year. Some mutinies were relatively insignificant, involving only a hundred men and lasting just a few weeks, but the major military revolts involved three or four thousand men and took a year, and sometimes two or three years, to pacify. These disorders are important for the historian not only because they lay bare the problems and pressures of the soldier's everyday life, but because they could give rise to serious political and domestic repercussions. A major mutiny, for example, might jeopardize the outcome of a war and could provoke unrest and even rebellion at home. Governments were always highly sensitive to the morale of their troops and many a political decision was influenced by the level of discipline (or indiscipline) among the armed forces.

There was already a strong tradition of organized mutiny among the Spanish troops on foreign service: several regiments had mutinied successfully in Italy during the 1520s and in the Netherlands during the 1550s. Sooner or later, when conditions became unbearable, the suggestion would be made that the time for protest had come again. In the middle of the night a group of discontented soldiers (often sworn comrades) would beat the alarm on their drums to assemble the troops and propose a mutiny. This was the critical stage of every sedition. Not all attempts at mutiny succeeded: on a number of occasions the ringleaders miscalculated the feelings of their comrades and were isolated, arrested and shot. For an appeal to mutiny to succeed, there had to be a general consensus among the troops that the proposed disobedience was entirely justified. Normally this meant that major Spanish mutinies only took place at the end of a campaign or after a battle, not before. Thus in April 1574 the High Command feared the outbreak of a mutiny among the Spanish veterans, who were owed three years' arrears of wages, when they were ordered to take the field against the invading army of Count Louis of Nassau. The Spaniards responded well however, and made a forced march of over two hundred miles to Mook, a town on the Maas south of Nijmegen. There, despite acute hunger (they had received no rations for three days), they fought and totally defeated the invaders (whose leaders, including Count Louis, were killed). Only then, as they stood elated on the field of victory, was the decision taken to mutiny for their just arrears – thirty-seven months' back pay. The veterans had performed their obligations to the full; they now felt that it was high time for the government to reciprocate.[5]

Once any group of soldiers had decided to mutiny, the officers and anyone else who would not join the movement were expelled from the camp. Regular officers were allowed to remain only if they agreed to waive their rank and serve on the same footing as everyone else. Troops from other units not caught up in the initial sedition, even those speaking a different language, were always free to join. Thus at the mutiny of Zichem, which began with four hundred Italians in July 1594, thirteen different languages were spoken by the 2800 veterans involved by the time it ended in July 1596. However neither the linguistic dissonance nor the distinctions of class and rank prevented the mutineers from united and purposeful action to achieve their ends.

The mutineers always elected their own officers. There was an *electo* or leader, a council to advise him and commissars to carry out his orders. Every man owed unswerving, blind obedience to these elected chiefs. All insubordination was punished with death.[6] On the whole, the leaders were ordinary soldiers. Some were educated but most were only semi-literate and a few could not even write their names. Almost all came from the rank-and-file. The soldiers did not have enough confidence in the officers and gentleman-rankers who joined the mutiny to entrust their entire destiny to them. Sometimes the *electo* or some of his advisers were NCOs (sergeants or *cabos de escuadra*), men accustomed to command and used to dealing with higher authorities, but often they were just privates with long service and correspondingly long pay-arrears.[7]

Having established their rudimentary political organization the mutineers turned their attention to self-defence. They had to secure control of a strongly fortified town or village, either by suborning its garrison (not a difficult feat when most garrisons were scandalously underpaid) or by direct assault and capture, so that they could safely defy the government without fear of counter-attack. Occupation of a fortified centre, preferably close to a political frontier, also enabled the mutineers to compel the neighbouring countryside to provide regular 'contributions' and food. Next, with defence and future income assured, the *electo* and his advisers got down to the business of negotiating with the government for the satisfaction of their claims. On the whole, these were not unreasonable and they were articulated with a surprising degree of sophistication in lengthy petitions.

First of all we ask and beg Your Excellency to give the order for us to be paid all the arrears of wages which are justly ours.

We ask Your Excellency, for the service of God and the good of all the soldiers, to ask His Majesty . . . [to provide] a wage which will allow the soldiers to feed and clothe themselves, for now the price of everything has increased so excessively that our wages are not enough even to buy food. We ask that while this matter is being discussed with His Majesty, Your Excellency should order victuals to be sold at a reasonable price which will allow the soldiers to live.

[We ask] that no Governor, Colonel or Captain should punish a soldier arbitrarily without the case first being considered by the Judge-Advocate, nor should degrading punishments like flogging be administered if the offence does not merit them.

Many soldiers have suffered and died because there was nowhere for them to be cured when they were sick. Most of them would have recovered if there had been medical assistance. We therefore ask Your Excellency to give us some help in this [and set up a field hospital].

Payment for services rendered, food at a price men could afford, no punishment without trial, basic medical care for soldiers in daily danger of death – these demands of the mutinous Spanish regiments in 1574 were hardly excessive. Their other grievances were equally reasonable. They asked that surgeons and chaplains should be provided to serve with the front-line units 'because many soldiers have died unconfessed for lack of anyone to cure or confess them'; that soldiers captured by the enemy should be exchanged for prisoners-of-war in Spanish hands; and that the arrears of soldiers who died in service should be paid to their next-of-kin.[8]

In all mutinies the payment of overdue wages was the principal point at issue. The amounts involved were certainly substantial. Whereas the wage-arrears claimed in 1647 by the mutineers of the English Parliamentary forces were calculated in weeks, those of the soldiers in the Spanish Netherlands ran into months. The mutineers of Antwerp in 1574, whose grievances are quoted above, were owed over three years' wages. The light cavalry mutinied in 1576 for seventy-two months' arrears – a total of six years' pay. A group of mutineers at Namur in 1594 claimed (with some exaggeration however) that the government owed them 'a hundred months' pay' (see the flysheet on page 114 below). These enormous outstanding arrears were the result of the chaotic structure of the army's finances. In the sixteenth century the Spanish army in the Netherlands very rarely issued a general pay to all its forces. With 70,000 men under arms, it seldom had the money to do so. Instead the government lived from hand to mouth, issuing a month's wages here, two or three months' there, in an effort to keep at least the front-line units content. Inevitably this meant that, for some of the time, some of the units were left with no pay at all. It was in these 'neglected' units that mutinies began.

The government's financial embarrassments also influenced the duration of most mutinies. When the numbers involved in a mutiny ran to two thousand men and more, immediate settlement of the mutineers' claim was out of the question. A special consignment of bullion had to be solicited from the central government in Spain (which at all times provided at least 75 per cent of the army's money). The mutiny of Antwerp in 1574 cost over one million florins to settle (£100,000 sterling at Elizabethan exchange rates). The first mutiny at Diest in 1590-1 cost 750,000 florins, the second in 1599-1601 1.3 million florins and the third in 1606-7 a further million.[9] Amounts of this magnitude were not easy for the central government to find, on top of all its other commitments. It could sometimes take a year. While the army's commanders waited for the money to come from Spain, a sort of interim agreement was worked out. The High Command promised to provide the mutineers with a regular sum (known as the *sustento*) every month until their outstanding arrears could be settled in full. In return the mutineers agreed to stop collecting contributions of their own from the countryside and promised to act as the official garrison of the town they had occupied. They also undertook to come to the assistance of loyal troops if these were in danger. Thus the mutineers of La Chapelle led the forces which relieved the beleaguered garrison of La Fère in 1596, and the mutineers of Diest fought in the forefront at the battle of Nieuwpoort (July 1600). They were still commanded by their *electo* however.

Mutual assistance of this kind sometimes hastened the final settlement of the mutineers' claims, but in a sense it was superfluous. Whether or not there was co-operation, almost every mutiny by troops of the Army of Flanders ended in complete success: each mutineer was paid in full and in cash.

Compared with their financial claims, the other grievances of the mutineers were easily dealt with. All demanded a full and free pardon for their actions during the mutiny; some asked to transfer to another unit (perhaps to escape retribution at the hands of their officers), while others demanded a safe-conduct to leave the Netherlands with their just rewards. Even the last presented no problem: the High Command was only too pleased to be rid of men who had displayed a talent for organizing and directing discontent. There were also the specific grievances (as in 1574-5, noted above), calling for the provision of cheap food, for a proper judicial system to protect the troops against the arbitrary power of their officers, for a hospital, field medicine and chaplains. The justice of these grievances was recognized and they were redressed by the High Command during the 1580s. A regular network of military judges and special courts grew up under a Judge-Advocate-General while a hierarchy of chaplains was instituted under a Vicar-General. At the same time a permanent military hospital was opened at Mechelen (it had 330 sick-beds by the 1630s) and each regiment was provided with a team of surgeons and barbers. In the 1590s the troops began to receive their daily bread (or rather a three-pound loaf every two days) and their clothes on credit, the cost being subsequently deducted from their wages. These welfare services were established largely on the initiative of Alexander Farnese, the prince of Parma, and they were important. They answered many of the complaints of the first generation of mutineers. However they left virtually untouched the central grievance: unpaid wages. Revolts among the troops therefore continued to occur, and they continued to last a long time.[10]

This longevity of the mutinies of the Army of Flanders posed a number of special problems for the troops involved. Above all they had to take steps to secure their internal discipline and morale, and to display to the outside world their corporate solidarity and their capacity to remain on strike until their demands were met. This was not easy. However justified and sophisticated the mutineers' behaviour might seem, the army's commanders remained convinced that they were dealing with 'lackeys and labourers', 'canaille', 'pay-grabbers and vagabonds', 'the vilest and most despicable people in the kingdom', 'low-born people who must be frightened and chastised for the sake of the future' and so on. The motives of such men were naturally assumed to be the basest possible: 'They do not mutiny through privation but for the hell of it and to steal whatever is going' wrote one observer; '[In time] necessity turns to corruption ... [and the soldiers] mutiny many times rather because they want to do so than because they have any just cause for it' wrote another.[11] There was no lack of evidence to give support to this hostile view. There were indeed certain soldiers who mutinied almost once a year to secure their wage-arrears, while many had been involved in more than three mutinies during their military career by 1609 (when they were all expelled from the army). In every mutiny there were also extremists. Their influence was responsible for some of the violence and some of the threatening flysheets which appeared in the early stages of each disturbance – the minatory *cartel* of 1594 printed overleaf is a good example of the genre.

Yet in the end almost everyone paid tribute to the discipline and self-control of the mutineers. With a few devastating exceptions (like the sack of Aalst and Antwerp in 1576) there was little unprovoked violence and even the most rapacious and sadistic officers were left relatively unscathed by their men. The *electo* of almost every mutiny published and enforced a strict legal code known as the Ordinance. The mutineers of Pont-sur-Sambre in 1593, Italians and Walloons, issued an Ordinance of twenty-one clauses on the first day of their mutiny, imposing severe penalties for theft and assault, for luxury and blasphemy.[12] No wilful damage to persons or property in the neighbourhood of the mutineers' camp was permitted; instead a careful assessment of local resources was made and a contribution-system organized, payable fortnightly in cash to the mutineers' treasurer.[13] The same strict discipline characterized most of the mutineers' military

Source: AGS, *Estado* 608 fo. 32. This is the only original *cartel* (fly-sheet) written by mutineers which is known to have survived. It was sent by the army's commanders to Spain as an indication of the low morale of the troops. A good deal of the menace lies in the child-like script of the soldier who wrote it. Very roughly translated it reads:

> They owe us a hundred pays and it seems to me that they don't care about us. Let them not be shocked at what they may see [if we revolt] since they treat us this way and don't pay us who work so hard. They even drag out from one month to the next the miserable hunger they impose upon us. They load up the donkey so much that they have to do it with kicks. By God's life I swear that those who are nearest must pay for it, since they take so little thought for us.

The Spanish text reads:

> Cien pagas nos deven i me parece que no hacen caso de nosotros no se espanten por cosas que uiren pus ansi nos tratan pu(e)s que no nos pagan lo que tanto trabajamos aun de una miser[i]a hanbre que nos dan nos la van alargando de mes a mes tanto cargan al asno que a coces echan la carga que por uida de dios que nos lo an de pagar los que mas cerca estuuieren pues tan poco se aquerdan de nosotros juro+
> ++

enterprises. Marching under their elected leaders and fighting beneath their own banner, they were a match for anyone. On occasion they displayed suicidal courage: at Antwerp in 1576 (the 'Spanish Fury') and again at Tienen in 1604 the mutineers, without waiting to make a breach with artillery, simply made a furious charge with scaling ladders on the walls of the obstreperous town. No officer would have dared to ask his men to undertake such a murderous mission.[14] As Cardinal Bentivoglio, papal nuncio in the Netherlands, grudgingly affirmed: 'Never has disobedience been seen which produced greater obedience.'[15]

A considerable part of the self-restraint and the foolhardy courage stemmed from the mutineers' conviction that they were right. A sense of the patent justice of their claims pervades almost all their known writings. The letters sent in their names to the government, the *carteles* or flysheets they circulated among themselves, the pamphlets they published all emphasized the righteousness of their cause. 'Anyone can see that we ask only for what is just and for what we so richly deserve' ran a flysheet composed by the mutineers of Antwerp in 1574 (they were owed thirty-seven months' wages at the time). These mutineers even devised their own slogan: 'Let us say with a loud voice that four-letter word which sounds so sweet in the ears of poor soldiers who have served so well: *TODO, TODO, TODO* (all, all, all).'[16] These men knew that they had earned their pay. They believed that their arduous and dangerous service over the years entitled them to a living wage and gave them the right to live.

The same sense of legitimacy underlay the self-confident tone which the mutineers adopted in their formal contacts with the outside world. To begin with, each mutiny had its own secretary who drafted the *electo*'s epistles and orders, carefully retaining a copy for the mutineers' archive. The secretary was also custodian of the official seal of the mutiny, used to authenticate correspondence, which usually bore some symbolic emblem or motto. Thus the mutineers of Zichem in 1594 had a seal which showed a queen bee followed by a swarm of drones encircled by the inscription *MENS EADEM OMNIBUS* ('the same mind in all)'. The three thousand mutineers of Hoogstraten in 1602 went even further and commissioned a special banner, inappropriately displaying the Virgin and Child, with the slogan *PRO FIDE CATHOLICA ET MERCEDE NOSTRA* ('for the Catholic faith and our reward'). They also dressed in green to distinguish themselves from the red badges of Spain and the orange of the States-General, they printed a pamphlet in several languages to justify their actions to the world and, like the mutineers of Zichem before them, they styled themselves 'The Republic of Hoogstraten'.[17] By such means the mutineers

115

attracted the attention of contemporaries – even playwrights: the mutineers of the 1590s were the subject of an entire play by Luis Vélez de Guevara (*Los amotinados de Flandes*, written in 1633) – and they earned the respect of their superiors. The government felt obliged to address its correspondence to 'The magnificent gentlemen, the honourable soldiers of the mutinied regiments', while abject commanders began their letters with engaging paternalism, 'Magnificent and honoured sons', and concluded, 'Your good father to love and serve you'. The mutineers thus achieved an ambition of the humble and the humiliated of all societies: they were acknowledged to be 'somebody'.[18]

Yet all this ostentation was a means not an end. Liable to attack by forces still loyal to the government, sometimes even driven to seek asylum with the Dutch, the mutineers valued every artifice which might bolster their morale and mpress the government with their collective solidarity. The mutineers of Hoogstraten or Zichem did not want to organize an independent city-state: they just wanted to be paid. Payment in full of outstanding wages was invariably followed by an immediate 'return to work'.

Like most civilian revolts of the early modern period, the military mutinies of the Spanish army reveal no evidence of any revolutionary purpose or politically conscious agitators. There is not a hint that any mutineers dreamed of overturning the established order, none that they even wished to influence the government towards making peace. The military proletariat in ferment with its elected leaders may bear a superficial resemblance to a soviet with its revolutionary committee, but there were no Levellers in the Army of Flanders and no Putney Debates. The mutineers were indeed more like strikers: they wanted to receive the wages they had already earned and a formal promise of better conditions of service in the future.

Nevertheless, the mutinies of the Spanish army in the Netherlands certainly did not lack political significance. Because they tied down the government's élite troops and involved such vast amounts of money, the outbreak of a major military revolt usually paralysed the army for a whole campaign, sabotaging any offensive and jeopardizing the security of loyal but isolated towns. In certain circumstances a mutiny could undermine the very foundations of the government's authority. In 1574 the Spanish Governor-General of the Netherlands, Don Luis de Requesens, lamented that the mutiny of his most seasoned troops at Antwerp called into question the whole basis of Spanish power. Speaking to a confidant,

> He insisted that it was not the prince of Orange who had lost the Low Countries but the soldiers born in Valladolid and Toledo, because the mutineers had driven money out of Antwerp and destroyed all credit and reputation, and he believed that within eight days His Majesty would not have anything left here.[19]

The outbreak of peasant revolts all over the South Netherlands (the consequence of an almost complete harvest failure) appeared to bear out the Governor's pessimistic view, but eventually the discontent died down and Requesens's prophecy was not fulfilled until 1576, in the wake of another major military revolt.

After a siege lasting eight months the Spanish field army forced the surrender of the seaport of Zierikzee in Zealand (21 June 1576). Once again, the troops had manifestly done their duty; now the cry went up for wage-arrears (forty months in some cases). The government in Brussels was in an impossible position. Requesens had died in March and the caretaker administration (the Council of State) which took over had neither the authority nor the funds to control the army. The king of Spain had already declared himself bankrupt (September 1575) and was unable to send any money to the Netherlands. There was thus no means of offering to the troops the pecuniary satisfaction which they desired and deserved – and the troops knew it! In July they abandoned their hard-won conquests in Zealand and streamed south in search of plunder and pay. On 25 July a group of three thousand Spaniards made a surprise attack on the loyal town of Aalst (Alost) in Flanders and sacked it with unusual

117

brutality. The reaction was swift and firm: the very next day the caretaker government published an edict which declared all mutineers to be outlaws who could be killed at will. Peasants in a number of villages were armed by their lords and organized into vigilante groups to protect their communities. Any troops in the neighbourhood were attacked. Stragglers and isolated detachments were regularly ambushed and even full companies of cavalry were set upon. To the propertied classes, total anarchy appeared dangerously near. The States of Brabant held an emergency meeting at Brussels and decided to levy troops on their own authority for protection against the mutineers and the peasants alike. They also summoned the Estates of the other provinces to join them, and within a month the self-appointed States-General had opened formal peace talks at Ghent with representatives from Holland and Zealand, the provinces in revolt since 1572. A tentative agreement to suspend hostilities, taken without reference to the king or the Council of State, was reached on 30 October – the 'Pacification of Ghent'. This made the position of the mutineers critical. Outlawed, attacked and now isolated by a cease-fire, the Spanish veterans decided on a perilous course of action. Only the city of Antwerp was rich enough to satisfy their financial demands and secure enough to guarantee their defence. Therefore on Sunday, 4 November, the Spaniards carried out a surprise attack on the city. Beneath their banner, which displayed Christ on the Cross on one side and the Madonna on the other, the mutineers stormed the city and sacked it. Eight thousand civilians were killed, often in the most barbarous manner, and perhaps one thousand houses were destroyed in this desperate action, known to posterity as the 'Spanish Fury'.[20]

The terrible holocaust perpetrated by 'the soldiers born in Valladolid and Toledo' destroyed the last vestiges of the king's authority in the Netherlands. On 8 November the 'Pacification of Ghent' was ratified by representatives of almost all the provinces of the Low Countries, again without reference to the king, bringing the war to an end. The sack of the richest city in northern Europe convinced every

Netherlander that peace had to be secured immediately and at all costs. Philip II's mutinous troops might have taken Antwerp, but they had lost the Netherlands in doing so.

Fortunately for Spain the circumstances of 1576 were unique. No subsequent group of mutineers repeated the outrages of the Spaniards at Antwerp; never again was a loyal town sacked by the troops who were supposed to be defending it, as Aalst and Antwerp had been. However the collective protests of the troops of the Army of Flanders continued to influence the strategic and political developments of the war. The outbreak of a mutiny among the forces in the field sabotaged the Spanish offensives of 1589, 1593 and 1600; the mutiny of the troops detailed to relieve Groningen in 1594 and Grave in 1599 led to the loss of these important towns; a major mutiny at Diest in 1607 seriously undermined Spain's bargaining position in the negotiations with the Dutch for a cease-fire. Even minor mutinies alarmed the High Command, and with some justice. A number of mutinous garrisons ended their disobedience by selling to the Dutch the places entrusted to their keeping (Crèvecoeur and St André forts north of 's Hertogenbosch in 1600; Ijzendijk and Sta. Clara forts in Flanders in 1604-5) and the government was always frightened that others, starved of their wages, would do the same. There was also the constant fear that a 'general mutiny' of the whole army would break out, as it had in 1576, threatening to bring civil revolution in its wake. Many political decisions were of necessity taken with this threat in mind.[21]

The mutineers of the Army of Flanders by no means stood alone. Similar disorders, of similar sophistication, affected most large military concentrations fighting far from their base. The mutinies of Queen Elizabeth's forces in Ireland and the Netherlands are an obvious parallel; so are those of the Habsburg troops in Hungary during the 'long' Turkish war (1593-1606.)[22] The widespread unrest in the Swedish army in Germany in 1633, 1635 and 1647-8 bore an unusually close resemblance to the mutinies of the Army of Flanders discussed above because, besides the similarity of organiza-

119

tion and aims, they had serious political repercussions: the insubordination of the Swedish troops in the 1630s ruined the prestige won by the victories of Gustavus Adolphus; and in the 1640s the mutinies delayed the signing of the peace of Westphalia.[23] The Polish army which invaded Muscovy in 1609 likewise ruined the political calculations of their masters when they decided to mutiny for their pay-arrears in January 1612 (but in the end they were besieged by the Muscovites until, starving, they ate first grass and then each other; the survivors surrendered at the end of the year). The Polish troops who remained on the home front organized 'military confederations' which for several years terrorized the local inhabitants and produced a constitutional crisis.[24]

Mutinies could also paralyse armies operating at home, although the commoner reaction of discontented soldiers serving in their own localities was desertion.[25] Thus the army of the English Parliament after the first civil war revolted against its conditions of service in 1647: 'Leveller' political and social grievances were prominent among the complaints of the field army (the 'New Model'); economic pressures (above all the delay in paying wage-arrears at a time of high prices) were foremost in the minds of the provincial units. Like the mutinies of the Army of Flanders, the collective disorders of the English provincial armies were organized overwhelmingly by the rank-and-file, not by dissident officers or professional agitators; and they followed a recognizable pattern of behaviour which was on the whole moderate and non-violent, culminating in the presentation of a formal petition demanding the redress of legitimate, limited grievances. Nevertheless, the mutinies seemed likely to produce social anarchy, and the fear of 'clubs and clouted shoes' played an important part in shaping Parliament's attitude towards its discontented troops between 1645 and 1647.[26]

The similarities between this pattern of 'military strike' all across Europe and the moderate demands, the conservative or atavistic motivation, the strict code of behaviour and the self-discipline which characterized popular revolts by civilian groups are obvious. They are surely more important than the differences. If the poor had a 'collective ideology', a 'moral economy', 'an inherited pattern of action with its own objectives and restraints', as E. P. Thompson has suggested,[27] then one would expect the pattern to be common to all revolts of the poor in early modern Europe – whether the participants happened at the time to be soldiers or civilians. Before the nineteenth century, the barriers between civilian and military life were so small that to cut off military history from general history in the field of popular unrest makes no sense at all.

6

This paper, like the other foray into naval history which follows in Chapter 7, was composed for a conference. I was one of a group of historians invited to a symposium held in London in December 1971 to celebrate the quatercentenary of the battle of Lepanto, the only substantial naval victory won by Christians over Moslems in the Mediterranean in early modern times. My brief was to explain how the campaign had been financed, setting Italian besides Spanish sources. After the paper, my colleague Dr Tony Thompson produced a number of documents, of which I was unaware, which complemented the accounts of the paymasters of the Grand Fleet which I had found. It seemed obvious that our knowledge should be pooled, and the following article is the result. Unfortunately, neither the proceedings of the London conference nor those of the international symposium held in Venice in 1971 have been published, and therefore our contributon to the Lepanto debate is rather isolated; however the financial intricacies surrounding any major campaign in early modern Europe were so complex that they seem to merit close study in themselves. If, at the end of this paper, the reader should feel none the wiser, he may take comfort from Philip II himself, who confessed on more than one occasion that he could never manage to understand matters of finance either (see the quotations from the King's letters in G. Parker, *Philip II* (Boston and London, 1978), pp. 123-4).

Lepanto (1571):
the Costs of Victory

The Holy League signed between Spain, Venice, and the Papacy on 25 May 1571, called for a Grand Fleet of 200 galleys, 100 round ships, 50,000 infantry, and 4500 cavalry, with the appropriate artillerymen and pioneers, to campaign for six months. The cost of this apparatus was not difficult for any courtier of 'moderate intelligence' to work out, and the duke of Sessa, one of Spain's foremost naval commanders, actually undertook the calculation as a form of occupational therapy during a period of bed-ridden and gouty idleness some two months before the battle. Sessa put the total for the campaign at 2,700,000 *escudos*, which, divided in the ratio 3:2 as stipulated in the alliance, would have cost Spain about 1.6 and Venice 1.1 million *escudos* – both very substantial sums. In the event, however, they were never paid. The costs of the Lepanto campaign were scaled down, redistributed and in part repudiated, so that ultimately it can be argued that, in real terms, the battle itself cost practically nothing at all.[1]

First there were reductions in time and numbers. The Grand Fleet was only mobilized for five and a half months (1 June to 15 November 1571), and although there were at least 211 Christian galleys and six galeasses in the battle, only twenty-six ships (instead of 100) and only 40,000 soldiers (instead of 54,500) took part. In addition, the papal contingent (twelve galleys and 3000 men) was paid for by the Pope directly, with some help from Florence. These economies brought the overall cost to be shared between Spain and Venice down to about two million *escudos*. A statement of expenses drawn up by the Spanish officials aboard the Fleet on 14 November 1571, put Philip II's actual contribution at 1,226,241 *escudos* (See Table 1).[2]

The accuracy of these figures is, of course, questionable. The account of 14 November was as much a political as a fiscal document. It was drawn up very quickly and in very general terms as a statement of the king's position prior to the settlement of the allied account. It was avowedly an estimate – so many items had passed through the hands of local officials in Naples, Milan, Spain and Sicily, that it was really impossible at that stage to know what provisions and supplies had been allocated to the Fleet, or how much they had cost – and it was an estimate unashamedly inflated in the king's favour. Even the Treasury officials had scruples, scruples which were allayed only by the conviction that the Venetians were not to be trusted an inch either.[3] However,

Table 1: Philip II's Lepanto Budget

		Gross cost of Lepanto	Regular defence cost	Source of Funds			
				SPAIN	NAPLES	SICILY	MILAN
Galleys at 800 escudos/month							
Spain	14 as 16	70,400					
Gian Andrea Doria	11 as 12	55,550					
Paolo Bautista Lomelin	4 ⎫						
Juan Ambrosio de Negron	4 ⎬	44,000					
Jorge de Grimaldo	2 ⎭						
Naples	30 as 31	138,600					
Stefano de Mari	2 ⎫						
Bendineli Sauli	1 ⎭	13,200					
Sicily	10 as 11	50,050					
				169,950	151,800	50,050	
		371,800	371,800				

Spanish, 9700						
Tercios of Naples	79,000					
Sicily	51,000	130,000	79,000			
D. Lope de Figueroa	59,075					
	(44,764)					
D. Miguel de Moncada	51,000	110,075	51,000			
Italian, 6000 in *coronelias* of S. Gonzaga from Lombardy Paolo Sforza from Urbino Count of Sarni from Naples	135,410		(45,410)	(45,000)		(45,000)
1000 from Sicily in 5 cos. 800 from Naples under Tiberio Brancaccio	38,164.5	(21,200)	(16,964.5)	(21,200)		
German, 7300	170,747.5	170,747.5		275,800		
Staff officers	33,731.5	33,731.5				
	618,128.5					
Shipping						
22 *naves*	121,412.5	134,062.5			122,250	
25 *fragates* & 1 *bergantin*	12,650					
Secret costs, postage, hospital services	30,250	30,250				
Artillery costs, wastage of victuals, overpays	72,000	72,000				
Totals	**1,226,241**	**567,764**	**783,191**	**275,800**	**122,250**	**45,000**

the Venetians accepted the Spanish estimate in broad outline and, by implication, they agreed to a contribution from the Republic of about 800,000 *escudos*. Probably this figure of two million *escudos* is as close as we can reasonably expect to come to the gross cost of the Lepanto campaign.[4]

By any standard Philip II's 1.2 million *escudos* was a very large sum, approaching 40 per cent of Spain's available income. But Lepanto was not just a Spanish enterprise. The burden was spread among all the Mediterranean states of the Monarchy. Of Philip II's share nearly one-third of the men, 80 per cent of the galleys, and possibly one-third of the money came from Italy. The greater part of the preparations, the procurement of provisions and supplies, naval stores and munitions of all kinds took place in Italy. Without oars, cables, and hardware from Milan and Naples, the Spanish galleys could not have been fitted out, nor equipped so cheaply; without the wheat and biscuit from Naples and Sicily to supplement the bad harvest in Spain and the deficiencies of the Venetians, Lepanto could not have taken place.[5] Forty-five of the galleys and the two élite *tercios* of Don Pedro de Padilla and Don Diego Enríquez were maintained and paid for by the revenues of the kingdoms of Naples and Sicily.[6] In addition, the five unattached companies (*compañías sueltas*) from Sicily and the Italian regiments of Sigismondo Gonzaga from Lombardy and the Count of Sarno from Naples were probably also paid by the Spanish dominions in Italy.[7] In all, Philip II's Italian states furnished about 443,000 *escudos* for troops and galleys alone, or 36 per cent of the total cost: 275,000 from Naples (22.5 per cent), 122,000 from Sicily (10 per cent), and 45,000 from Milan (3.7 per cent). Regarded as an imperial rather than as a purely Spanish enterprise, Lepanto was only a moderate burden – 1.2 million *escudos* representing only about 13 per cent of the nine million or so which the king received each year from his Mediterranean possessions. Moreover, the burden was distributed more or less equitably in proportion to each province's share of the revenues.[8]

Table 2 demonstrates the remarkable coincidence between

the taxable strength of Naples and Spain and their contributions to the battle, in contrast to Milan which apparently paid less than its share, and Sicily which paid somewhat more. Nor does the 10 per cent share in the 'visible' Lepanto budget by any means measure the full extent of Sicily's participation in the activities of the Grand Fleet. Professor H. G. Koenigsberger's evidence on Sicily demonstrates that the years 1571-7 were a time of enormous strain

Table 2: Philip II's Revenues, c. 1571

STATE	REVENUES IN *escudos*	% OF TOTAL	CONTRIBU-TION TO LEPANTO IN *escudos*	% OF TOTAL
Spain	5,600,000	63	783,191	63·8
Naples	1,950,000	22	275,800	22·5
Sicily	690,000	7·7	122,250	10
Milan	650,000	7·3	45,000	3·7
Total	**8,890,000**	**100**	**1,226,241**	**100**

on the island's finances. During the period 1.6 million *escudos* were spent on naval preparations and defence, an average of over 250,000 a year. An additional donative of 100,000 *escudos* was granted in 1571, and during the years 1571-3 Sicily contributed a total of 1.2 million *escudos* – quite apart from the loss of tens of thousands more in taxes waived on the grain supplied to the Fleet and to the Venetians under the terms of the League. The royal governor of the island, Terranova, was fully justified when he claimed that, in proportion to its size, no other kingdom had done as much.[9] For Naples too, the official figure of 275,000 *escudos* was certainly a bare minimum: in February 1571 the kingdom promised a donative of one million *escudos*, payable over two years, and by April the viceroy already had 900,000 *escudos* available for use on the Fleet.[10]

These were all large sums, but they still left Spain to provide almost two-thirds of Philip II's share of the campaign costs. Fortunately, the Pope came to the rescue. For most of the sixteenth century the Kings of Castile collected two important clerical taxes, the *cruzada* (the proceeds from the sale of indulgences in Spain) and the *subsidio* (a clerical income tax). These two taxes, together worth between 750,000 and 850,000 *escudos* annually, could only be collected with Papal authorization and had to be applied exclusively to the fight against the Infidel. In 1567 the Pope created a new tax on the Spanish Church to help the king finance the war in the Netherlands, the *excusado* (the tithe of the third richest man in every parish). However, Pius V's scruples over indulgences and Philip II's refusal to enter a League against the Turk, to which the Pope was passionately attached, in addition to serious jurisdictional conflicts and disagreements over foreign policy, strained relations between them. The *cruzada* was suspended after 1566, the *excusado* was not collected, and the *subsidio* was due for renewal in 1571. When in March 1570 the Turkish attack on Cyprus led the Pope to approach Philip again about joining a League against the Sultan, the king made it clear that Spain's participation would be impossible without the 'Three Graces' (as these taxes were always called).[11] In July 1570, Pius issued the bulls authorizing the collection of the three taxes (the *excusado* on rather better terms than in 1567) and in return the king agreed in principle to the League.[12] News that the 'Three Graces' were again conceded to the king had an immediate effect on his credit: bankers were at once willing to advance money against promise of repayment from one of the new taxes with a sure yield – 400,000 *escudos* were borrowed from the Genoese in May at low interest and were at once used to prepare the Fleet.[13] The total annual yield of the 'Three Graces', something in excess of a million *escudos*,[14] was substantially greater than the 783,191 *escudos* which was Spain's share of the Lepanto enterprise!

The cost of Lepanto to the Spanish Monarchy was thus by no means an intolerable burden. Venice was not nearly so fortunate. Her share of the bill, perhaps 800,000 *escudos*, was smaller than Philip II's but her revenues were also far less.[15] The Republic's income in 1571 amounted to 2,000,000 Venetian ducats (or 1.75 million *escudos*), of which 700,000 ducats came from the city, 800,000 from the Italian mainland and 500,000 from Venice's seaborne empire.[16] Venice's overseas possessions were too small, too distant, and too poor to shoulder much of the burden of manning and equipping the Grand Fleet as Philip II's dependencies had done. On the other hand, the Pope offered little help. In March 1570, Pius confirmed the claim of the Seigneury to levy a tax on the landed property of the Venetian clergy – the *décimo al clero* – to further the Republic's naval construction. This appears to have been worth about 50,000 ducats a year, just over 6 per cent of the total cost of the Venetian fleet.[17] Here again, Venice was left worse off than Spain. The conclusion is inescapable that in real terms the Republic paid far more for the victory of Lepanto than Philip II.

Even these modifications, far as they are from what had originally been anticipated, give a misleading impression of the true cost of the campaign. The allied battle fleet was not built for the occasion from scratch. On the contrary, both Venice and Spain maintained very considerable permanent forces for the defence of their Mediterranean possessions. Between 1545 and 1633 the Venetian navy always numbered a minimum of 100 light and twelve great galleys, to which six galeasses were added after 1565. This establishment number was often surpassed: over 130 Venetian galleys were involved in the 1571 campaign, while in 1581 the Republic had in its service 146 light and 18 great galleys. The cost of this regular defence force was enormous – 489,320 ducats in the uneventful year of 1587, over 600,000 in the more turbulent 1590s.[18] The greater part, perhaps 60 per cent, of the cost of Lepanto to Venice was thus a recurring charge which would have been incurred whether or not there was a battle fought: perhaps only an extra 300,000 ducats were required from Venice to convert defence into offence.

The position of the Spanish Monarchy was the same. The Venetian envoy in Madrid was right when he pointed out that Philip II should not consider the galleys as costing him anything extra as they had to be paid for the whole year round.[19] It is true that the ninety-six or so galleys which the King was maintaining in October 1571 was the highest number that he – or possibly any king of Spain – had ever had in service, but this was largely independent of Lepanto. Philip II was committed to maintain a minimum of 100 galleys as a condition of the *subsidio* grant from as early as 1561, a number still not attained in 1571. Some fifteen new galleys were indeed added to the squadrons of Sicily, Naples and Spain during 1571, and new contracts were made with private owners, but the 1571 fleet was still only a point on the curve of recovery from the disasters of Djerba and La Herradura in 1560 and 1562; it was far from being a peak.[20]

Table 3: The Growth of Philip II's Mediterranean Fleet, 1562-77

Squadron	Nov. 1562	1567	17.3.1571	7.10.1571	1574	1576	1577
Spain: in Spain	7	10⎱	24	⎰18?	37?	40?	33
in Italy	7	15⎰		⎱14	14		
Naples	8	14	29	33	54	44	32
Sicily	10	10	11	10	22	22	14
Gian Andrea Doria	12	11	11	11	12	12	12
Other contractors	11	19	10	10	16	16	11
Total fleet	**55**	**79**	**85**	**96**	**155**	**134**	**102**

The real 'extraordinary' burden of the Lepanto campaign for Spain lay in the troops aboard the Fleet; yet only two-thirds of the 25,000 paid men provided by Philip II were raised specially for the campaign.[21] The 9700 Spanish infantry at Lepanto were divided into four *tercios*: the *tercio* of Naples under Don Pedro de Padilla, the *tercio* of Sicily under Don Diego Enríquez, a *tercio* under the command of Don Lope de Figueroa, known as the *tercio de Granada*, and a *tercio* raised mainly in the crown of Aragon under Don Miguel de Moncada. All four *tercios* had been serving in the war against the Morisco rebels in Granada which finally petered out in the early spring of 1571, and without exception they were so depleted and in such poor condition that the companies had to be almost entirely re-recruited.[22] Actually, while the *tercios* of Figueroa and Moncada were in effect new *tercios*, those of Padilla and Enríquez were not: they were permanent and regular units, in normal circumstances based in Naples and Sicily and paid for out of Neapolitan and Sicilian revenues. They served outside Italy only during specific emergencies (like the Morisco revolt) and they would undoubtedly have had to be reinforced and shipped back to Italy regardless of Lepanto. A document drawn up in May 1571, at the time of their embarkation for Italy, credits the *tercio* of Naples with 3277 men and that of Sicily with 2152 – some 54 per cent of the total number in the four *tercios*.[23] Besides these two regular units, each galley normally carried a special task-force of fifty soldiers, provided by the king, during the summer campaign season. These too would have been provided with or without Lepanto. The *tercios* of Naples and Sicily usually supplied the soldiers for the galleys of the Italian squadrons, but the 1900 men required for the remaining thirty-eight galleys and the 1000 men of the five un-attached Italian companies from Sicily, who apparently served permanently with the galleys of Sicily, should also be added to the list of regular troops.[24] The recurring account for Philip II's Mediterranean fleet then stands as follows:

Table 4: Philip II's Lepanto Budget: Recurring Costs

83 galleys	371,800
54 per cent of 9700 Spanish foot	130,000
1000 Sicilian infantry	21,200
1900 other infantry	44,764
	567,764 escudos

Recurring costs thus represented about 46 per cent of Philip II's share of the expenses of the Lepanto campaign.

A final balance-sheet of the 'visible' costs of Lepanto for the two principal Christian powers would thus show a net cost to Venice of about 300,000 ducats above her normal defence budget, partially offset by a papal grant worth 50,000; while Philip II spent about 660,000 *escudos* more than his ordinary

131

outlay on defence, receiving in return papal concessions, payable in Spain, worth over a million. In addition, the victory brought the allies a booty of some 400,000 *escudos*, half of which went to Spain, half to Venice and the Papacy. The Christians captured 130 vessels, 390 guns, and 3486 Turkish slaves; they lost 17 galleys of the Papal and Venetian fleets, and suffered a great deal of damage and the loss of many oarsmen. Net profit cannot have been less than 3500 *escudos* per galley, the value of the bare hulls and the artillery. Although much of the booty must have been redistributed in rewards and gratuities, it should not be ignored in this account.[25]

But it is not enough to leave the matter here. There is a counterfactual problem also. Lepanto was not fought in a vacuum; it was merely a high point in half a century's confrontation between the Spanish and Ottoman empires. It was the Christian response to a period of the most intense Moslem military and naval pressure. There were, indeed, few years between 1551 and 1578 when Spain could be confident that the Turkish navy would not come west in force. More than 600,000 *escudos* had to be spent on the relief of Oran in 1563. The Sultan besieged Malta in 1565, and so terrified the west that Philip II's plans for the defence of the Mediterranean the following summer involved the levy of 30,000 men at an estimated cost of 1,400,000 *escudos* – well over double the extraordinary expenditure on the 1571 campaign. Similarly expensive preparations had to be undertaken by the Venetians during these crisis years. There followed a brief respite between 1567 and 1569, but with the fall of Cyprus to the Turks in September 1570, massive *defensive* preparations for 1571 would have been inevitable.[26]

Lepanto itself did nothing to increase the security of the west. Even in the mid-1570s, the persistent threat from the enemy fleet made it necessary for Philip to raise 9000 men for the defence of Sardinia, together with all the victuals and munitions they required, and, in addition, to enlist 10,000 to 12,000 more as a special strategic reserve to be ready to go wherever they might be needed.[27] In the context of the general defence budgets of these years, therefore, even the 'extraordinary' expenditure on the League was a recurring charge. Lepanto was not so much an unusual burden as a redirection of resources. In the short term at least, it was a triumphant vindication of those who argued that attack was not only the best form of defence, but also the cheapest.[28]

7

Probably the most important new 'sister-discipline' of history
is scientific archaeology. The techniques which have been
evolved over the past century or so for excavating and
evaluating prehistoric and classical sites, for which there is
little or no written evidence, have more recently been applied
to the medieval and post-medieval periods, for which local
documentary sources are abundant. Each discipline needs
the other, for there are things which mere finds can never tell
(such as ownership or exact purpose), and other things on
which mere documents will always be silent (such as physical
appearance and exact mechanics of operation); and yet
contacts between archaeologists and historians are still often
infrequent and fraught with suspicion. However, one area in
which contacts are both numerous and enlightening is
nautical archaeology. Documents can provide the excavator
with lists of the exact cargo, the number and nationality of
the crew and the equipment of a given wreck, all indicating
what should be at the site of the wreck and in what quantities.
Other documents may reveal exactly where a given ship went
down and how much of its cargo was salvaged; others still,
especially when illustrated, may permit the reconstruction (or
identification) of an object of which only a few deformed
fragments have survived.

The article which follows was prepared for the conference
on the wrecks of the Spanish Armada organized by the Coun
cil for Nautical Archaeology at the University of Kent a
Canterbury in April 1974. The gathering included both
historians and underwater archaeologists and both groups
emerged convinced of the need for close co-operation with
the other. Although this paper was delivered at the im
probable hour of nine on a Sunday morning, its counter
factual approach – assessing what might have happened if the
Armada had managed to land its invasion army – stimulated
the archaeologists in the audience to produce much informa
tion previously quite unknown to historians. Excavations o
the Armada wrecks found to date reveal that the great flee
was carrying a train of fifty-pounder siege-guns (almos
certainly too cumbersome ever to be fired at sea), a forest o

134

scaling ladders (pine trees with their branches sawn off about a foot from the trunk) and bundles of brushwood suitable for filling up moats. This new evidence lends the strongest support possible to the view that the Armada was sent actually to invade England (and not, as some historians have argued, merely to parade in the Channel and encourage negotiations to be undertaken); it also shows that the fleet was superbly equipped to achieve its primary purpose. I am most grateful, therefore, for the comments and books of my friends in nautical archaeology: Colin and Paula Martin, Robert Sténuit and Sydney Wignall.

If the Armada had Landed

If a Spanish army had ever landed in England at all, that event would have occurred on the 7 August 1588. The weather was not unfavourable, the sea was smooth . . . For aught that Leicester, or Burghley, or Queen Elizabeth knew at the time, the army of Farnese might, on Monday, have been marching upon London.[1]

And if the Spanish forces aboard the Armada *had* managed to land, 'Farnese' had clear orders. He was to lead his troops through Kent, take London by storm (preferably with Elizabeth and her ministers still in it) and hope that the enemies of the Tudor regime in the north, in the west and in Ireland would rise in rebellion and aid the invaders to master the kingdom. However Philip II realized that success on this scale was somewhat unlikely. He had therefore devised an alternative plan. If there were no native rising, or if London could not be taken, Parma was to use his presence on English soil to force Elizabeth to make three concessions. In descending order of importance these were: toleration of Roman Catholic worship in England, the surrender to Spain of all Dutch towns held by English troops (especially Flushing, which commanded the sea-approaches to Antwerp), and perhaps the payment of a war-indemnity.[2]

Could this Grand Design have worked? All historians agree that chance played a considerable role in the outcome of the battles in the Channel between the Armada and the English fleet. The Dutch, suspecting that Elizabeth was about to conclude a separate peace with Spain, refused to join in the fray until 1 August, keeping back in harbour the vital fly-boats which prevented Parma's troops from effecting a rendezvous with the fleet from Spain.[3] Until the fireships stratagem on 8 August the Armada was still in good order and possessed far more powder and shot than the English fleet. If Medina Sidonia had succeeded, against all the odds, in landing the army of invasion on England's shores, what could have been achieved? Were the means provided by the Prudent King equal to the ends he had in mind?

The first historian who seriously considered these questions, Sir Walter Raleigh (in his *History of the World* of 1614), had no illusions. Writing some twenty-five years after the Armada, he was convinced that the English were 'of no such force as to encounter an Armie like unto that, wherewith it was intended that the prince of *Parma* should have landed in *England*'.[4] Philip II intended the invasion to be carried out by the finest troops in his army, selected principally from the forces already in the Low Countries to suppress the Dutch Revolt, supplemented by contingents from the Armada itself.[5] An assault force of some 17,000 men was embarked in the ports of Flanders to await the arrival of the great fleet. There were 4000 Spaniards, 3000 Italians, 1000 Burgundians, 1000 from the British Isles (mainly Catholic exiles) and 8000 Germans and Walloons. These men were the cream of the most famous and formidable army in Europe. The English, particularly those who had already fought in the Netherlands, were terrified of them. Sir Roger Williams, third-in-command of the army at Tilbury, held up the Army of Flanders as a shining example to others: 'To speake troth,' he wrote, 'no Armie that euer I saw, passes that of the Duke *de Parma* for discipline and good order.' And Williams had good reason to know, since he had fought with the Spaniards in the Netherlands from 1574 until 1578, and against them thereafter. The earl of Leicester, commander-in-chief of Elizabeth's forces, was likewise filled with apprehension at the threat of an invasion by the Flanders veterans against whom he had fought for two years without success. They were, he informed Lord Burghley sadly, 'ye best soldyers at this day in Christendom'.[6]

The Army of Flanders, which had been fighting with scarcely a break since 1572, had been moulded into a superbly experienced fighting force. Some veterans had been on active service for thirty years and they were commanded by officers who had risen through the ranks. They were successful and self-confident following their conquests in Flanders and Brabant during the previous decade, culminating in the capture of the important port of Sluis in August 1587 in the teeth of a spirited defence by England's best troops and most experienced commanders (including Sir Roger Williams). Parma's army on the eve of the Armada venture, according to an eye-witness, contained 'neither women nor children, and few of the soldiers were raw recruits. They were powerful men, well-armed and of martial aspect, highly trained and always ready to obey and to fight.' They were the 'asphalt soldiers' of the sixteenth century.[7]

Despite this panegyric, however, there were inevitably some weaknesses in the Army of Flanders. In the first place, not all the troops under Parma's command were so experienced. Second, some of the best men had to be left behind to defend the Netherlands against the Dutch. There were, indeed, hardly enough troops to go round: the Army of Flanders had suffered heavy losses during the winter of 1587-8. Much of the province of Flanders, where the prospective invasion force was billeted, had been devastated and depopulated by the heavy and bitter fighting of the 1580s; only one-tenth of the arable land was under cultivation; many towns and villages lost over one-half of their population.[8] The troops, lodged in deserted barns or makeshift shelters, without a regular supply of food, were severely afflicted by cold and hunger. The less experienced men sustained particularly heavy losses. In the summer of 1587 some 9017 Italian footsoldiers, specially recruited for the Enterprise of England, marched to the Netherlands. They drew favourable comments from all who saw them along the way on account of their rich apparel and their magnificent equipment; yet by April 1588, after a mere six months in the Low Countries, there were only 3615 men left. The rest – two-thirds – were gone, either through death, disease or desertion. The fate of the Spanish troops specially raised for the invasion of England was scarcely better: the *tercio* (regiment) of Don Antonio de Zúñiga numbered 2662 men in July 1587 but only 1500 men in April 1588.[9]

It was a tribute to Philip II's foresight that, despite such heavy losses, in the end the duke of Parma still had enough men at his disposal. The 17,000 men required for the invasion were all assembled at the ports of Flanders by the end of July 1588 and they included some of the best troops in Europe. The king had also ensured that sufficient resources were available to maintain his forces. Despite the cynicism of friends and enemies alike, Philip II succeeded in channelling an unprecedented supply of money to his armies and his allies in northern Europe. The leaders of the French Catholic League were persuaded to stage a campaign in northern France in 1587, which effectively scotched the threat of French action in support of England, and the leaders of the League received 1,500,000 ducats from Spain between 1587 and 1590; over the same period the Army of Flanders received some 21,000,000 more; in addition, the total cost of the Armada itself to Philip II must have exceeded 5,000,000 ducats (there were about four ducats to the pound sterling, so the total outlay was almost £7,000,000).[10] All these sums were paid in cash. Philip II's heart was in the Enterprise of England and he sent the duke of Parma 'larger provisions than any man can remember' in 1587 and 1588 in order to expedite preparations in the Netherlands for the combined operation with the great fleet.[11] There is every reason to suppose that, had the invasion taken place, adequate funds to sustain Parma and his troops would have been forthcoming. The money was there: between 1590 and 1598 over 30,000,000 ducats was poured from Spain into the Army of Flanders' campaigns in France.[12] There might even have been the papal largesse of 1,000,000 ducats, promised for the day when the first Spaniard actually landed on English soil (again, during the 1590s, the Papacy spent heavily on aid to the Catholic League in France).

The only apparent deficiency in Parma's invasion force was his lack of siege artillery. His barges and flyboats were simply too weak and insubstantial to carry heavy guns across from Flanders. However, Philip II had anticipated this problem. The Armada carried a complete siege train of great fifty-pounder guns. There were perhaps forty-eight of them, mounted on mobile field-carriages, together with scaling ladders and other siege tackle which would have been disembarked for use on land.[13] Moreover the guns were embarked on ships which possessed large lighters and proper derricks, so that the guns could be easily brought ashore. Parma's army would have enjoyed full artillery support.

This was an advantage of critical importance, since there were very few towns and castles in south-east England which were capable of withstanding a heavy battery. The fortifications of most places in Elizabethan England, indeed, were extremely poor. According to one disgruntled old soldier, the Queen's ministers 'are perswaded according to the opinion of the Lacedemonians, that fortifying of towns doth more hurt than good'.[14] Admittedly, Henry VIII had done a good deal to improve the defences of the Kent coast, with five forts between the Downs and Rye (at Sandown, Deal, Walmer, Sandgate and Camber), and five more along the Thames estuary. But all these new defences (as a visit to the still extant castles of Camber and Walmer shows) were constructed with thin circular walls and curved, hollow bulwarks. Only solid quadrilateral bastions, protected by wide moats, were capable of withstanding heavy bombardment and in the south-east only Upnor Castle, built between 1559 and 1567 to defend the new naval dockyard at Chatham, had those. Upnor alone was far too small to stop the duke of Parma and his army. The larger towns of Kent, Canterbury and Rochester still had only their antiquated medieval walls, while Rochester Castle, commanding the main crossing over the Medway, was thoroughly decayed. There seem to have been no defence works at all between Margate, the projected landing area for the Armada, and the Medway. Philip II had deftly selected his adversary's weakest point.[15]

With so few physical obstacles in his path, Parma could have moved fast. When in 1592 he invaded Normandy with 22,000 men, the duke covered sixty-five miles in six days, despite tenacious opposition from the numerically superior forces of Henry IV and the earl of Essex.[16] Even in the face of similar resistance, the Spaniards might reasonably have covered the eighty miles from Margate to London in a week. Such a rapid advance would have brought the advantage of surprise, and also the windfall of copious food supplies: the fields of Kent were just being harvested; the crops would provide the invaders with all the food they needed. Even at London, the Army of Flanders would have found little to hold them up: the city was still defended by its medieval walls. They had scarcely changed since 1554 when Sir Thomas Wyatt's rebel army, 'not in any good order or array', marched through Kent, crossed the Thames at Kingston and advanced with impunity through Westminster until they were able to march down Fleet Street to Ludgate.[17] In military terms, London presented far less of a challenge than Antwerp, a city defended by an enceinte of walls five miles in circumference and built to the most sophisticated modern designs. Yet the Army of Flanders captured Antwerp, after a year's siege, in 1585.

However, as Parma was well aware, the state of a town's physical defences was not always the decisive factor in wartime. Several places in the Netherlands with poor, outdated fortifications had, thanks to the determination of the besieged population, managed to avoid capture; conversely, several towns protected by magnificent fortifications had fallen to the Spaniards before their time because their citizens, their garrisons or their commander succumbed to the bribes of the genial yet astute duke of Parma. It is by no means certain that the defenders of every English town and castle would have resisted the Spaniards to the last man. After all, Queen Elizabeth's troops in the Netherlands had a distinctly uninspiring record in that respect: in September 1582

Sir William Semple betrayed Lier to the Spaniards; in November 1584 the English garrison of Aalst sold their town to Parma for 45,000 ducats; in January 1587 Sir William Stanley and Captain Roland Yorke, together with over 700 men under their command, defected to Spain, thus betraying the places entrusted to their care (Deventer and a fort overlooking Zutphen); finally, in April 1589 the English garrison of St Geertruidenberg sold themselves and their town to Parma for 60,000 ducats.[18] With few exceptions, the defectors proceeded to fight for Spain against their former comrades. One can protest that many of the men were Irish or Anglo-Irish Catholics, and thus *ipso facto* unreliable; but it remains true that all had been recruited by, or with the consent of, the English government and had been sent abroad specifically to fight for the Protestant cause in Holland. Elizabeth and her advisers, moreover, pinned their hopes on the comrades of these traitors, recalling 4000 from Holland to form the nucleus of the army which was intended to defend London. Its quartermaster-general was the brother of Roland Yorke; its third-in-command was Sir Roger Williams who had fought in the Army of Flanders for four years.[19] One cannot exclude the possibility that some of these men might have been prepared to sell strongholds in England to Parma, as their fellows had sold strongholds in the Low Countries.

Elizabeth, however, had no choice. She was forced to depend on the veterans from Holland because there were very few other experienced troops on hand in whom she could trust. The London-trained bands, who had been drilling twice weekly since March, were probably capable of putting up a good fight (although some doubted it) but little could be expected from the militia of the inland shires, which was only ordered to mobilize on 2 August – especially since these units were ordered to march to Tilbury in Essex whereas the Spaniards were intending to land at Margate in Kent! Preparations were desperately behind-hand all over. The fortifications of Tilbury, centrepoint of the projected resistance to the invaders, were only begun on 3 August; 000 of the veterans summoned back from Holland remained wind-bound at Flushing until the 6th. In Kent, the troops at

Dover (most of them raw recruits) began to desert in considerable numbers when the Armada came into sight off Calais (perhaps through lack of wages but more probably through fear). In any case, there were only 4000 men in all, a ludicrously inadequate force to throw into the path of the seasoned Spaniards.[20] Not only were there not enough men; even the available forces were in the wrong places. On 6 August, the day before the Armada was due to land, the commander of the Queen's forces in Kent admitted that the Isle of Thanet, the very place which (unknown to him) had been selected for the landing, was virtually undefended because the officer in charge of it was absent.[21] The impressive defences erected on the Isle of Wight or around the Norfolk coast would have been of little use against an invasion mounted through Kent.[22]

Much of this confusion and unpreparedness arose from the failure of the government to decide on the correct strategy to employ against the invaders. The commander-in-chief, Leicester, had no powers to issue orders to troops outside the county of Essex until 2 August, and in his absence a controversy over the appropriate strategy broke out between the general officer commanding in the south-east, Sir John Norris, and the local commander in Kent, Sir Thomas Scott. Only a fortnight before the Armada arrived off Calais, Scott was still arguing that it was better to spread out his forces along the coast and 'answer' the enemy 'at the sea side', while Norris wished to withdraw all but a skeleton force inland in order to make a stand at Canterbury and there 'staye the enemy from speedy passage to London or the harte of the realme'.[23] It seems clear that Elizabeth, unable to raise loans either at home (because of a trade recession) or abroad (because most bankers thought that Spain would win), was forced to delay every stage of her counter-invasion plan until the last possible moment in order to save money.[24] Perhaps too, she believed that the Armada would never set sail, that the problems contingent upon getting 130 ships and 30,000 men to sea simultaneously and in battle order would prove to be beyond the capacity of Philip II's Spain. Elizabeth was not alone in this. In Paris, early in July 1588, even the friends of Spain were still laying odds of six to one against the great fleet ever reaching the Channel; in Flanders, the duke of Parma acted even in late July as if the junction between his forces and the fleet would never take place; while in Corunna the duke of Medina Sidonia advised the king to call the whole venture off after a severe storm had damaged his ships.

But of course the Armada *did* reach the Channel, and had Parma landed on the Isle of Thanet early in August 1588 he would have been opposed by untrained troops without clear orders, backed up by only a handful of inadequately fortified towns. The invasion's success would therefore have hinged mainly upon the spirit of the ordinary citizens of south-east England. How determined would the defence of London and the Home Counties have been?

Certainly there was considerable hatred of the Spaniards in these staunchly Protestant areas, a hatred stoked up by evocative propaganda and by such hair-raising accounts of their cruelty as George Gascoyne's *The Spoyle of Antwerp* (London, 1576) and the English version of Bartolomé de las Casas's *Destruction of the Indies* (published in 1583).[25] But where there was hate there was also fear – fear that the formidable power of Spain and her Catholic allies 'might swallow up little *England*, as the ravenous Crocodile dooeth the smallest fish'. And this fear lasted far beyond 1588.[26] Everything depended upon the balance between fear and hate among the ordinary soldiers and citizens of England. Would they have been able and willing to fight on the beaches and in the streets for Elizabeth Tudor, a monarch with no obvious successor, and her ramshackle church which even in the 1590s 'the common people for the greater part' still called 'the new religion'?[27] Or would 1588 have been like 1688, with the mass of the population standing idly by, indifferent to the character, nationality and religion of their ruler? Or would 1588 have perhaps been like 1940 when, at the height of the Blitz, even Churchill admitted in a cable to Roosevelt on 15 June: 'A point may be reached in the struggle where the present ministers no longer have any control and a pro-German government would be called into being to make peace, and might present to a shattered or a starving nation

143

an almost irresistible case for entire submission.'

Yet another possible sequence of events, had the Armada turned out differently, was set out in the prologue to a recent quasi-historical novel:

On a warm July evening of the year 1588, in the royal palace of Greenwich, London, a woman lay dying, an assassin's bullets lodged in abdomen and chest. Her face was lined, her teeth blackened, and death lent her no dignity; but her last breath started echoes that ran out to shake a hemisphere. For the Faery Queen, Elizabeth the First, paramount ruler of England, was no more.

The rage of the English knew no bounds . . . The English Catholics, bled white by fines, still mourning the Queen of Scots, still remembering the gory Rising of the North, were faced with a fresh pogrom. Unwillingly, in self-defence, they took up arms against their countrymen as the flame lit by the Walsingham massacres ran across the land, mingling with the light of warning beacons the sullen glare of the *auto-da-fe*.

The news spread; to Paris, to Rome, to . . . the great ships of the Armada, threshing up past the Lizard to link with Parma's army of invasion on the Flemish coast . . . The turmoil that ensued saw Philip ensconced as ruler of England; in France the followers of Guise, heartened by the victories across the Channel, finally deposed the weakened House of Valois. The War of the Three Henrys ended with the Holy League triumphant, and the Church restored once more to her ancient power.

To the victor, the spoils. With the authority of the Catholic Church assured, the rising nation of Great Britain deployed her forces in the service of the Popes, smashing the Protestants of the Netherlands, destroying the power of the German city-states in the long-drawn Lutheran Wars. The New-Worlders of the North American continent remained under the rule of Spain; Cook planted in Australasia the cobalt flag of the throne of Peter.

Speculation on this scale – 'the Walsingham massacres' and

all – is useful because it brings out the enormous gains which would have accrued to Spain had the invasion of England resulted in total triumph, with a Spanish Infanta on Elizabeth's throne and Spanish soldiers and seminaries in every major town.[28] Of course a victory of this magnitude was improbable; but even the occupation of Kent alone might have given Spain important advantages. Parma could have exploited his conquests, together with the threat of another Catholic rising in the north or in Ireland, to extort from Elizabeth the three key concessions demanded by Philip II: withdrawal from the Netherlands, toleration for the Catholics of England, and a war-indemnity. It must be remembered that the English government was negotiating with Parma throughout 1588 on the first point (talks were only broken off, somewhat abruptly, when the Armada arrived off Calais).[29] Everything suggests that Elizabeth was anxious for a peace with Spain; with Parma on English soil, peace would perhaps have seemed inexcusable. And had the Queen made peace with Spain, abandoning the Dutch Republic, there is every reason to suppose that the Dutch would have been constrained to make a settlement in their turn. Once again, the matter had already been discussed. In December 1587, at Elizabeth's insistence, the States-General debated at length whether they should send a delegation to the Anglo-Spanish peace conference to be held at Bourbourg in Flanders. Although most of the deputies from Holland, Zealand and Utrecht were firmly against negotiations, there were a number of dissenting voices (most notably the town of Gouda); while the inland provinces which had to bear the brunt of the war against Spain (Gelderland, Overijssel, the Ommelanden around Groningen and most of Friesland) spoke out strongly in favour of a settlement. Opinion in the Netherlands was sharply divided. Queen Elizabeth's special envoy, appointed to convince the Dutch of the need to negotiate, informed the Queen that 'The Common Wealth of these Provinces consisting of divers Parts and Professions as, namely, Protestants, Puritans, Anabaptists and Spanish Hearts, which are no small number; it is most certain that dividing these in five parts, the Protestants and the Puritans do hardly contain even one part of five'. And, the envoy continued, only the 'Protestants and Puritans' favoured a continuation of the war.[30] The controversy over war or peace grew more and more acrimonious until the defeat of the Armada settled the matter; but had the Enterprise of England succeeded, the young Republic could hardly have gone on fighting Spain single-handed for long. Pressure for a compromise would have become irresistible. Medina Sidonia would not have sailed in vain.[31]

Perhaps, however, all these scenarios are too favourable to Spain. It is perfectly possible that, had Parma managed to occupy a slice of Kent in August 1588, he would *not* have started to negotiate. He, or his master, might have insisted on going for total victory. After every major success in the struggle against the Dutch (for example after Maastricht in 1579 or after Antwerp in 1585), Spain refused all talk of compromise and tried to score further successes. It was the same in France after 1589. Inevitably, this policy led to a stalemate: Spain poured her money into the war in order to gain a town here and lose a fortress there. If the invasion of England had become bogged down, the Dutch Revolt and the French wars of religion would have continued, sapping Spain's resources, pushing her towards another bankruptcy.

'One can always play a parlour-game with the might-have-beens of history,' wrote E. H. Carr in 1964. 'But they have nothing to do with history.' It is true that any – or none – of the scenarios discussed above might have resulted had winds or incompetence kept the Dutch ships in Flushing and the English fireships in Dover. We do not know, and no amount of speculation or calculation can enlighten us. But a counterfactual approach still has its uses. It is essential when the historian wishes to assess the feasibility of a course of action or a policy, and this is particularly desirable in early modern times when the obstacles which complicated any major military or naval operation were so enormous and imponderable. It is easy to underestimate or ignore the problems posed by distance, by stunted naval technology, by the scarcity of credit facilities, to an enterprise like the Spanish Armada. By insisting on the mistakes and the over-sights of Philip II and Medina Sidonia one can reduce the whole project to a futile, crack-brained and over-ambitious adventure. Yet in all complex undertakings of this sort – as the allied landings at Anzio or in Normandy in 1943-4 showed – the balance between success and failure is precarious. If we are to make an accurate and realistic evaluation of the Armada project, we must remember the strengths as well as the weaknesses: the selection of an ideal invasion area; the formidable planning and immense resources which brought the fleet from Spain and the army from the Netherlands so close together; the fact that the occupation of even a part of Kent – carefully exploited – could have brought enormous benefits to Spain.[32] If, on that Monday morning, 7 August 1588, the Army of Farnese had been marching towards London, everyone today would regard the invincible Armada, despite its deficiencies, as Philip II's masterpiece.

III

Spain in
the Netherlands

8

Francisco de Lixalde, the Paymaster-General of the Spanish Army of Flanders from 1567 until his death ten years later, has become a figure of some interest to historians. Dr Albert Lovett of University College, Dublin, published an article in the 1971 issue of the Dutch journal *Tijdschrift voor Geschiedenis*, which argued at some length that certain accusations of corruption made against Lixalde by the Castilian Audit Office were groundless. For Dr Lovett, Lixalde was just an honest but overworked bureaucrat whose worst offence was to get his sums wrong. This conclusion seemed to be quite unsupported by the evidence which I had accumulated for my book on the Army of Flanders, and I set about verifying the facts given by Dr Lovett (several of which proved to be entirely wrong), checking Lixalde's sums (which were always wrong in his favour), and collating the Spanish sources with some Dutch material which Dr Lovett did not cite. The results of this microscopic enquiry seem to merit reprinting here, without Dr Lovett's original article, for three reasons. First, they illustrate some of the pitfalls which may claim the unwary student of Habsburg financial history: an ingenious and unscrupulous official could embezzle fairly large amounts of public money and cover his tracks with considerable success, so that subsequent historians may fail to spot the frauds perpetrated. Second, the Lixalde case reveals a good deal about the administrative methods and assumptions of the Spanish officials concerned with the Netherlands. Finally, wrestling with the sordid misdeeds and base aspirations of obscure men reminds us that history, even the history of a great organism such as the empire of Philip II, is made by faceless bureaucrats as well as by omniscient statesmen and heroic generals. The saga of Francisco de Lixalde tells us as much, in its way, about the workings of Spanish imperialism in the Netherlands as a biography of the Duke of Alva or the Prince of Parma.

Corruption and Imperialism in the Spanish Netherlands: the Case of Francisco de Lixalde, 1567-1612

Francisco de Lixalde has certainly caused a great deal of ink to flow. His accounts as Paymaster-General of the Spanish army in the Netherlands from 1567 until 1577, which involved over twenty-three million *escudos* and included 475 separate receipts and no less than 10,345 individual payments, were written out and audited four times before they were finally closed in 1612. Just one draft of Lixalde's first four years (1567-71) covered two thousand sheets of paper. An abstract of the first version of the account has been printed twice (once by Lixalde himself in 1576, and again in 1902) and the innumerable close-written folios of the remainder fill almost twenty-two fat foolscap *legajos* (bundles) of documents at Simancas. Finally, in 1577, there was a full-scale legal enquiry by the magistrates of Antwerp into the prominent part played by Lixalde in the notorious 'Spanish Fury' in which eight thousand persons lost their lives and many more lost their property.

Recently, Dr A. W. Lovett of University College, Dublin, discussed the Lixalde case in some detail.[1] He drew attention to the fact that Lixalde's story illustrated a good many of the formidable administrative problems created by Philip II's decision to suppress the revolt of the Netherlands by force. He pointed to the haste with which the principal civil servants of the new Army of Flanders were appointed,[2] to the persistent failure of the court of Spain to ensure an adequate supervision of the Military Treasury (*pagaduría*) in the Netherlands, and to the fruitless attempt of the first Paymaster, Francisco de Lixalde, to have his accounts audited before his death. For Dr Lovett, Lixalde was essentially an overworked bureaucrat: 'The confusion surrounding his accounts probably owed little to incompetence and less to corruption. It represented, rather, the difficulties of administrative adjustment to the new circumstances . . . of permanent

152

warfare in the Low Countries.'³ Even after a lapse of four
hundred years, this judgement seems excessively charitable.
After all, as Dr Lovett admitted, Lixalde's accounts were
only closed in 1612 – thirty-five years after his death – when
his heirs agreed to pay a sizeable fine of 13,000 ducats to the
Castilian Treasury in return for an undertaking that all
further investigations into the Paymaster's affairs would
cease.⁴ This was an unprecedented step: the incorruptible
Audit Office of the Spanish Exchequer (the *Contaduría
Mayor*) was rarely, if ever, bought off in this way again. And
the payment by Lixalde's heirs was all the more remarkable
because it contradicted the claim made by the Paymaster
himself in August 1576 that the king owed him the sum of
112,929 *escudos*.⁵ What had happened to change a large
credit balance into a considerable deficit? Had the overworked Lixalde inadvertently done his sums wrong? After
such a long lapse of time it is impossible to be absolutely
sure – especially since the 13,000 ducats changed hands
specifically to prevent the truth from being established – but
the surviving evidence suggests that Lixalde was guilty of
extortion and corruption on a considerable scale.

As Dr Lovett wrote, almost every Paymaster in the
Spanish Netherlands was suspected of malversation at some
time – 'Accusations of corruption went with the job' (p. 18) –
but, for all that, a quite unusual number of charges were
levelled at Lixalde. In September 1567, only one month after
his arrival in the Netherlands, rumours began to circulate
that the Paymaster was making an illicit profit on the exchange rates at which he received and disbursed the various
coins current in the Low Countries. In October this was
broadened into the more serious allegation that both Lixalde
and the Duke of Alva's secretary, Juan de Albornoz, were
using public money in their keeping to speculate on the
Antwerp stock market. However the principal witness against
the two men, Gerónimo de Curiel, Philip II's Factor at the
Antwerp Fairs, was ambushed and stabbed by two friends of
Albornoz to prevent him from giving evidence. The charges
were dropped. Again, in 1570, Lixalde and Albornoz were
accused of smuggling English goods into the Netherlands

during a time of embargo; but once more they were exculpated.[6] Finally, the Paymaster's actions during the sack of Antwerp in 1576 were the subject of a legal enquiry. Some days before the Spaniards' furious attack on the city on 4 November, Lixalde – who had lived in Antwerp for some years – moved all his valuables into the citadel, which was controlled by reliable Spanish units. Then he returned to his house in the *Beddestraat* to await the onslaught. As soon as the local militia was defeated and the city open to sack, members of Lixalde's household, led by his brother-in-law Martin de Maller clad in armour from top to toe, began to plunder the neighbouring houses. Servaes Bas, a sixty-year-old dealer in second-hand clothes, was dragged from his house into the Paymaster's residence next door where Lixalde's wife was waiting. A halter was placed round his neck and the household discussed whether to strangle him or run him through. In the end avarice triumphed and Bas was simply given a red mark on his forehead while his house was plundered even down to the contents of his children's *spaerpotken* (piggy bank). Margrite Wips, another resident of the *Beddestraat*, reported that members of the Paymaster's household, aided by Spanish troops, burst into her house shouting 'Geld, geld, croonen, croonen', (money, money, ducats, ducats) and when she replied that she had none they took straw out of the beds and set fire to it. She was only allowed to put out the flames when she produced two silver dollars from her purse. In all, fifteen surviving residents of the *Beddestraat* and adjacent streets testified that they had been robbed and harassed by the members of Lixalde's household, and that their stolen goods had been taken to the Paymaster's lodgings. Alas, that was the last they saw of them, for the Paymaster's family evacuated all their booty when the Spanish army left the Netherlands in April 1577.[7]

It was not an edifying tale but, as it happened, the Spanish auditors who examined Lixalde's official accounts knew nothing of it. The 13,000 ducat fine did not arise from any of these misdemeanours. Instead the *Contaduría Mayor* uncovered an even larger swindle perpetrated by Lixalde, this time on the Spanish Treasury. There was a long-established custom among Spanish troops on foreign service that a permanent military hospital should be established to care for and cure all ailing soldiers, to which each man contributed one *real* (about one-thirtieth of his wages, or less) each month. This *real de limosna* was deducted from all wages by the Paymaster-General before the men were paid. Lixalde's accounts, however, made no mention of it.

In November 1603 the *Contaduría Mayor* demanded an explanation from the Lixalde family: why had the Paymaster not deducted the *limosna*? The family's lawyer replied (correctly) that at the mutiny of Antwerp in 1574 the government had tried to deduct the money for the Hospital from the thirty-seven months' wages which were owed to the Spanish troops, but that the mutineers had refused to pay it. From this concrete example he proceeded to argue (incorrectly) that the Paymaster had never deducted the *real de limosna* from any troops:

> The said Paymaster never deducted the said *limosna* nor was he obliged to, because he had no authority to do so nor could he do it by any custom established in the Army of Flanders because he was the first Paymaster of a royal army formed in those provinces.[8]

The *Contaduría Mayor* did not believe a word of this. They reasoned *a priori* that Paymasters of Spanish armies had always deducted the *limosna*.

> In all departments which have to do with the Spanish infantry and cavalry it has always been, and is, as sure and as certain as . . . law that by the said custom the *limosna* which any soldier owed to the Hospital was deducted from the wages he received.[9]

To support this view, the government auditors pointed to Lixalde's own admission in his printed *tanteos* that he had

155

made certain direct payments in 1571 and 1572 'to the royal hospital to cure sick and wounded soldiers'. They also drew attention to the facts that one of Lixalde's predecessors, García de Portillo, had been ordered to deduct the *limosna* in 1552,[10] and that Lixalde's nephew and immediate successor in office, Martín de Unceta, had deducted the *limosna* from the day Lixalde died.[11] Finally, the *contadores* found a small bundle of receipts signed by individual soldiers for their wages (running from 1567 to 1572) which stated unequivocally that the money for the hospital had been deducted from their pay.[12]

The available evidence gives the clear impression that the Paymaster had deducted the *real de limosna* from the Spanish troops in the Netherlands between 1567 and 1572 without declaring it in his accounts. He must therefore have pocketed the proceeds. Lixalde, however, was hoisted with his own petard. After 1572 he was unable to continue with this particular fraud because the Spanish troops were seldom paid any wages at all. When in April 1574 they mutinied for three years of back pay, they refused to pay the *limosna* on the grounds that insufficient medical care had been provided. In the end the government accepted this and no *limosna* was deducted.[13] But the *Contaduría Mayor* knew nothing of this. Having established to their own satisfaction that Lixalde had cheated for some of the time, they assumed that he must have cheated throughout the whole of his ten years of office. In 1612 the auditors therefore added up all the wages paid by Lixalde to the Spanish troops between 1567 and 1577 and calculated that he should have deducted no less than 441,880 *reales* – over 40,000 ducats – in *limosna* for the hospital.[14] The fascimile on page 163 illustrates the various stages in this process. Now by ancient tradition, any mistake or fraud discovered in a public account submitted to the *Contaduría Mayor* incurred a fine of three times its own amount (the *pena de tres tanto*). Lixalde's 'mistake' over the *limosna* for the hospital would therefore produce a fine of some 120,000 ducats. At the same time, careful scrutiny of the various entries in Lixalde's account gradually eliminated his original

156

claim that the crown owed the Paymaster 112,929 *escudos*. In the end, a royal debt of 643 *escudos* was all that remained.[15] Small wonder, then, that Lixalde's son and heir, who had already spent 60,000 ducats in legal fees,[16] decided to propose a settlement 'out of court'. His offer was accepted by the government for a number of reasons: first, some of the relevant papers of the Lixalde case had been lost at the sack of Antwerp;[17] second, most of the officials connected with the accounts were dead; third, the cost of the two auditors permanently employed on the Lixalde case was becoming a burden (they had been at work for thirty-one years and were in receipt of a specially high salary on account of the complexity of the work). Outweighing all these factors, however, in the government's eyes, was the fact that Lixalde had only left an estate worth 22,000 ducats at his death. The crown conceded that it could not fine the Paymaster's heirs a penny more than they had received from Lixalde, so that finding further frauds in his accounts was largely superfluous.[18] After some haggling over the final figure, it was agreed that the heirs should pay the crown 13,000 ducats and in return enjoy the Paymaster's inheritance, fully assured that they would never again be liable for any debt arising from Lixalde's account. The agreement was signed on 27 September 1612.[19]

There are a number of lessons to be learned from the Lixalde story. Of course it illustrates the fallibility of documents and even of statements on oath made to financial and legal tribunals – although it also demonstrates the ability of the same bodies to smell a rat through even the most elaborate disguises. More important, it manifests the principal structural weakness of the Spanish regime in the Netherlands. Lixalde's case by no means stands on its own. Many other members of the duke of Alva's administration were either accused or convicted of corruption and misgovernment. Juan de Navarrete, paymaster of artillery and then senior accountant (*Contador del Sueldo*) of the army, was suspended from office for a year for negligence but died before his criminal misuse of public funds in Flanders was discovered. Juan de

Albornoz, Alva's private secretary, was imprisoned when he returned to Spain in 1574 while charges of corruption against him were examined. There was even a move to try the duke himself for the excesses which were alleged to have occurred during his administration in the Netherlands. However, all the charges were in the end dismissed: Alva returned to a pre-eminent place at court; Albornoz was allowed to enjoy his ill-gotten gains at large.[20]

Corruption was rife in the Spanish administration in the Netherlands after 1567, and it stemmed ultimately from two failings at the heart of the Habsburg system. First, there was no formal training for civil servants: the men who staffed the royal administration usually came from the private secretariat of one of the King's ministers. The households of the great ministers were well known as the 'seminary' in which future generations of public servants were formed, but they were formed with a sense of loyalty to their patron which often overrode their sense of duty to the crown. This was a serious weakness, and it was compounded in the Spanish Netherlands by a second failing: the lack of any institutional checks on the military administration. At first there was only one: the Inspector-General (*Veedor General*). Single-handed, this official was expected to control abuse in an army of up to 80,000 men. Of course he could not, especially since the post was often unfilled. Lixalde, for example, was only subjected to the scrutiny of a *Veedor* for thirty months of his ten years in office (March 1567-June 1569 and July-August 1572).[2] The situation was clearly unsatisfactory, and it is surprising that the king did nothing to amend it. After all, a whole hierarchy of institutions existed in Spain and Spanish America specifically to restrain unscrupulous royal officials. It was a source of wonder to other European governments and their advisers:

> The king of Spain . . . possesseth in much peace many lands far remote from Spain, abounding in riches and all manner of delights. Whose viceroys, presidents and officers of charge change often place and have no continuance to

158

breed a faction. Besides that when new come in place the old are not dismissed before inquiry have been thoroughly made of all manner of their demeanours, according to which they are returned to Spain either with due commendation or blame, which they must answer before their sureties and pledges first given for their allegiance be also set free.[22]

In Spain and Spanish America, throughout the sixteenth century, when an official's tour of duty came to an end, a *residencia* followed – a period of several weeks during which the official continued to reside in the area where he had held his position while all those who had a complaint to make against him were allowed to do so in the presence of a local judge specially appointed for the purpose (the *juez de residencia*). To control abuse of power by military personnel in each large province the crown also established local tribunals (known as *audiencias*) composed of local lawyers and vested with wide-ranging powers of audit (*cuenta*) and inspection (*visita*) under the general supervision of the Council of the Indies or the Council of Castile.[23] But these valuable institutions were never planted either in Spanish Italy or in the Spanish Netherlands; and in Spanish America they were allowed to decay. The reason is not hard to find. During the reign of Philip II the conviction grew in governing circles that the Indians, the Italians and the Netherlanders were all inferior, subject peoples. One writer in 1557, himself a Spaniard, observed that the Castilians in particular 'put so high a value on their own achievements and so low a value on everyone else's, that they give the impression that they alone are descended from heaven and the rest of mankind are mud'. Likewise the French ambassador at Philip II's court in Brussels noted in 1559 that 'Nothing here is well-said, well-done or well-thought unless it comes in Spanish and from a Spaniard'.[24] For many Spaniards, Indians were 'animals who do not even feel reason, but are ruled by their passions'; 'their base and imperfect character requires that they should be ruled, governed and guided to their appointed

159

end by fear more than by love'. The Italians were hardly better: 'For these Italians, although they are not Indians, have to be treated as such, so that they will understand that we are in charge of them and not they in charge of us.'[25] This disdain explains in large measure the brutal behaviour of the Spanish troops and others in Italy – it should be remembered that the 'Black Legend' of Spanish arrogance and cruelty originated in Italy.[26] It was the same in the Netherlands. The Spanish troops who served in the Low Countries acted as if they were conquerors in occupied territory, at least until the end of the sixteenth century, and their misbehaviour became legendary even in Spain, where it gave rise to a telling proverb: *Estamos aquí o en Flandes?* (Are we here or in the Netherlands?) meaning 'What a dreadful way to behave!' The Spanish officers of the Army of Flanders had a similarly low opinion of the Netherlanders. The Duke of Alva dismissed the magistrates of Brussels as 'scum', excoriated the entire civil service as incompetent or wicked (or both), and dismissed the nobility as poltroons of only 'average and a little below average' capacity.[27] The only solution to the Low Countries problem, according to Alva, was to 'create a New World' in the Netherlands.[28]

There were, of course, many Spaniards who did not share this view, criticizing Alva and his lapidary attitudes just as Fray Bartolomé de las Casas had attacked Spanish brutality in America during the reign of Charles V.[29] But, as Dr Lovett himself has demonstrated admirably in another article, the opponents of Alva's point of view never entirely succeeded in convincing the king.[30] Philip II could never bring himself to trust his Low Countries vassals; above all he would never agree to set natives of the Netherlands above Spaniards. Low Countries institutions such as the *Chambres des Comptes* (*Rekenkamers* – Audit Offices) or the *Grand Conseil de Malines* (*Grote Raad van Mechelen* – the supreme court of appeal in the Netherlands) were never allowed to interfere with Spanish administrative personnel.[31]

Lixalde, Albornoz and the other fraudulent officials of the duke of Alva's regime were thus, as it were, the price which Spain had to pay for her 'Master Race' mentality.

Without adequate training or supervision, it is hardly surprising that unscrupulous or weak-minded bureaucrats should have taken advantage of the ample opportunities for profit afforded them by the Spanish system. The Lixalde case is only unusual in that it shows *in detail* how easy it was to be a corrupt official in the Habsburg Netherlands – and almost get away with it!

The main entry concerns the 27,414 *escudos* paid to the *tercio* as its wages for April and May 1567 (paid by order, or *nómina*, of the duke of Alva, dated 9 June 1567). It is the notes of the auditors at the top and in the right-hand margin which are of special interest however:

[Top centre]

> *Notta: por c[ed]la de su mag[esta]d de xxvij de set[iembr]e de dcxij [= 1612] se tomo medio y concierto con Ju[an] Baut[ist]a de Lex[ald]e cav[aller]o del auito de S[an]tiago hijo y her[eder]o del d[ic]ho pag[ad]or por el q[ua]l mando su mag[esta]d que no se prosiguiese mas en la qu[en]ta del d[ic]ho pag[ad]or y la dio por acavada y q[ue] haviendo pag[a]do xiijU d[ucad]os se le diese finiquito della en la forma y segun se dize en la nota q[ue] esta en pliego de or si juncto a este.*

[Top right]

> *Ojo = nota = que se ha de aueriguar el desquento del ospital porque en las libranças ordenaron los contadores del ex[erci]to al pag[ad]or que descontase un real de cada soldado y el que da estas quentas dize que aunq[ue] lo desconto que lo boluio a entregar a los mayor-domos del ospital que ha de mostrar recado dello.*

[Centre right]

> *Ojo = nota = Q[ue] Xpoual [=Christoual] de Ypeñarrieta, del cons[ej]o de hazi[en]da y cont[adur]ia m[ay]or della de su m[a]g[esta]d, siendo contador de la comision de flandes junto con Ju[an] Lopez de Aliri, glosaron la datta de lo pag[a]do al tercio de Sicilia, qu[e] esta a lo ultimo de toda la ynf[anter]ia sp[año]la en este libro y en cada p[a]r[ti]da sacaron cargo al d[ic]ho pag[ad]or Lexalde desta limosna del ospital. Y asi en la misma conformidad se ha de descontar la deste tercio por ser del mis[m]o t[iem]po y genero qu[e]el como tanbien so son los t[e]r[ci]os de Lombardia, Cerdeña y Flandes y el de la Liga, a qu en asimis[m]o se ha sacado cargo de la d[ic]ha limosna en pliego aparte que [e]sta antes deste en este libro por Menor. Y por el pareçe q[ue] monta toda esta limosna cccc°xljU dccc°lxxx° r[eal]es. [= 441,880 reales;* the sum of 6374 reales in the left hand margin was the sum which the auditors thought Lixalde should have deducted from the pay given to the *tercio* of Naples on 9 June 1567.]

[Bottom right]

> *= Notta = Tanbien queda en este libro antes deste pliego una copia autentica de una orden qu[e] e duq[ue] de alua dio en el campo çesareo en prim[er]o de novi[embr]e de dlij [= 1552]; y el original se ynbio al Tribunal; por donde consta la antiguedad q[ue] ay p[ar]a descontarse esta limosna y asimis[m]o queda acqui un auto del Tribunal dado al pie de petiçion de la p[ar]te del pag[ad]or y del fiscal de su mag[esta]d el año de dcvj [= 1606] p[ar]a q[ue] se descuente la d[ic]ha limosna q[ue] se hallo sobre un caxon de papeles de la p[ar]te qu[e] estuaabierto en xxij deste press[en]te mes de octu[br]e de Mdcxj años =*

FACSIMILE. First sheet of the *pliego de asiento* with the *tercio* of Naples for 1567 (AGS CMC 2a época/29).

9

It can be said in defence of the frauds and malfeasance of the early years of the Spanish regime in the Netherlands described above that it was committed by men placed in an impossible position: they had expected to serve in their posts, hundreds of miles from their families and homes, for no more than a year, but they were required to remain in the Low Countries for ten. However lucrative the opportunities for illicit profit, they did not want to stay. As the emergency arrangements introduced in 1567 were prolonged for one year after another, the pleas from the various members of Alva's administration to be allowed to go home became more strident. The situation improved little under the duke of Parma and his short-lived successors (1578-96), and it was only with the creation of a permanent political system under the Archdukes Albert and Isabella that public and private probity returned to the government of the Catholic Netherlands. The normal structure of checks and balances was restored both in the military administration (run by Spaniards and Italians) and in the civil departments of state (run mainly by Netherlanders); and, under this reformed polity, a new and distinctive 'South Netherlands' nationality emerged which proved strong enough to resist all efforts to incorporate the country in either its Dutch or its French neighbour.

The Decision-making Process in the Government of the Catholic Netherlands under 'the Archdukes', 1596-1621

Philip II's immediate reaction to the revolt of the Netherlands in 1572 was a major effort to reconquer the rebellious provinces by force, an effort which he continued for over twenty years. Towards the end of his life, however, with the final victory still not in sight, the King became aware of the defects of his approach and determined on a supreme gesture of conciliation. He decided that the Netherlands should be handed over, not to his son the future Philip III, but to his daughter Isabella, who was to marry her cousin Albert, Archduke of Austria and (since 1596) the King's Governor-General in Brussels. In August 1598 Albert assumed the sovereign power in Isabella's name and in April 1599 they married. Thenceforth 'the Archdukes' governed together as sovereign rulers of the South Netherlands. But what did this transfer of power mean? How did it affect the functions of the administrative bodies which were responsible for ruling the Netherlands, and especially of the three senior institutions the Council of State, Council of Finance, and Privy Council – commonly referred to as the 'Collateral Councils'? These are unfashionable questions, for administrative history has become an unfashionable subject. And yet some understanding of the workings of the institutions of government is vital. We do not fully understand how any government of an early modern state made decisions, because we do not fully understand how the governmental processes worked. The purpose of this paper is therefore mainly informative: to ascertain how far the decisions of the archdukes were formed by the collateral councils and, indeed, whether their decisions were made in Brussels at all. Were the archdukes in fact 'independent'?

The powers of the three Collateral Councils were neither fixed nor clearly defined. On the whole, their actions were determined by tradition but tempered by expediency. The Council of Finance, to begin with, was responsible for the yield of the sovereign's lands and taxes in the Netherlands; but both the raising and the spending of most sources of revenue were decentralized to a significant extent. The local collectors spent a large amount of the money they received on the spot, and only the residue was transferred to the central treasury. Decentralization was most extensive in the case of the taxes voted by the provincial Estates – the *aides* or *beden*: first, the council had to secure the consent of the Estates of each province to the imposition and allocation of each *aide*;[1] and, after 1590, there was a greater degree of participation

165

by the Estates in the expenditure of the money raised.[2] In some regions, indeed, such as Flanders and Brabant, the Council had to tolerate the co-administration of the provincial Estates at every level: even the accounts of the *aides* collected were audited by a special committee consisting of several representatives of the estates but only one delegate of the sovereign. The royal Audit Office, responsible to the Council of Finance, was altogether excluded.[3] When in 1600 the States-General, representing all the provincial Estates, voted a larger *aide* than ever before, the government had to agree that the proceeds would be applied first and foremost to the payment of the troops stationed in each province and that any surplus would be handed over directly to the treasurer of war who was responsible for military expenditure.[4]

However, the government's ordinary receipts from the crown lands and from *aides* were not nearly enough to cover its expenditure, mainly because of the cost of the war with the Dutch. There were therefore a number of extraordinary sources of revenue, among which the most important were the remittances from Spain, averaging over £1,000,000 sterling each year. In an effort to extend its competence to all matters of finance, the Council tried to gain control of this important source of income, but it failed.[5] The money sent from Spain to the Netherlands central Treasury steadily diminished, and instead a separate administration manned exclusively by Spaniards was set up. There was a *pagador general* (Paymaster-General) and *contadores* (accountants) after 1567, a *superintendente de hacienda* (financial controller) from 1578 and a *junta de hacienda* (finance committee) from August 1595, all appointed by the king and possessing almost complete control over the provisions sent from Spain. This money was ear-marked for military expenditure, and principally for the Spanish and Italian troops. Despite the sovereign status of the archdukes, the *junta* continued to control the army's funds, ignoring the Collateral Councils and owing obedience and responsibility solely to the king of Spain.[6]

Where the Council of Finance watched over the material

interests of the sovereign, the Privy Council acted in the sphere of *grace, justice et police* – *police* in early modern times including the important duty of promulgating government edicts.[7] However, the fact that the Council prepared and proclaimed acts of legislation did not necessarily mean that it had taken the initiative in proposing them. The idea could, and often did, come from one of the other councils or from one of the sovereign's personal advisers. The Privy Council was only required to clothe the archdukes' commands in legal language. To take two examples: a placard issued by the Council on 16 November 1599 which declared that the 'new Dutch guilder' should have the same current value as the 'guilder of account' merely embodied the findings of an extensive enquiry by the Council of Finance among its Mintmasters and Auditors.[8] Similarly, in March 1603 the Privy Council had to draw up and issue a placard which gave legal force to certain mercantile policies devised by Juan de Gauna, one of the archdukes' Spanish advisers, despite the fact that the Collateral Councils had expressed disapproval of the scheme. Gauna had the support of Philip III of Spain and the Brussels government therefore had to concur.[9]

But publishing edicts was only a small part of the Privy Council's business. Thanks to its powers of justice it controlled the entire complex of law enforcement in the Catholic Netherlands and Franche-Comté. The annual appointment of magistrates in cities and castellancies took place at its behest, even though its choice was limited to the list of names put forward by a handful of local worthies (normally the senior cleric, the senior judicial officer and the local military commander).[10] The Council also filled vacancies in the Great Council of Mechelen and the 'Provincial Councils' (each acting as the royal court of justice for its province), although again it was customary for the Council to make its selection from a list of three or four names submitted by the body concerned (and in cases where it desired to nominate an outsider it did so only after consultation with the subordinate institution).[11] In addition the Privy Council was able to intervene directly in the administration of justice, both positively and negatively. All law courts (and especially the

Great Council of Mechelen, the senior tribunal of appeals) and the 'Provincial Councils' operated under the constant scrutiny and pressure of the government. The Privy Council could and did stop cases being heard in an inferior court simply by asking for information about the suit: until further instructions came from the Council, no verdict could be reached. Sometimes the Council sent one of its members 'to intervene in the resolution of the case pending there [*pour entrevenir à la resolution du procès y pendant*]'.[12] Such interference was regarded as perfectly normal (indeed the lower courts on certain occasions asked the Council for advice – for instance when there was no agreement among the judges upon a verdict).[13] The Privy Council could also delay and even disrupt the normal course of justice in any lower court by the arbitrary use of an impressive range of judicial instruments which all legal tribunals had to respect. It could delay the hearing of a case until further notice, by letters of *staet ende surceancie* (which suspended civil legal claims until further notice) and *atterminatie ende respijt* (which prorogued actions for debt and split repayments into a number of instalments). It could issue letters of *abolitie* (pardon), *gratie ende remissie* (which saved sentenced murderers from execution), or *rehabilitatie* (which reversed a previous sentence).[14] All were freely and frequently used.

This sort of conduct by a government department would be unacceptable today, but in the Habsburg Netherlands the executive and the judiciary were one and the same. The Privy Council in fact administered justice itself almost every day. In the first place, the Council considered itself to be the appropriate tribunal for the personal suits of all those connected with the palace and court of the sovereign, a group known to the law as the *escroes*. Not unnaturally, since the Privy Council was so conveniently situated and also supreme, the *escroes* made sure that it heard every civil suit in which they were involved.[15] Second, and more important, because it provided a better legal title, with no risk of an appeal to a higher court, all sorts of outside people and institutions appealed to the Council for a ruling. It was this above all that stimulated the Privy Council to extend its jurisdiction during the reign of the archdukes. If a greater degree of centralization in the judicial system meant a safer legal judgement, everyone was happy to accept centralization.[16] The same thing happened with ecclesiastical cases. The Council took an interest in all types of suit – from those involving disputes over clerical property (*de petitorio*) and possession (*de possessorio*) to mere canonical controversies – but again it acted in response to popular demand: more and more clerics tended to seek justice from the central tribunal. The 'usurpation' was not the result of empire-building by the court.[17]

However, the history of the Privy Council under the archdukes was not simply one of jurisdictional 'gains'. There was one loss as well. The Spanish troops who arrived in the Netherlands in 1567 were accompanied by their own legal officers and police force, the *auditores* and *barracheles de campo*. As the size of the armed forces in the southern provinces increased to seventy and eighty thousand men, a fully-fledged superstructure of legal tribunals grew up to handle the litigation, both civil and criminal, in which the soldiers were involved. This development took some time, but with the appointment of the first *superintendente de la justicia militar* (superintendent of military justice) in 1595, the separation of jurisdictions was complete. In the early years of the archdukes it became established that even if only one of the parties was a soldier, the case went to the military tribunals, not the civil courts. Moreover the Spanish *superintendente* acquired the right to hear appeals against sentences passed by Netherlands military tribunals. The Privy Council, like all other Netherlands institutions, was almost totally excluded.[18]

Traditionally, the Council of State was senior in status to the other two collateral bodies. It was certainly different in structure. In theory it was the most important of the councils, concerned with internal, external and defence policies at the highest levels,[19] but in practice its authority was limited by two factors. In the first place its meetings and its powers were more closely controlled by the head of state.[20] Second, founded only in 1531, the Council had not had time to consolidate a firm hold on any sector of public policy. In foreign affairs and defence especially, it had to endure increasing competition from the so-called 'Spanish Ministry', the nucleus of Spanish advisers in the Netherlands, many of them summoned specially by the archdukes from Spain.[21] Between 1599 and 1609, indeed, only one 'Belgian' councillor had any appreciable influence on high policy – Jean Richardot – and even he was excluded from all military matters (which were reserved for Spaniards).[22] The main difference between the Council of State and its two sister institutions was that the former was only an advisory body while the Privy and Financial Councils actually took decisions.[23] In a way, this was inevitable. Because the Council of State dealt with matters of the greatest importance, the archdukes were bound to take an interest; conversely, the abundance and the technical nature of the matters referred to the other two councils made it impossible for the archdukes to make a personal decision on every issue and the Privy and Financial Councils therefore resolved a good many matters for themselves, without interference from the archdukes. Very often the sovereigns only signed an order to authenticate it, and they rarely disregarded the advice offered by one of the Collateral Councils or followed the opinion of a minority. There is an inescapable impression that the sovereign's signature was often a formality.[24] On the other hand, the Archdukes made sure that a number of important issues never appeared on the Councils' agenda. The Council of State, in particular, was not allowed to discuss many issues of foreign and defence policy; instead these were handled informally by the sovereigns in consultation with their personal advisers, some of them Netherlanders like Richardot or Matthias Hovius (archbishop of Mechelen) or Louis Verreycken (the *Audiencier*), but most of them Spaniards.[25] The 'Spanish ministry' included some confidants who came in the entourage of the archdukes (such as Albert's confessor, fray Iñigo de Brizuela) together with other officials attached to the army and appointed by the king (such as Juan de Mancicidor, secretary of state for war, and Ambrogio Spinola, *maestre de campo general* and *superintendente de hacienda*).[26] These men – 'alcuni domestici et privati' as a

170

papal nuncio put it – were consulted by the archdukes informally either individually or in *juntas* (committees) whenever the need arose.[27] However, really important matters in foreign and defence policy always had to be referred back to the king of Spain. The truce talks with the Dutch in 1607-9 were a case in point. Richardot, the chief minister of the 'Belgian' government was forbidden by Philip III to send agents to the Hague to discuss peace until 1606 (and only then when Ambrogio Spinola, the king's chief adviser in the Netherlands, had become convinced that further fighting was futile). When the talks did start in 1607, although Richardot was allowed to participate, the Collateral Councils remained expressly excluded.[28]

Spanish influence in the Netherlands was strongest in questions of defence and foreign affairs. In these matters the archdukes, although they took one or two decisions on their own, were normally bound hand and foot by the 'Spanish ministry' in Brussels, acting on the direct commands of the Spanish king and his entourage. It was the king who controlled military operations in the Netherlands and who appointed and removed the officers of the Army of Flanders. Although for the sake of appearances military personnel were appointed by patents from the archdukes as well as by letters from the king, the archdukes could not act first in military patronage. And in many issues of foreign affairs they were never allowed to act at all. For the peace-talks with England in 1603, Philip III appointed Juan Fernández de Velasco, Constable of Castile, to conduct negotiations for himself and the archdukes; Albert and Isabella were instructed to maintain 'good mutual contact' – and to accept whatever the Constable was able to secure for them. The Spanish delegation, Richardot complained, 'behaved themselves more as our masters than as our companions'.[29] It was the same again during the truce talks with the Dutch in 1607-9: Philip III appointed Spinola and Mancicidor (the chief Spanish minister in Brussels) to represent him, and he saw to it that everything was dealt with by them, despite their difficulty in understanding any of the French and Dutch spoken by the other side.[30] If he chose to do so, the king could also intervene in other areas besides defence and foreign policy. Foreign trade was from time to time subject to Spanish intervention. Thus in October 1598 the archdukes were ordered to forbid all commercial relations with the Dutch; despite protests and hardship among southern merchants – the archdukes' own subjects! – Spain's views prevailed.[31] Again in 1603 an unpopular order arrived from the king: all foreign trade except that with Spain was to bear a new value added tax of 30 per cent. Again local protests, and even complaints from France and England, were ignored and the tax was imposed (although in time the archdukes connived at exemptions and evasion in order to protect local trade).[32]

One might have expected that, with the conclusion of the truce in 1609 and the reduction of the armed forces that followed, Spanish pressure on the Netherlands would abate. It did not. During the Cleves-Julich emergencies (1610 and 1614), the Bohemia-Palatinate crisis (1618-20) and the manoeuvres over renewing the Truce (1619-21), Philip III's control remained undiminished. It was the same in smaller incidents. In 1616, for example, the inspector-general of the Army of Flanders, a Spaniard, personally insulted the archduke Albert; there was nothing the 'sovereign' could do, however, except plead with his brother-in-law, Philip III, to recall the offensive minister. The truth was that Philip III could not afford to relax his grip. The transfer of power to the archdukes in 1598-9 had been only temporary: if they died without children – and it became increasingly clear that they would – the Catholic Netherlands were to revert immediately to Spain. If there was nevertheless a change in the relationship between Spain and the archdukes' Netherlands after the conclusion of the Truce, it was not because Philip III had softened, but because until 1609 every effort and every action of the government had of necessity been part of the war effort against the Dutch. There had been neither time nor money for anything else. After 1609 the archdukes were free to initiate new domestic policies to restore a measure of prosperity to their devastated country, and in such internal matters Philip III – who of course stood ultimately to benefit – was content to give a free hand to the archdukes and their Collateral Councils.

To some extent, the activity of the Collateral Councils therefore remained confined to matters of secondary importance, and in the main their daily routine was determined, prosaically enough, by the quantity and the content of the correspondence and memoranda received at any given time – from envoys abroad, from foreign princes or ambassadors, from subordinate tribunals and officials, and from the provincial Estates – and by the volume of 'Requests' pending.[33] The Request was the normal way by which inferior institutions and private individuals brought a matter to the government's attention: most of the state's actions and even some of its legislation (placards and ordinances) stemmed from a private Request and there is no doubt that this practice stimulated an extension of state activity and promoted greater centralization.[34] Requests were almost always addressed to the archdukes but in fact they were sorted out by an official secretariat headed by the 'president' (chairman) of the Council of State, and then directed (where necessary) to the appropriate Collateral Council.[35] A member of the Council was entrusted with the investigation of the matter and the preparation of a report, and he sought information from institutions such as the Provincial Councils and Audit Offices which, in their turn, consulted the relevant local authorities and finally the individuals concerned.[36] A dossier was then drawn up on the basis of the advice received from these various sources and presented to the Council, which scrutinized the report and made a recommendation to the sovereign. Normally the Council accepted the advice of lower courts in its decisions and in its recommendations to the archdukes, and normally the archdukes in turn accepted the advice of the Council, although pressure from court dignitaries or others close to the archdukes could always influence the final decision.[37] The Collateral Councils expended a great deal of their time and energies on the 'Requests'.

On the whole the government relied to a surprising extent

173

upon local institutions for advice in taking decisions. It also depended upon them to publish and execute those resolutions. The Council of Finance regularly called on the Audit Offices to communicate its orders to the minor revenue-collectors.[38] Placards and ordinances of the government were delivered to the supreme court in each province (the Provincial Council) by the court's messengers, and indeed government legislation only acquired the force of law after the Provincial Councils had noted and registered it and affixed their 'lettres d'attache'.[39] Sometimes these councils postponed publication of a placard or suppressed certain clauses. Normally they then contacted the Privy Council to discuss the point at issue, although sometimes they might just keep quiet. Thus in April 1596 the Privy Council noticed that the Council of the province of Luxemburg had still not published the ordinance, issued almost ten years before, which prohibited study at a foreign university.[40] The Audit Offices, as well as the Provincial Councils, had to confirm grants (*octroyes*) and remissions (*abolitie; gratie ende remissie*) before they were valid.[41]

The same deference to local institutions coloured many of the executive commands of the central government. Most orders were meant to resolve only a specific situation – they were rarely general or absolute – and even then most of them ended with a phrase such as: '*ten zy dat ghy hebt eenighe legittime redenen oft oorsaecke ter contrarien*' (unless you have any legitimate reasons or causes to the contrary).[42] This elastic formula was hardly the cachet of despotism. Besides the inclusion of such flexible safeguards in most executive commands, many individual government orders contained manifold exceptions which virtually undermined their effect. This was particularly so in the various attempts to regulate the economy. For example, on 12 October 1598 the Privy Council issued a placard which forbade merchants to buy butter, cheese, grain or livestock from the producers in the countryside; thenceforth all farmers were to sell their goods on the open market in person. This measure provoked an immediate storm of protest from the butchers' guilds in several cities and so the Council almost at once 'interpreted' the placard in a way which gave the meat trade certain exemptions from its terms.[43]

Of course, in the seventeenth century, a number of the measures which appealed to governments were so unrealistic that it was quite impossible to apply them, but even some quite straightforward acts had constantly to be re-issued – a sure sign that they were not being enforced. The classic case is the series of placards on the currency issued by the Privy Council after 1600 in the hope of making the value of real money in the South Netherlands correspond to the value of money-of-account without altering the intrinsic worth of the coins in circulation. Every attempt failed – although the Council kept on trying. Even the laws of princes could not overcome the laws of the market.[44]

The seventeenth century was undoubtedly a time of absolute monarchy, and to some extent the archdukes could be termed 'absolute' rulers. But there were two important bridles on their independence of action. First, and more obviously, there was the political influence of the king of Spain and the Spanish ministry in Brussels on foreign policy, defence, military justice and finance. The king had the power to order with one hand that the war with the Dutch should continue yet withhold with the other the funds necessary to wage it. But the king could be persuaded, even manipulated, and might change his mind. On a number of occasions the archdukes, aided by Spinola, brought him round to their point of view – they even persuaded him to agree to a cease-fire with the Dutch in 1607 and to a long truce in 1609. In the other spheres of their 'sovereign power' the Archdukes were far more free of Spanish interference, but here a second limitation on their 'independence' came into play, less obvious but more effective: the subordinate institutions and officials of the South Netherlands. The archdukes could only govern with their tolerance and consent – that is, by involving themselves in what political sociologists would call a 'participative decision-making process'. Although there was a considerable expansion in the activity of the central organs of government, this was only permitted where it corresponded to the needs of society. Beyond that, the local institutions

175

protected themselves and their subjects with implacable tenacity. Particularist feeling had always been especially strong in the Netherlands it is true – that was what the Dutch Revolt had been about for many people – but the strength of provincialism all over Europe in early modern times can hardly be exaggerated. The great confrontations between governments and the governed all over Europe in the middle decades of the seventeenth century proved it. If the archdukes chose to respect the feelings of their 'inferior magistrates' and rule with their consent, it was a sign of political wisdom: they could not have governed effectively in any other way.[45]

10

The last essay in this book is, appropriately enough, an attempt to evaluate the economic and social costs of Spain's long involvement in the Netherlands. The task of quantifying phenomena in the pre-statistical age is notoriously difficult – apart from deliberate fraud among those compiling the figures (see Chapter 8 above), the surviving data are often incomplete and, even if complete, were recorded for entirely different purposes from those of the modern student – and my conclusions have been the subject of some dispute. In particular, they have been criticized for overstating the deleterious effects of the Eighty Years' War on the Dutch Republic; but they have recently received strong support from an important article published by Dr Jonathan Israel, who is preparing a monograph on the conflict of the Dutch and Spanish empires between 1621 and 1648, and from Professor Ivo Schöffer, who has completed a large-scale survey of the trade of the Dutch East India Company between 1602 and 1795. I have incorporated those of their conclusions which are already available in print in the pages that follow, but in all other respects it is the same as the article which appeared in the *Festschrift* published in memory of David Joslin, formerly Professor of Economic History at Cambridge, who had persuaded the university's Ellen MacArthur Fund to make two grants to enable me to prolong my research in foreign archives. Historical research abroad, for young British scholars at least, is usually an expensive and solitary affair, especially when the topic concerns the economic and social history of early modern Europe, since it is normally necessary to extract serial data from such vast quantities of record that bulk microfilming is impracticable. David Joslin was one of those who recognized this special need.

War and Economic Change:
the Economic Costs of the Dutch Revolt

In 1580 the States-General of France commissioned a royal official, Nicolas Froumenteau, to ascertain the costs of the civil and religious wars fought since 1559. Froumenteau scanned the civil, ecclesiastical and judicial records of each diocese of France in search of statistics, and his report – which took up 591 closely printed pages – even included an estimate of the total number of French women raped between 1559 and 1580 (no less than 12,300 of them). Froumenteau's was a remarkable achievement. It was also unique: nothing else quite like it was composed in early modern times. For other wars in other areas historians have had to do their own sums.[1]

Unfortunately, since the volume of surviving archival and literary material is so vast, there have been many studies published on individual communities or areas but few syntheses or general surveys. Generalization is hampered by the fact that the experience of each community tends to be unique, some registering total dislocation, others only a slight disturbance. A recent survey of the economic consequences of the Thirty Years' War in Germany, for example, counted ten local studies published between 1910 and 1943 which suggested that Germany was in decline before the war began as against twenty-four which supported the view that the war dealt a catastrophic blow to a previously booming economy. The discussion remains open.[2] The debate over the economic consequences of the Dutch war of liberation (1568-1648) has followed much the same course. The view has been advanced by some scholars that the economy of the South Netherlands was permanently crippled and that of the North decisively stimulated by the conflict; others hold that the war was not nearly so influential, that Holland gained less and 'Belgium' lost less than had been supposed. A number of regional and local studies have been produced to support each interpretation.[3]

178

The aim of the present essay is to examine and correlate the various sources which bear on this question and to consider the effects of the war upon some of the numerous participants. The Eighty Years' War was, *par excellence*, a war of intervention. Throughout early modern times the Netherlands were the 'cockpit of Europe' and almost every European state became involved in the Dutch struggle for independence at some time. Several German princes sent occasional subsidies; Elizabeth of England sent at least fifteen million florins to the Low Countries between 1585 and 1603; and Henry IV of France sent ten million florins between 1598 and 1610. These sums were considerable, but they could hardly compare with Habsburg Spain which often sent as much as that in a single year, and sometimes more. Then there were manpower costs. England, France, the German states, Spain and Italy as well as the Netherlands provided a steady supply of troops and the cumulative loss of life, civilian and military, must have been considerable – although not, perhaps, as high as the estimate of the Spanish writer Quevedo who, through the mouth of an imaginary Dutch sea captain informing the ignorant Indians of Chile about the Revolt, wrote:

> The harsh spirit [*ánimo severo*] of Philip II placed the bloody punishment of the two noblemen [Egmont and Hornes] above the retention of all those provinces and lordships . . . In wars lasting sixty years and more we have sacrificed more than two million men to those two lives, for the campaigns and sieges of the Netherlands have become the universal sepulchre of Europe.[4]

It is with the Netherlands as a 'sepulchre', of money, material and morale as well as of men, that this essay is concerned; and inevitably, therefore, attention will be focused primarily upon the three areas which were most affected, economically speaking, by the Dutch Revolt: modern Belgium, the Iberian peninsula, and the Dutch Republic.

179

I

Perhaps the least disputable economic consequence of the Dutch Revolt was a catastrophic fall in the population of the South Netherlands.[5] We have a relatively large amount of information concerning the demographic decline of 'Belgium' between 1572 (the outbreak of continuous fighting) and 1609 (the Twelve Years' Truce), and with scarcely an exception there is clear evidence that almost every community in Flanders and Brabant lost between a half and two-thirds of its inhabitants. Moreover this long-term development, illustrated in Figure 1, in most cases masks an even sharper fall in the decade 1578-88. The demographic experience of the small Flemish village of Evergem – the subject of Figure 2 – appears to have been all too typical. Rural areas suffered particularly severely. In southern Flanders it has been estimated that only 1 per cent of the farming population remained on their land throughout the crisis decade of the 1580s, while further north, around Ghent, the area under cultivation fell by 92 per cent over the ten years. It was the same story in Brabant where farms were destroyed, crops burned and entire families of peasants murdered by the soldiers and freebooters.[6] Only the provinces which defected to Spain without a blow in 1577-9 – Artois, Hainaut and French Flanders – appear to have escaped the devastation.

The proximity of heavy fighting also had an adverse effect on industrial production. Heavy capital equipment was wantonly destroyed by the troops of both sides. The cloth works of Hondschoote, far and away the largest in the Netherlands, changed hands six times between 1578 and 1582, when they were burnt to the ground by French soldiers. The town's population fell from 18,000 in the 1560s to 385 in 1584. Figure 3 (below) shows the severe slump in its production. Other textile centres virtually ceased to produce during the 1580s and some of them never recovered.[7]

Thus far, therefore, the traditional picture appears correct. Flanders and Brabant, the ancient heart of the Low Countries, formerly the most prosperous provinces, were totally ruined.

180

In 1585 and 1586 it proved impossible even to sow crops in many areas through shortage of labour.[8] However the South Netherlands did not remain at this low level for long. After about 1600 the character of the war in the Low Countries changed. The battle-line was dramatically shortened by the

Figure 1: The Depopulation of Flanders and Brabant, 1570-1600. (For sources see page 273 below.)

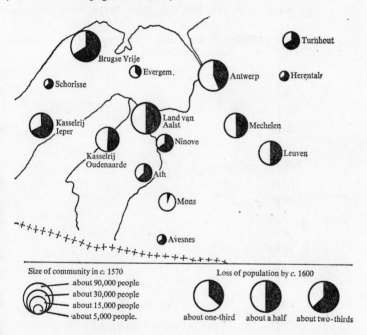

victories of Maurice of Nassau in the 1590s and hostilities were gradually limited by the system of 'contributions' (whereby a community paid protection money to the enemy in return for a guarantee that it would not be molested) and 'convoy and licence money' (dues paid to the Dutch to allow ships to sail to Antwerp). These conventions, although deplored by many professional soldiers on the Spanish side, did create the conditions of security which were the essential prerequisite of any economic recovery. Gradually, the

181

Spain and the Netherlands

population increased anew. The parish registers of the southern towns reveal a substantial increase in the number of baptisms recorded between the 1590s and the 1640s: over 90 per cent up at Lier and Leuven, 82 per cent up at Mechelen, and 76 per cent up at Ghent.[9] The former metropolis of Antwerp, whose population fell from almost 84,000 in 1582 to 42,000 in 1589, had recovered to about 54,000 in 1612. Antwerp merchants began to trade again with Italy and Spain and even with the Spanish and Portuguese overseas

Figure 2: The Population of the Village of Evergem (just North of Ghent), 1571-1601.

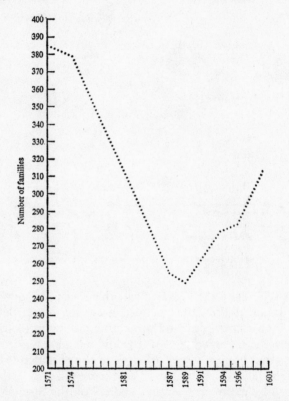

Source: A. de Vos, 'Dertig jaar bevolkingsevolutie te Evergem (1571-1601)', *Handelingen der Maatschappij voor Geschiedenis en Oudheidkunde te Gent,* XIV (1960), p. 122.

182

empires.[10] Almost 600 South Netherlands merchants are known to have traded with the Iberian powers and their empires between 1598 and 1648. Silk, sugar and other 'colonial' goods flowed into Antwerp in considerable quantities after 1589, while the vast sums spent by the king of Spain on his army in the Netherlands, most of it sent from

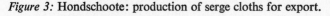

Figure 3: Hondschoote: production of serge cloths for export.

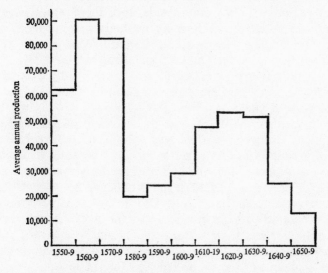

Source: E. Coornaert, *Un centre industriel d'autrefois. La draperie-sayetterie d'Hondschoote, XIVe-XVIIIe siècles* (Paris, 1930) – based upon the statistical appendix at the end.

Castile, also brought prosperity to some bankers, sutlers and military contractors in the 'obedient provinces'.[11] There was considerable industrial recovery too. As Figure 3 shows, even Hondschoote produced almost as many broad-cloths in the 1620s as in the 1550s: almost 60,000 were turned out in some years, most of them exported to Spain through Ostend and Dunkirk. Ghent too produced large quantities and many varieties of textiles in the first half of the seventeenth century: 29,000 linen cloths were brought to market in 1636, of

183

which 20,000 were exported to Spain.[12] In many towns new activities grew up to compensate for the demise of the old – silk, lace, tapestries, glass-making, jewellery, diamond-cutting and printing – while in general there was a shift of emphasis from quantity to quality. The profits made from these enterprises are reflected to this day in the rich town houses of Antwerp, Ghent, Brussels, Berghes and elsewhere constructed between 1600 and 1670. One-eighth of Ghent – 1260 houses – was rebuilt or refaced in stone during this period.[13] In the countryside, too, there was recovery. The improvements in farming methods became legendary and an English observer, Sir Richard Weston, wrote in 1644-5 that between Dunkirk and Bruges 'I saw as rich a countrie as ever my eies beheld, stokt with goodly wheat and barlie, and excellent meadow and pasture'.[14] Rural Flanders had come a long way since 1586.

Yet neither the degree nor the duration of the recovery must be exaggerated. The war continued to take its toll. Taxes were required in ever-increasing quantities to finance the war – about four million florins a year between 1600 and 1640 – diverting capital from productive investment and impoverishing the taxpayers. The 70,000 and more troops who regularly fought for Spain in the South Netherlands, mainly foreigners, were expensive in other ways too: quite apart from the malicious damage they so often committed, the soldiers all had to be fed and lodged in billets at the Netherlanders' expense. The areas near to the theatre of military operations therefore recovered very slowly. Some relatively sheltered areas also failed to thrive. The population of the rural areas around Ieper, for instance, declined steadily throughout the period of the Twelve Years' Truce, while the cloth works at Dixmuide, Eecke, Menin, Poperinghe and other lesser centres never fully recovered from the destruction of the 1580s. Further south, the city of Mons, which had weathered the storms of the later sixteenth century with relatively little loss, began to decline fairly rapidly after 1600. Its population in 1593 was 17,239, but it had fallen to 13,944 by 1625. For Mons and the other large towns along the southern border, the war which broke out between Spain and France in 1635 brought widespread devastation and industrial collapse.[15]

Thus, if it is possible to overestimate the 'crisis' caused by the Eighty Years' War in the South Netherlands, it is equally easy to exaggerate the recovery. The southern provinces never fulfilled the promising destiny which seemed to beckon during the reign of Charles V. They remained an economic backwater from 1572 until the coal and steel boom of the early nineteenth century made Belgium the first continental country to experience an industrial revolution.

II

If the costs of the Dutch Revolt to the South Netherlands were severe, they were scarcely less deleterious for the other dominions of the King of Spain. In the opinion of Don Fernando Girón, an experienced councillor of Philip IV, 'The war in the Netherlands has been the total ruin of this monarchy'.[16] This view was echoed in the highest quarters. In 1604, for example, Philip III succinctly summarized the effects of the Low Countries Wars upon Spain as follows:

My uncle [the Archduke Albert, ruler of the Netherlands] is well aware of the extent to which my kingdoms [of Spain] resent the continuation of such great provisions as he has been sent, seeing that all the money which arrives from the Indies goes into them, and that since this does not suffice the people of Spain have always to pay extraordinary taxes; these are the fruits of the war that they see, together with the absence of their sons, brothers, dependents and relatives, who either die or return wounded, without arms, sight or legs, totally useless; and having yielded the promise of their lives there, their parents, brothers and relatives have to support them here.[17]

Spain sacrificed an unacceptably large number of her young men upon the altar of the Netherlands war. Recruiting for the Spanish army removed perhaps 8000 men a year from Castile when Spain was at war: they went to defend the African garrisons, Italy and the Netherlands and to man the Mediterranean and Atlantic fleets. Between 1567 and 1574, some 42,875 soldiers actually left Spain to fight in Italy and the Netherlands alone – an average of over 5000 a year even though none left in 1569 and 1570 because of the war of Granada. In the period 1631-9 over 30,000 Castilians were sent to the Army of Flanders alone: over 3000 a year.[18] This military drain of manpower was far more important than, for example, the emigration to the New World, at least in quantitative terms, although of course not all the troops sent to the army were permanently lost: as the king pointed out, many returned when they were unfit for further service, 'wounded, without arms, sight or legs, totally useless'. The human waste associated with the war in 'Flanders' also revolted a man of letters like Quevedo, who found fault with a popular saying of Golden Age Spain: *No hay más Flandes* ('There's no place like Flanders'): 'We condemn those who in some light conversation say *No hay más Flandes* in praise of some pleasure . . . because up to now we have seen nothing worthy of note to come from that country except eyes torn or squint, or broken arms and legs.'[19]

Overshadowing these 'social costs' of the war, however, was the far more debilitating haemorrhage of Spanish treasure and the virtual destruction of the Castilian economy in order to finance the war against the Dutch. Figure 4 illustrates the two great 'waves' of Spanish spending in the Netherlands, the first stretching from 1586 until the truce in 1607, the second from 1621 until 1640. They corresponded to the two massive thrusts of Spanish imperialism in Europe under Philip II and under Olivares. But this flexing of Spain's imperial muscles was only achieved at a terrible cost. Philip III was quite correct to claim that more was sent to the Netherlands than arrived legally on the New World treasure fleets. His father, Philip II, had voiced exactly the same complaint, with equal justice, in 1578:

[The war has] consumed the money and substance which

has come from the Indies, while the collection and raising of revenues in these kingdoms has only been done with great difficulty because of the dearth of specie in them (since so much is exported) and because of the damage which this does and causes to the commerce and trade on which the yield of our taxes depends.[20]

There was no exaggeration in this amazing claim. Between 1571 and 1575 the total 'royal' receipts from the Indies came

Figure 4: Money received from Castile by the Paymaster-General of the Army of Flanders.

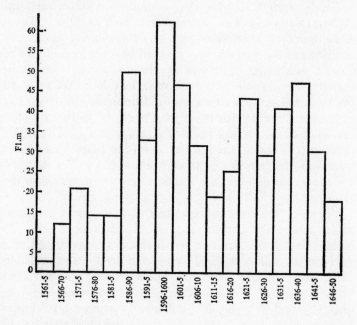

(For sources see page 274 below.)

to 3.9 million ducats; over the same quinquennium the Pay-master-General of the Army of Flanders received some 9 million ducats from Castile. In the same period, the Pay-master-General of the Mediterranean fleet received a further five million ducats, bringing Philip II's total outlay on 'imperialism' to around fourteen million. This pattern was repeated in subsequent years: the crown regularly spent more in the Netherlands than it received from the Indies. Between 1566 and 1654, the Military Treasury in the Netherlands received a minimum of 218 million ducats from Castile, while the crown received only 121 million ducats from the Indies. This vast shortfall, together with the rest of the government's needs, was made up in the end by the Castilian taxpayers. As one outraged delegate in the *Cortes* of Castile expostulated in 1586: 'However much money comes [from the Indies], this kingdom has less!'[21]

The Spanish Habsburgs left virtually no stone unturned in their efforts to finance the subjugation of the Dutch. Taxes were increased repeatedly and it was generally agreed by travellers in the early modern period that the population of Castile was taxed more heavily than any other people in Europe. Modern calculations have shown that while prices in the sixteenth century rose three-fold between 1500 and 1590 in Castile, taxation rose more than five-fold, so that by 1590 one-third of the average peasant's income in a good year was consumed in tax. In the last decade of the century new taxes were imposed (above all the *millones*, a new excise tax) and harvest yields fell, so that taxation bit even deeper into the economy.[22]

Yet even the most savage and onerous fiscal measures could not make current income match expenditure. To bridge the deficit caused by Habsburg imperialism the government was compelled to borrow on a grand scale. In 1557, at Philip II's accession, the Castilian national debt stood at thirty-six million ducats; in 1598, when the king died, it stood at eighty-five million. Two years after Philip IV's accession, in 1623, the total public debt had risen to 112 million ducats – the equivalent of at least ten years' revenue; two years after his death, in 1667, the debt stood at 180 million. This five-fold increase in a little over a century was caused in large measure by Spain's insistence on heavy military spending in the Low Countries: the periods of fastest increase in the debt corresponded with the periods of greatest expenditure in the Netherlands.

These costs of the war in 'Flanders' were felt by all (or almost all) parts of the Habsburg empire, but there were two areas which suffered especially heavy damage: Old Castile and Portugal. *Castilla la Vieja*, more or less the Duero basin, was famous in the early sixteenth century for its wool. Some of it was made into cloth locally, mainly at Segovia, but most – often two-thirds – was exported via Burgos, Santander and Bilbao to northern Europe, especially to the Netherlands. This trade was crippled by the Dutch Revolt. In 1570, some 17,000 sacks of wool were exported through Santander; by 1622 this total had fallen to 605 sacks. It was the same story in Bilbao: the port insurance registers reveal that shipments to the Netherlands, having risen steadily throughout the earlier sixteenth century, ceased abruptly in 1572-3 when the Sea Beggars closed the Scheldt to Spanish shipping. The entire economy of Old Castile, which had centred for so long on the wool trade, was seriously dislocated. Wealth and population drifted to the south on an increasing scale. By the 1590s Old Castile, the ancient heart of Spain, was in full decline.[23]

As Professor C. R. Boxer has written, the struggle between Spain and the Dutch in many ways deserves to be called the 'First World War' since it was fought out in Africa, America and Asia as well as in many parts of Europe. From the 1590s onwards the Dutch organized expeditions of trade, war or piracy to many parts of the Iberian empires overseas. Regular trade was carried on with the Guinea Coast after 1592 and with the Caribbean after 1594; in all, perhaps 150 ships were involved annually. In 1615 the first Dutch fleet entered the Pacific and ravaged the west coast of Mexico and Peru before sailing on to attack the Philippines. Later expeditions followed, co-ordinated after 1621 by the Dutch West India Company. This upsurge of hostilities on the high seas around America inevitably led to an increase in Spanish defence spending there. Heavier (and more expensive) escorts were needed for fleets and costly fortifications were required on land. Already in 1624 the viceroy of Peru spent 200,000 *pesos* on defence; in 1643 he spent 948,000 (the *peso* was worth a little more than a ducat). It was the same in Mexico. The government there sent 1,500,595 *pesos* to Spain in the four years 1618-21, but it sent 1,653,253 to the Philippines to pay for the islands' defence.[24] This was all money which could otherwise have been shipped back to Spain (and used to finance military operations in the Netherlands).

But at least the Castilian seaborne empire lost little of its overseas territory: just a few small islands in the Caribbean. Portugal and her empire suffered far greater losses. The first Dutch attacks on Portuguese possessions came in 1598-9 when the islands of Príncipe and São Tomé in the Gulf of Guinea were raided by a fleet of seventy-two Dutch ships. In 1605, ten years after their first expedition to the Far East, the Dutch captured some of the major spice islands; in 1612 they took their first stronghold in West Africa (Fort Nassau); and in 1630 they invaded Brazil. Despite setbacks and defeats, the Dutch consolidated and extended their bases on all three continents and by the 1650s Portugal had lost for good her control of Asia and Africa and only held on to Brazil, thanks to a revolt by the native Catholic population (Indians and Negro) against the Calvinist invaders. The costs of this dogged, global struggle were enormous: an ever-increasing burden of taxation was laid upon the inhabitants of Portugal and her colonies, while the need to organize convoys, escorts and fortresses for the defence of trade tended to strangle the commerce they were meant to protect. Although no doubt the Dutch would sooner or later have come into conflict with the Portuguese over the right to trade in the Indian Ocean, there can be little doubt that Philip II's war with the Dutch caused the struggle to break out earlier and more destructively than it might otherwise have done.[25]

III

These impressive Dutch conquests overseas, like the capture
of innumerable towns and villages in Gelderland, Limburg,
Brabant and Flanders, were not achieved at all cheaply. On
the contrary, the need to finance operations at home and
abroad, on land and sea, represented an enormous, continual
and constantly rising charge on the North Netherlands. In
the first place there was defensive expenditure: garrisons,
militia and, above all, fortifications. A comparison of the
detailed maps made of many Dutch towns by Jacob van
Deventer in the 1550s with those made by Johan Blaeu a
century later reveals a total transformation: the defences of
almost every town, large and small, had been totally rebuilt
to conform to the latest standards and refinements of military
science. The cost must have been enormous.[26] Then there
was the need to finance operations against the enemy. From
3.2 million florins in 1591, the first year in which the Dutch
mounted an offensive campaign, the annual cost of the
Republic's armed forces rose to 8.8 million florins in 1607,
13.4 million in 1622, and 18.8 million in 1640.[27] Prolonged
military expenditure on this scale compelled the Dutch
government to impose heavy taxes on its subjects – far more
onerous than the duke of Alva's 'Tenth Penny' which had
done so much to start the Revolt. Riots, caused for the most
part by tax increases, broke out in several Dutch towns: at
Utrecht in 1610 (over beer duties); at Alkmaar, Haarlem,
Enkhuizen and Amsterdam in 1624 (over an excise on butter,
and involving the killing of several citizens by the troops
called out to quell the troubles); and so on. It was partly to
avoid such ugly scenes that the Republic endeavoured to
finance as much of its war-effort as possible by raising public
loans. In 1651 the debt of the province of Holland alone
stood at 153 million florins. Fortunately for Dutch trade,
throughout the seventeenth century there was enough
capital in Amsterdam alone to float government loans and
finance trade and industry without pushing up interest rates.
The government was able to borrow at 10 per cent in the

191

1600s, at 5 per cent in the 1640s and at 4 per cent after 1655.[28]

There is no doubt that a substantial part of this capital-seeking investment was provided by merchants exiled from the South Netherlands who sought refuge in the North. Of the 320 largest depositors in the Amsterdam Exchange Bank in 1611, over half were southern refugees. Surviving tax registers from 1631 reveal that about one-third of the richest Amsterdammers were of southern origin. Some 27 per cent of the shareholders of the Amsterdam chamber of the Dutch East India Company in 1602, including the three largest subscribers, were Walloon or Flemish exiles, and they provided almost 40 per cent of the company's total capital. It was the same story in the West India Company later on: at least half of the sixty-six directors who ran the company between 1622 and 1636 are known to have come from the South Netherlands.[29]

The refugees from the south were important for their numbers as well as for their wealth. 1283 persons from the southern provinces – 780 from Antwerp alone – became citizens of Amsterdam between 1580 and 1606. Most of them were heads of households who may have brought their families with them. Many other southern exiles came to the city and either did not need or could not afford to purchase citizenship. An analysis of marriages celebrated at Amsterdam between 1586 and 1601 reveals that 1478 bridegrooms, 16 per cent of all men married in the city in those years, came from the south (and 788 of these came from Antwerp).[30] The stream of refugees, mainly but not entirely from the south, was an important factor in the growth of the towns of Holland and Zealand: Amsterdam grew from almost 31,000 people in 1585 to 120,000 in 1632; Leiden, with its famous cloth works, rose from not quite 13,000 in 1574 to 65,000 in the 1640s. But very few parts of the Dutch Republic underwent a demographic boom on this scale during the Eighty Years' War. Even in Holland, the population of the northern areas appears to have increased less rapidly after 1569 than before. The military operations and political upheavals of 1572-9 took a heavy toll, and the picture was much worse in the eastern provinces of the Republic which were involved in the fighting for far longer. In Overijssel a large number of farms were laid waste and up to 20 per cent of the agricultural land was abandoned. In the Veluwe, south-west

Figure 5: Dividends paid to shareholders by the Dutch East India Company 1602-49. Open columns represent dividends paid in spices; hatched columns represent dividends paid in cash.

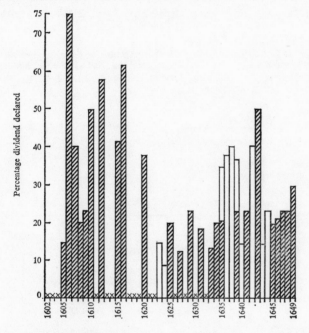

(For sources see page 274 below.)

of Overijssel, the population does not appear to have grown at all, while further south in the town and 'meierij' (district) of 's Hertogenbosch there was a marked decline.[31]

Yet despite the decay in the landward provinces, seen from Holland – and particularly from Amsterdam – it was hard to resist the impression that the war with Spain had made a decisive contribution towards the unparalleled prosperity of the Republic in the seventeenth century. The Amsterdam magistrate, C. P. Hooft (1547-1626), was quite explicit in his claims that the 'war of Liberation' had had a beneficial effect on the economy of his country. 'It is known to all the world,' he wrote, 'that whereas it is generally the nature of war to ruin the land and people, these countries on the contrary have been notably improved thereby.' Naturally, Hooft had in mind the newly burgeoning trade with the East and West Indies which was based on Amsterdam. Many men besides him were captivated by the rich cargoes of

Figure 6: Dutch and Portuguese ships sailing to the East Indies 1570-1670. It must, of course, be remembered that not all the ships sailing to the East were the same size; nevertheless the trend of the trade of both nations emerges clearly enough.

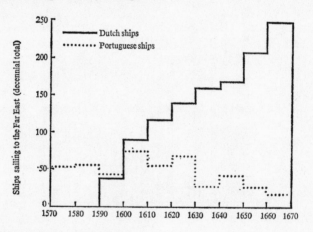

(For sources see page 275 below.)

spices brought from Asia and the sugar brought from Brazil.[32] In particular, the return of the 'second voyage' to the East Indies under Jacob van Neck in 1599 created a tremendous impression. 'So long as Holland has been Holland,' wrote one contemporary, 'never have such richly laden ships been seen here.' The profit on the venture was some 400 per cent.

Undoubtedly the economic gains from breaking the Spanish and Portuguese monopolies on extra-European trade were great, but they must not be overestimated or antedated.

194

Although the gains were often spectacular, for many years they were also sporadic. As Figure 5 shows, between 1611 and 1632 (a period of twenty-two years), the Dutch East India Company declared only ten dividends. Large dividends were only paid regularly after 1634. Likewise, as Figure 6 shows, the rate of growth in the East India trade was slower in the war decades (1620-49) than both before and after. Dutch commerce with other areas outside Europe was even less successful. Trade with the West Indies (*sc.* America), although it started earlier, never really got off the ground at all. Although between 1599 and 1605 almost 800 ships arrived off Punta de Araya in Venezuela to collect salt, there were heavy losses in 1605 at the hands of the Spanish navy and the erection of a fort by the Spaniards in 1622 prevented further activity. After 1622 all Dutch trade to America was controlled by a special trading and paramilitary organization, the West India Company. Major fleets, heavily armed, were sent to the Caribbean from 1623 onwards and to Brazil after 1624. In 1628 the company's ships captured the treasure fleet of New Spain in Matanzas Bay, Cuba, and some twelve million florins (3,300,000 *pesos*) of silver and merchandise were brought back to Holland. The company declared a bumper dividend of 75 per cent and its stock rose from 115 points to 206, but in the event this was practically the only dividend the West India Company ever issued! At all other times the profits it made, whether from the lucrative Guinea slave trade or from the even more lucrative Brazilian sugar trade, were immediately absorbed by the costs of conquering and defending its strongholds in Brazil. In 1647 the company estimated it made 400,000 florins profit from Brazil, but spent 1,100,000 florins on its defence. Operations there even required regular contributions from the States-General: 1,200,000 were provided between 1623 and 1626 and 700,000 florins annually from 1631 until 1644, when the sum had to be increased still further on account of the revolt of the native population of Brazil. By 1640 the West India Company's debt stood at eighteen million florins and in September of that same year the last of its large trading fleets sent to the Caribbean was destroyed by the Spaniards off Cuba. Dutch

Brazil was steadily lost between 1645 and 1654 and the company's stock fell from 100 points in 1642 to 14¼ in 1650. After 1660 it stood at just three points until the unhappy company was liquidated in 1674. Those who had invested in this branch of Dutch imperialism lost their money.[33]

It is therefore hard to substantiate the numerous extravagant claims about the importance to the Republic of the trade with the East and West Indies, the only sector of the Dutch economy which clearly developed from the war with Spain. Undoubtedly some influential and voluble Amsterdammers were enriched, and undoubtedly Amsterdam became able to corner the supply of many exotic products, thus increasing its importance as a commercial centre. But this is no reason to believe the special pleading of the directors of the two chartered companies to the effect that their enterprises were 'the foremost source . . . of the prosperity of an incalculable number of inhabitants of our Republic'.[34] Impartial observers all agreed that the soul of Dutch trade in the seventeenth century was in reality the seaborne commerce with the Baltic, normally referred to as the 'mother trade' of the Dutch economy because it gave birth to so many other activities. A survey of Dutch shipping in 1634 gives an unmistakable picture:[35]

The fishing fleet	2,250 boats
Trade with the Mediterranean and Baltic	1,750 boats
Trade with the East and West Indies and Guinea	300 boats
Total	4,300 boats

The relatively small part of the Republic's shipping resources devoted to extra-European trade – 7 per cent of the total – seems even smaller when one recalls that a round trip to the East Indies took two years, often with a ballast or bullion cargo on the way out, while ships bound for the Baltic could make two, three or four voyages a year. Only ten to twenty ships sailed to the Far East every year, compared with between 1000 and 2000 annually passing through the Sound into the Baltic and out again to Spain and southern Europe. 'The importance and magnitude of the trade [with the Baltic] is so great that it alone is the soul of business affairs, upon which all other trades and dealings depend,' observed the States of Holland in 1646, and there is a wealth of evidence to support them. It occupied many hands; it supplied grain to feed a large part of the Dutch population; it supplied domestic industries with vital raw materials; and it provided a strong incentive to build more and bigger ships.[36]

However, to a considerable extent this vast and important trade depended on the re-export of Baltic goods, and especially grain and timber, to Spain and Portugal, in return for the purchase of Iberian salt which was required by both Holland and the Baltic states. Of 1068 ships which left Amsterdam between 1591 and 1602 declaring that they were bound for Spain or Portugal, 434 also declared that they intended to sail straight from there to the Baltic. 314 of these ships were going south for salt which they would carry direct to the ports of North Germany and Poland. Spain and Portugal were crucial to the health of Dutch trade to the Baltic. It is therefore pertinent to enquire how far this 'mother trade' of the Dutch economy was helped by the war with Spain. The answer is clear: hardly at all. After 1572 the growing contacts between North Netherlands merchants and Spain ceased abruptly. Although there was some clandestine recovery after a year or so, the commerce of Holland, Zealand and Friesland with the Iberian peninsula was frequently disrupted by Spain's periodic decisions to prohibit all trade with the 'rebels' (1585-6, 1595-6, 1599, 1601, 1603-4 . . .) or by the hostility of the Inquisition towards the Dutch, which often led to confiscations and imprisonment. After the expiration of the Twelve Years' Truce, Spain waged economic warfare against the Republic far more effectively. Dutch trade to the Baltic declined seriously during the 1620s, thanks to Spain's boycott of Dutch vessels (coupled after 1626 with Sweden's destructive campaigns in Poland). Even in the 1630s, when a run of unusually bad harvests in Spain and Portugal increased the demand for Baltic grain, Dutch vessels were forced by Spanish hostility to carry their cargoes to Bordeaux, where English and French shippers took them on to the Iberian ports. The 'mother trade' of the Dutch economy only regained its pre-Truce level with the revolt of Portugal against Philip IV in 1640, which reopened the peninsular market to Dutch ships. The Spanish embargo policy also affected other sectors of the Republic's economic life: little salt, merino wool, cochineal or indigo – all goods produced in the Iberian world for which it was difficult to find a suitable substitute – reached Holland between 1621 and 1641, causing a rise both in prices and, it would seem, in unemployment.[37]

These difficulties naturally favoured the merchants of other countries who could offer more or less the same services as the Dutch. Thus the 'obedient provinces' gained to some extent – even though they were obliged to pay 'convoy and licence money' to the Dutch in order to use the port of Antwerp – and many Antwerp firms continued to deal with Spain, Portugal, Italy and the overseas colonies (*cf.* pp. 182-3 above). The English too developed a lively trade with Spain during the reign of James I and in the 1630s, as did the French (Amiens sent vast quantities of cloth to Seville between 1600 and 1635); but above all it was the Hanseatic merchants, especially the men of Hamburg, who profited.[38] From the 1580s onwards their ships made the 'Westfahrt' in ever-increasing numbers and from the 1590s they too began to trade direct with Brazil and the Canaries. About 100 ships from Hamburg alone sailed to the Iberian peninsula annually in the 1590s. It was all trade lost by the Dutch.[39]

The war hampered Dutch trade in other ways. The formation of a war fleet in Dunkirk after its recapture by Spanish forces in 1583 constituted a serious menace to Dutch shipping. There were perhaps fifty privateers based on the port during the 1590s and they took a regular toll of Dutch ships. In the 1620s and 1630s, some fifty to sixty privateers (half of them government owned) were the scourge of shipping in the North Sea and no less than 1835 vessels, mainly Dutch, were captured or sunk between 1626 and 1634. (By way of comparison, between 1623 and 1636 the Dutch West India Company captured or destroyed only 547 Spanish or allied ships.) The cost to the Dutch in higher rates

of insurance, in convoy and escort charges, and in direct loss
was considerable. Further south, the Spanish squadrons
which patrolled the Mediterranean also claimed a number of
prizes. Scarcely less deleterious was the disruptive effect of
Spanish naval action against the Dutch herring fishery: the
small fishing centre of Maassluis alone lost 212 herring
'busses' between 1631 and 1637; its larger neighbour,
Schiedam, saw its fleet diminish by half between 1625 and
1635. The total cost of the ships and gear lost by the herring
industry during the 1620s and 1630s has been estimated at
twelve million florins – equivalent to a whole year's main-
tenance for the Army of Flanders – much of it taken by the
privateers of Philip IV based on Dunkirk and Ostend (who
also pocketed the considerable ransoms charged for Dutch
fishermen captured in action).[40]

A brief survey of Dutch commerce during the period of the
war with Spain thus supports the verdict of Dr F. Snapper,
that until 1627 at least 'war brought more loss than profit to
Holland's seaborne trade'.[41] The growth of the Republic's
overseas commerce was substantial between 1572 and 1635,
it is true; but there is every reason to suppose that it would
have been greater still if a permanent peace with Spain had
been arranged. Recovery to the level of prosperity of the
'golden years' during the Truce did not occur until France
declared war on Spain in 1635 and Portugal rebelled in
1640: the first simultaneously diverted the Hispanic war
effort away from the North Netherlands and eliminated one
of the Republic's chief competitors for Spanish trade (the
English Civil War soon eliminated another); the second
delivered an important intercontinental market – Portugal
and her overseas empire in Africa, America and Asia – into
the hands of Dutch merchants. Dutch trade was at last free
to prosper and develop untrammelled by the fortunes (and
misfortunes) of war.

IV

It is tempting to suppose that all these losses must have produced some gains for the participants elsewhere – after all it seems fairly clear that in the seventeenth century at least conflicting economic aspirations were the main reason for the continuance of the war.[42] However, apart from the towns of Holland, which drew immense benefit from the influx of men and money from the south, and apart from the handful of *hoofdparticipanten* (major shareholders) in the East India Company, it is hard to point to any single group even in the Dutch Republic who made substantial profits *which they would not have made without the war*. True, there were the numerous generals and administrators in Spanish service who were given a landed estate in the Netherlands as a reward for their services, and the sutlers, arms manufacturers and financiers on both sides who served the military machine and made a profit from it. But any enumeration of individuals can only be misleading, as a perceptive French writer observed at the time, since: 'For every two soldiers who find wealth in the wars, there are fifty who acquire only injuries or incurable illnesses. To win favour in the sight of their sovereign they squander all their money.' Even the duke of Alva, who did so much to precipitate the revolt of 1572, plunged his estates deep in debt by assuming command of the Army of Flanders.[43]

It must be admitted that most of the money and resources which the various combatants poured into the war in the Netherlands were, in economic terms, entirely unproductive. There was little or no technological spin-off; the men paid to fight were men lost to agriculture and industry; the taxes raised to pay for the armies yielded little return (at least to the belligerent states) in the shape of increased demand for goods and services. The war was, in many ways, conspicuous expenditure on a monstrous scale by the various governments of Europe.

As so often in war, it was the neutrals who made the real gains. England, Sweden and Germany in particular acquired

200

trade, export markets and skilled refugees which they would otherwise not have had. The bankers of Genoa and Portugal who financed the war for Spain made a fortune at the expense of the Castilian taxpayers. The independent principality of Liège, an enclave in the Spanish Netherlands, burgeoned after 1572 as local armourers and industrialists met the rising demand of both sides in the war for powder, arms and artillery. The prosperity of individual towns like Frankfurt-am-Main, whose community of 600 Dutch refugees included most of the wealthiest citizens, owed much to the Netherlanders who brought their capital and expertise into exile with them. It was on the periphery of the great conflict, not in Spain or the Netherlands, that the true economic beneficiaries of the Eighty Years' War were to be found.[44]

The participants' 'gains', if we may call them that, were not really economic at all. Spain was fighting in the sixteenth century to preserve the absolute authority of the king and the religious monopoly of the Roman Catholic Church in the Netherlands. In the end she succeeded in ten out of the seventeen provinces inherited by Philip II. In the seventeenth century it seems that Spain fought more to save her overseas empire from falling into the hands of the Dutch, and here too there was partial success. Although in 1640 Portugal had been lost as well as most of her empire, in 1648 the Peace of Münster stipulated that the Dutch would not 'journey to or trade in the harbours and places' which belonged to the king of Spain (clause six). This was a major victory, albeit tempered by the fact that by 1648 the Indies no longer produced the treasure nor required the European goods which had made them such a priceless trading partner in the sixteenth century. The Dutch West India Company was giving up relatively little. The only tangible gains which Spain made from the war were therefore political and religious.

One can say almost the same for the Dutch. They too had fought for the right to govern themselves and to worship in the Calvinist manner, and in both these aims they succeeded, although it must be remembered that the benefits were only shared by a minority of the Dutch population. On the political

201

plane, only the provinces which sent representatives to the States-General had a share in the decision-making processes of the Republic, and the citizens of North Brabant, North Flanders and Limburg were therefore unenfranchised. And even in the provinces which had States of their own, power rested securely in the hands of the 2000 or so families who formed the town oligarchies (the 'regent class'). The major gain of the oligarchs from the 'war of liberation' was that control by the central government was removed; after the revolt, each provincial and municipal administration became its own master. The religious 'gains' of the Dutch were also far from being universally shared: they were enjoyed only by the 2000 or so ministers and the congregations of the 'Reformed religion' which even in 1650 still unquestionably constituted a minority of the total population, outnumbered by the combined forces of Roman Catholics and Anabaptists.

No historian is really entitled or qualified to measure in economic terms whether such intangible achievements in the end vindicated the human and material sacrifices. There is no doubt that the Spanish and Dutch leaders fully realized the economic costs of their policies and considered them justified. But there is equally little doubt about the scale of the sacrifice. While one must not – to adapt an aphorism of Professor Postan – ascribe to the war what was due to the eighty years, it seems clear that the prolonged conflict generated by the Revolt of the Netherlands served to retard the growth of the northern republic (and particularly of its landward provinces), to inflict permanent damage on the economy of large areas of the Spanish empire, and to ruin for two centuries the prosperity of 'Belgium'. These were the harsh material consequences of the *ánimo severo* of Philip II. They must not be forgotten in assessing the significance of the Dutch Revolt. It was not perhaps entirely in the spirit of cant and humbug that those who drafted the Peace of Münster in 1647-8 began their preamble:

Let all persons know that, after a long succession of bloody wars which for many years have oppressed the peoples,

subjects, kingdoms and lands which are under the obedience of the Lords King of Spain and States-General of
the United Netherlands, the aforesaid Lords, the King
and the States, moved by Christian piety, desire to end the
general misery and prevent the dreadful consequences,
calamity, harm and danger which the further continuation
of the aforesaid wars in the Low Countries would bring in
their train . . . They invite and call upon other princes and
potentates to allow themselves to be moved by the same
pity and to avert the mishaps, destruction and disorders
which the heavy plague of war has made men suffer for so
long and so heavily.[45]

Notes

Preface

1. A. H. Layard, *Discoveries in the Ruins of Nineveh and Babylon* (London, 1853), p. 663.

1. Spain, her Enemies and the Revolt of the Netherlands, 1559-1648
(Originally published in *Past and Present*, XLIX [1970], pp. 72-95.)

The following abbreviations are used in the notes to this chapter:

AGS E.   Archivo General de Simancas (Spain), sección de Estado (with *legajo* and folio).

AGS CMC   *Ibid.*, sección Contaduría Mayor de Cuentas (with *época* and *legajo* – none of the bundles have been foliated).

ANP 120 AP   Archives Nationales, Paris, Private Papers of Sully.

BPU Favre   Bibliothèque Publique et Universitaire, Geneva, section des Manuscrits, Collection Edouard Favre (with volume and folio).

CODOIN   *Colección de Documentos Inéditos para la Historia de España*, 112 vols., Madrid 1842-92.

IVdeDJ   Instituto de Valencia de Don Juan, Madrid, Manuscript collection (with *envío* and folio).

1. J. W. Smit, 'The present position of studies regarding the Revolt of the Netherlands', *Britain and the Netherlands*, ed. J. S. Bromley and E. H. Kossmann, I (London, 1960), pp. 11-28.

2. The latter omission is particularly surprising in view of the abundance of the materials for study, many of them printed. For a survey of this material and its present location, see G. Parker, *Guide to the Archives of the Spanish Institutions in or concerned with the Netherlands, 1556-1706* (Brussels, 1971).

3. E. Gossart, *Espagnols et Flamands au XVIe Siècle: l'Etablissement du Régime espagnol dans les Pays Bas et l'Insurrection*

(Brussels, 1905), p. xi. The refrain was repeated but hardly elaborated by L. van der Essen, 'Een punt van methode betreffende de studie van de Opstand der Nederlanden in de XVIe eeuw', *Mededelingen van de Koninklijke Vlaamse Akademie . . . Letteren*, X (1948), no. 3.

4. Pierre Chaunu, 'Séville et la Belgique, 1555-1648', *Revue du Nord*, XLII (1960), pp. 259-92.

5. *Ibid.*, p. 274.

6. *Ibid.*, pp. 259-61.

7. *Ibid.*, pp. 280-2.

8. The growth of the Netherlands state debt under Charles V is analysed by F. Braudel, 'Les Emprunts de Charles-Quint sur la Place d'Anvers', *Charles-Quint et son Temps* (Paris, 1959), pp. 191-201; the debt in 1565-6 is given in the very important 'Mémoire en matière des finances pour M. de Montigny' printed by H. A. Enno van Gelder, *Correspondance française de Marguerite de Parme: supplément*, I (Utrecht, 1941), pp. 190-3.

9. IVdeDJ 68/309, 'Cuenta con Gerónimo de Curiel y Francisco de Lixalde', for the money received by Curiel, the government's Factor at Antwerp, and by Margaret of Parma; AGS E. 513/174, minute of Philip II's address to the Netherlands Council of State in 1556 in reply to Emanuel-Philibert of Savoy's 'Remonstrance', which gives a figure (provided by the Spanish Treasury) of 'eleven million ducats which amounts to twenty-two million florins' sent since 1551.

10. F. Braudel, *La Méditerranée et le monde méditerranéen à l'époque de Philippe II*, II, 2nd edn. (Paris, 1967), p. 281: letter of Philip II to the duke of Sessa, Governor of Milan, 8 Apr. 1559.

11. See J. F. Guilmartin, *Gunpowder and Galleys: Changing Technology and Mediterranean Warfare at Sea in the Sixteenth Century* (Cambridge, 1974), pp. 123-34.

12. For figures on the growth of Spain's Mediterranean fleet, see the table in ch. 6, p. 130 below.

13. For the aristocratic preponderance on the Council of State at this time *cf.* M. Baelde, *De Collaterale Raden onder Karel V en Filips II (1531-1578). Bijdrage tot de geschiedenis van de centrale instellingen in de XVIe eeuw* (Brussels, 1965), pp. 67-87.

14. These aims were stated baldly and succinctly by Egmont in his final *Recuerdo* (Memorial) to Philip II dated 24 Mar. 1565: printed by Enno van Gelder, *Correspondance française*, I, pp. 51-4.

15. P. Rosenfeld, 'The Provincial Governors from the Minority of Charles V to the Revolt', *Standen en Landen*, XCII (1959), pp. 1-63, esp. pp. 28-33.

16. C. Weiss, *Papiers d'Etat du Cardinal de Granvelle, 1546-65*, IX (Paris, 1852), pp. 279-80: Viglius to Granvelle, 14 June 1565.

17. J. S. Theissen, *Correspondance française de Marguerite de Parme . . . 1565-67* (Utrecht, 1925), p. 59.

18. *Ibid.*, p. 91. See also, for a fuller account of these events, G. Parker, *The Dutch Revolt* (London, 1977), ch. 2.

19. L. P. Gachard, *La Correspondance de Philippe II sur les affaires des Pays Bas*, I (Brussels, 1848), p. 358: Gonzalo Pérez to Armenteros, 30 June 1565: 'Of Egmont's Instruction neither Tisnacq nor Courtewille knew anything, and neither Ruy Gómez nor I knew anything about the letter they wrote from Valladolid [on 13 May].'

20. AGS E. 528 (unfol.), Armenteros to Pérez, 11 Oct. 1565.

21. One letter of 17 Oct. (in French) is published by Theissen, *op. cit.*, pp. 99-103; many of the king's notes expressing his concern for its exact wording are printed in Enno van Gelder, *op. cit.*, I, pp. 121-4. One letter of 20 Oct. (in Spanish) is printed in CODO IN, IV, pp. 326-36. See also, on this intricate episode, P. David Lagomarsino, 'Court factions and the formation of Spanish policy towards the Netherlands, 1559-1567' (Cambridge University Ph.D. thesis, 1973), pp. 168-206.

22. The letter of 31 July 1566 is printed by Enno van Gelder, *op. cit.*, II, pp. 269-74. The king's declaration that his concessions were extorted by force was made on 9 Aug. 1566 and is to be found in AGS E. 531/52-3.

23. The shrewd French ambassador in Spain saw this as a leading consideration in Alva's delayed departure: C. Douais, *Dépêches de M. de Fourquevaux . . . 1565-1572*, I (Paris, 1896), p. 202: Fourquevaux to Charles IX, 15 Apr. 1567: 'One of the purposes of the duke [of Alva]'s delay has been to see whether the Turk will send his fleet.' The English ambassador shared this opinion: on 25 March 1567 he informed his government that

Alva was 'assured that the Turke will not bende towardes Christ-
endome this yere' (Cambridge University Library, Ms. Mm-3-8/
110, Dr Man to Cecil, 25 March 1567).

24. On all this, see G. Parker, *The Army of Flanders and the
Spanish Road, 1567-1659* (Cambridge, 1972), chs. 2 and 3, and
ibid., *The Dutch Revolt* (London, 1977), pp. 99-105. See also A. C.
Hess, *The Forgotten Frontier* (London, 1978), ch. 5.

25. On Brederode, H. A. Enno van Gelder, *Van Beeldenstorm tot
Pacificatie* (Amsterdam, 1964), pp. 68-9. (I am most grateful to
Mr A. C. Duke for bringing this reference to my attention.) For
Orange, G. Groen van Prinsterer, *Archives ou Correspondance
inédite de la Maison d'Orange-Nassau*, 1st ser., I, 2nd edn. (Leiden,
1841), p. 369, Orange to Count Louis, 3 Apr. 1565. For further
sources which reveal the extent of Dutch awareness of events in
the Mediterranean, see G. Parker, *The Dutch Revolt*, p. 286 note
46.

26. E. Charrière, *Négociations de la France dans le Levant*, III
(Paris, 1853), p. 61, M. de Grantire de Grandchamp to Charles IX,
14 Mar. 1569. It will be remembered that in 1568-9 France and
Spain were allies. The 'preceding letter' mentioned by the ambassador has, alas, not yet been found. See also ch. 3, pp. 68-9, below.

27. E. Charrière, *op. cit.*, III, pp. 477-82: bishop of Dax to
Charles IX, 4 and 8 May 1574. (The italics are mine.) The bishop's
assertion that Charles IX had sent unofficial aid to the Dutch from
November 1572 is intriguing: while it would seem likely that some
subsidies were sent, I doubt whether the French Treasury could
have managed a *regular* monthly payment.

28. Full figures for Spanish spending in the Netherlands and in
the Mediterranean, together with the effect on the king's peace of
mind, are given in G. Parker, *Philip II* (Boston and London, 1978),
p. 122.

29. IVdeDJ 67/121: Don Luis de Requesens to Don Juan de
Zúñiga (his brother), 30 Oct. 1575.

30. AGS E. 562/150 *bis*: Don John of Austria to the king, 21 Nov.
1576.

31. On the pathetic divisions within the Republic after 1585 *cf.*
A. M. van der Woude, 'De crisis in de Opstand na de val van
Antwerpen', *Bijdragen voor de Geschiedenis der Nederlanden*,
XIV (1959-60), pp. 38-57 and 81-104. For two examples of Spanish

incredulity at the unwavering resistance of the States, attributing the blame to England, *cf.* AGS E. 589/15, Philip II to Parma, 29 Nov. 1585 and *ibid.*, f. 120, Parma to Philip II, 31 Dec. 1585. Naturally the English in Holland agreed with this appraisal: they too believed that without their help the Republic could not survive: *cf.* the letters of Leicester to Burghley and Walsingham analysed in the *Calendar of State Papers, Foreign Series (Elizabeth)*, XX, pp. 38-42.

32. The Treaty of Nonsuch is given a prominent place in the important, recent study of Charles Wilson, *Queen Elizabeth and the Revolt of the Netherlands* (London, 1970). See also ch. 3 below, pp. 70-2.

33. AGS E. 601/113: Juan Bautista de Tassis to Philip II, May 1591.

34. The size of these subsidies is interesting, especially when compared with the Spanish contribution. According to W. A. Shaw, *Report on the Manuscripts of Lord De L'Isle and Dudley Preserved at Penshurst Place* (Hist. Manuscripts Com. Rep. no. 77), III (London, 1936), p. xlv, the total amount spent by Elizabeth in the Netherlands between 1585 and 1603 was £1,486,026 sterling, or 14.86 million florins – over half sent between 1585 and 1590. According to D. Buisseret, *Sully and the Growth of Central Government in France* (London, 1968), pp. 82-3, France paid £12,783,000 Tournois to the Republic between 1598 and 1610, or 10.22 million florins. After 1604 the French subsidy was a regular standing charge – *partie ordinaire* – of the French budget (ANP 120 AP 10 ff. 77v and 96 for example). Even so, these sums form only a fraction of what Spain was paying. Spain often sent more in one year than France or England sent in ten.

35. On French intervention in the Mantuan war, see J. Humbert, *Les français en Savoie sous Louis XIII* (Paris, 1960); on the economic costs of the war after 1621 to the Dutch, see ch. 10 below, and also J. I. Israel, 'A conflict of empires: Spain and the Netherlands 1618-1648', *Past and Present*, LXXVI (1977), pp. 34-74.

36. See Israel, *op. cit.*, pp. 67-71; see also ch. 2 below.

37. The figures are displayed in a diagram on p. 187 below.

38. On the question of Castilian debt *cf.* the excellent articles of A. Castillo, 'Los juros de Castilla: apogeo y fin de un instrumento de crédito', *Hispania*, XXIII (1963), pp. 43-70, and 'Dette flottante et

dette consolidée en Espagne', *Annales, E.S.C.*, XVIII (1963), pp. 745-59.

39. Perhaps it would be fairer to state that Castile and her defence came first, when necessary. In 1578-80 and after 1640 this view was advanced in preference to expenditure on Flanders or on a war with France: see Archivo Histórico Nacional, Madrid, *Estado libro* 969, unfol., Don Miguel de Salamanca to Olivares, 14 July 1641: 'primero es procurarse ajustar las cosas de España que conservar otras provincias'. (Just one example among many.)

40. On the great debate over the question in 1544 *cf.* F. Chabod, 'Milan o los Países Bajos: las discusiones sobre la "alternativa" de 1544', *Carlos V: Homenaje de la Universidad de Granada* (Granada, 1959), pp. 331-72. On later debates concerning the relative importance of the Netherlands against Italy, see AGS E. 556/101, 'los tres' to the king, 12 Feb. 1573; duque de Berwick y Alba, *Epistolario del III duque de Alba*, III (Madrid, 1952), pp. 300-1: Alva to Gabriel de Zayas, 7 Mar. 1573; L. Didier, *Lettres et négociations de Claude de Mondoucet, Résident de France aux Pays-Bas, 1571-4*, II (Paris, 1892), pp. 338-9: Mondoucet to Henry III, 23 Oct. 1574.

41. *Cf.* P. Brightwell, 'Spain and the Origins of the Thirty Years' War' (Cambridge University Ph.D. thesis, 1967), chs. III-V.

42. AGS E. 3337/133: 'Voto del Conde Duque', 13 Dec. 1632. See also Bibliothèque royale de Bruxelles, Ms. 16147/33v, marquis of Aytona to count-duke of Olivares, 26 Apr. 1629: 'acudamos primero a lo de italia que a lo de flandes.'

43. P. Chaunu, 'Une histoire religieuse sérielle', *Revue d'histoire moderne et contemporaine*, XII (1965), pp. 3-34. *Cf.* pp. 3-5: 'Ce qui est révolutionnaire, disons plus simplement novateur et fécond, c'est l'étude sérielle des phenomènes.'

44. When it was first published, this article provoked a 'Comment' from Dr Albert Lovett of University College, Dublin, which suggested that I had made improper use of some documents, and in particular of a calculation by Pero Luis Torregrosa, an experienced Treasury official, concerning the revenues of the crown of Castile for 1574 (see *Past and Present*, LV [1972], pp. 154-9). Dr Lovett suggested the document belonged instead to 1571. Since the custom of the journal is to publish a simultaneous 'rejoinder' by the original author, I had to write a reply without going back to Spain to verify Dr Lovett's assertions. Not entirely to my surprise, when I went to Spain again I discovered that he

had entirely misrepresented the document (Instituto de Valencia de Don Juan, *envío* 24 fo. 16). There is a holograph postscript to the calculations which states: 'Un memorial imbio a v.s. con esta, que si no me engaño lo imbie a v.s. el año de 1571; y agora e acrecentrado otras cosas que me an occurido.' The figures were revised in accordance with the latest estimates sent by the Treasury to the deputies of the Castilian *Cortes*; it is therefore perfectly proper to use them as a basis for calculating the budget of Philip II for 1574, since that was the precise purpose for which they were compiled. The rest of Dr Lovett's objections to my article were answered in the 'rejoinder' of 1972; for a discussion of Dr Lovett's own historical endeavours, see ch. 8.

2. Why Did the Dutch Revolt Last So Long?
(Originally published in *Transactions of the Royal Historical Society*, 5th series, XXVI [1976], pp. 53-72.)

1. For an effort to quantify these costs for the major belligerents see ch. 10 below.

2. Population figures from G. Parker and C. Wilson, eds., *Introduction to the Sources of European Economic History, 1500-1800*, I (London, 1977), pp. 81-4; and J. de Vries, *The Dutch Rural Economy in the Golden Age* (New Haven and London, 1974), pp. 74-101.

3. G. Groen van Prinsterer, *Archives ou Correspondance inédite de la Maison d'Orange-Nassau*, 1st series, IV (Leiden, 1837), pp. 2-6: a despairing letter from William of Orange to his brother, Count John of Nassau, written at Zwolle on 18 October 1572, announced that the prince was sailing forthwith to the only province remaining loyal to his cause, Holland, 'pour maintenir les affaires par delà tant que possible sera, ayant deliberé de faire illecq ma sépulture'.

4. Of the 800 Netherlands Protestants recorded in the various 'Books of Martyrs' as having perished in the course of the sixteenth century, 617 (or 70 per cent) were Anabaptists; their total losses through Habsburg persecution must have numbered many thousands. Not surprisingly, as early as July 1572, the Anabaptists declared their support for Orange and provided money for his army. (G. Brandt, *The History of the Reformation and other ecclesiastical transactions in and about the Low Countries from the beginning of the eighth century down to the famous Synod of Dort*,

---

Spain and the Netherlands

inclusive, I [London, 1720], p. 295.) This was, of course, a bribe. In the 1560s Orange, like most other princes, had persecuted and even executed Anabaptists. For some of the reasons which underlay this intolerance, *cf.* W. Kirchner, 'State and Anabaptists in the sixteenth century: an economic approach', *Journal of Modern History*, XLVI (1974), pp. 1-25.

5. *Epistolario del III duque de Alba*, ed. the Duke of Alba (Madrid, 1952), III, p. 261, Alva to the King, 19 Dec. 1572: 'Degollaron burgueses y soldados sin escaparse hombre nacido.' The policy of 'beastliness' almost worked in Holland too: news of the massacre of Naarden spread fast and three magistrates from Haarlem came to offer the surrender of their town on 3 Dec., the day after the massacre; the Spanish commander, however, unwisely insisted on unconditional capitulation and this the town refused to do. Other towns also showed a willingness to negotiate but would not throw themselves on the Spaniards' mercy. *Cf.* the eye-witness account of a Catholic living in Amsterdam, the Spanish headquarters at this time: *Dagboek van Broeder Wouter Jacobszoon, prior van Stein*, ed. I. H. van Eeghen, I (Groningen, 1959), p. 90.

6. Owen Feltham, *A brief character of the Low-Countries under the States. Being three weeks observation of the Vices and Vertues of the Inhabitants* (London, 1652), pp. 1 and 5.

7. Queen Elizabeth sent perhaps 1200 men unofficially in the months of April and May 1572, but then withdrew them. The support of the Flemish and Walloon churches in England was smaller but steadier: the correspondence of the churches pullulated with details on the aid in men and money sent over to the Low Countries. *Cf. Ecclesiae Londino-Batavae Archivum*, ed. J. H. Hessels, II (Cambridge, 1889), e.g. nos. 112, 115, 123, 129; III part I (Cambridge, 1897), e.g. nos. 195, 197, 257, 367, 380. The Scottish government also sent substantial aid.

8. F. Snapper, *Oorlogsinvloeden op de overzeese handel van Holland, 1551-1719* (Amsterdam, 1959): 989 Dutch ships passed out of the Sound in 1574, but only 840 in 1575 and 763 in 1576 – clear evidence of the growing impact of the war.

9. Feltham, *op. cit.*, pp. 83-5.

10. The bastions of most of the large towns of Holland appear clearly in the contemporary drawings executed by the English soldier, Walter Morgan. His collection of drawings (All Souls' College, Oxford, MS. 129) has now been published together with

212

the journal of the war in Holland which he wrote: D. Caldecott Baird, *The Expedition in Holland 1572-74. From the manuscript of Walter Morgan* (London, 1976).

11. A partial census of Antwerp in 1584 revealed 3248 Protestant and 3011 Catholic households, out of a total of 10,176 households covered by the census (perhaps 60 per cent of the city's population). *Cf.* the interesting and important article of A. van Roey, 'De correlatie tussen het sociale-beroepsmilieu en de godsdientkeuze te Antwerpen op het einde der XVIe eeuw', in *Sources de l'Histoire religieuse de la Belgique* (Louvain, 1968), pp. 239-58.

12. *Nueva Colección de Documentos Inéditos para la Historia de España*, V (Madrid, 1894), p. 368, Requesens to the king, 6 Oct. 1574; Archivo General de Simancas, Estado 560 fo. 33, Requesens to the king, 7 Nov. 1574.

13. On mutiny and desertion *cf.* G. Parker, *The Army of Flanders and the Spanish Road. The logistics of Spanish victory and defeat in the Low Countries' Wars, 1567-1659* (2nd edn., Cambridge, 1975), chs. 8 and 9; and ch. 5 below.

14. D. B. Quinn, 'Some Spanish reactions to Elizabethan colonial enterprises', *Transactions of the Royal Historical Society*, 5th series, I (1951), pp. 1-23. On the cost of all this to Spain – the defence of Florida against the French cost 180,000 ducats in 1565-66 alone – *cf.* P. E. Hoffman, 'A study of Florida defence costs, 1565-85: a quantification of Florida history', *Florida Historical Quarterly*, LI (1973), pp. 401-22; and K. R. Andrews, *Elizabethan Privateering: English Privateering during the Spanish War, 1585-1603* (Cambridge, 1964).

15. For a few examples among many: Archivo General de Simancas *Estado* 550 fos. 115-16, 'Parescer' (opinion) of secretary of war Juan Delgado, 1574, 'Flanders' or the Mediterranean; Estado 554 fo. 89, king to duke of Alva, 18 Mar. 1573; Instituto de Valencia de Don Juan (Madrid), *envío* 109 fo. 59, secretary of state Gabriel de Zayas to Don Luis de Requesens, 8 May 1575 (a copy of the same letter is at Estado 565 fo. 79).

16. As early as January 1566 Orange made enquiries about raising troops in Germany (Groen van Prinsterer, *Archives*, II, pp. 23-5: letter to Count Louis of Nassau, 25 Jan. 1566); in Aug., Count Louis signed a contract with a German military enterpriser to raise 1000 horse for service against the king in the Netherlands (*op. cit.*, pp. 257-8, 'Accord' of 30 Aug.); and in Feb. 1567 he actually came to the camp of the Imperial army at Gotha in

Saxony and tried to recruit soldiers (M. Koch, *Quellen zur Geschichte des Kaisers Maximilian II*, II [Leipzig, 1861], pp. 36-7, letter to the Emperor dated 19 Feb. 1567). On Orange's efforts to persuade the Emperor and princes to intervene in the Netherlands troubles in 1566-7, *cf.* Groen, *op. cit.*, II, pp. 27-30, 178-80 and 299-302, and III, pp. 1-6, 9-10, 26-40 and so on.

17. Orange wrote to his brother John: 'il a ainsy pleu à Dieu pour nous oster toute espérance que pouvions avoir assise sur les hommes' (Groen van Prinsterer, *Archives*, III, pp. 501-10 and IV, p. cii, letter of 21 Sept. 1572).

18. See pp. 29-32 and 68-70 above.

19. The new fortifications, the 'houten redoubten', and the campaign plans of 1605-6 are described and illustrated by the eyewitness P. Giustiniano, *Delle Guerre di Fiandra, libre VI* (Antwerp, 1609), pp. 228-9 and figs. 14 and 25. There is some correspondence about their construction in Algemeen Rijksarchief, the Hague, *Staten-Generaal* 4748. The classic account of how to construct fortifications in the cheapest way possible was by the mathematician Samuel Marolois, *Fortification ou Architecture militaire* (Amsterdam, 1615). Marolois was military adviser to the States 1612-19.

20. Instituto de Valencia de Don Juan, *envío* 51 fo. 31, Mateo Vázquez to the king with holograph royal reply, 31 May 1574. This document is cited, with others, in an unacceptable translation by A. W. Lovett, 'Some Spanish attitudes to the revolt of the Netherlands', *Tijdschrift voor Geschiedenis*, LXXXV (1973), pp. 17-30, at pp. 24-5. Dr Lovett has also produced a study of the 'arch-secretary': *Philip II and Mateo Vázquez de Leca: the Government of Spain, 1572-92* (Geneva, 1977).

21. Archivo General de Simancas, *Estado* 2855, unfol., 'Sumario de los 4 papeles principales que dio el presidente Richardot'; Instituto de Valencia de Don Juan, *envío* 51 fo. 1, Mateo Vázquez to the king with holograph royal reply, 8 Feb. 1591.

22. Orange to Counts Louis and John, 5 Feb. 1573 (Groen van Prinsterer, *Archives*, IV, pp. 49-51). *Cf.* also Orange to Marnix, 28 Nov. 1573 (L. P. Gachard, *Correspondance de Guillaume le Taciturne*, III [Brussels, 1851], pp. 88-93). Precisely the same two demands were made at the peace negotiations at Breda in 1575 (*cf.* E. H. Kossmann and A. F. Mellink, *Texts concerning the Revolt of the Netherlands* [Cambridge, 1975], pp. 124-6); at St Geertruidenberg in 1577 (G. Griffiths, *Representative Government in*

Western Europe in the Sixteenth Century [Oxford, 1968], pp. 454-62); and at Cologne in 1579 (Kossmann and Mellink, *op. cit.*, pp. 183-7).

23. Kervijn de Lettenhove, *Relations politiques des Pays-Bas et de l'Angleterre sous le règne de Philippe II*, VII (Brussels, 1889), p. 397, Dr Thomas Wilson to Walsingham, 27 Dec. 1574; Archivo General de Simancas, Estado 561 fo. 95, the king to Don Luis de Requesens, 9 Aug. 1574.

24. W. J. M. van Eysinga, *De wording van het Twaalfjarige Bestand van 9 april 1609* (Amsterdam, 1963), ch. 1; J. den Tex, *Oldenbarnevelt*, I (Cambridge, 1973), pp. 199-201.

25. Archivo Histórico Nacional (Madrid) Estado 3285, unfol., *voto* of the Count-Duke of Olivares, 1 Sept. 1628.

26. *Cf.* the opinions of various Spanish ministers printed by G. Parker, *The Army of Flanders* (2nd edition), p. xiv and pp. 127-34. There was also an 'ideological floodgates' theory, which argued that if heresy were allowed to prevail in northern Europe all heretics would attack the possessions of Philip II. 'Much . . . will be risked in allowing the heretics to prevail,' the king wrote in 1562: 'For if they do, we may be certain that all their endeavours will be directed against me and my states.' (Quoted by H. G. Koenigsberger, 'The statecraft of Philip II', *European Studies Review*, I [1971], pp. 1-21, at p. 13.)

27. Archivo Histórico Nacional, Estado 3285, *ubi supra*.

28. P. J. Blok, 'De handel op Spanje en het begin der groote vaart', *Bijdragen voor Vaderlandsche Geschiedenis en Oudheidkunde*, 5th series, I (1913), pp. 102-20; J. H. Kernkamp, *De handel op den Vijand 1572-1609*, 2 vols. (Utrecht, 1931), gives a good account of Dutch trade with the Iberian peninsula during the war period, but it will be superseded in due course by the work of Dr Jonathan I. Israel. See his important article: 'A conflict of empires: Spain and the Netherlands 1618-1648', *Past and Present*, LXXVI (1977), pp. 34-74.

29. On English policy and profits, *cf.* K. R. Andrews, *Elizabethan Privateering: English Privateering during the Spanish War 1585-1603* (Cambridge, 1964), *passim*.

30. C. C. Goslinga, *The Dutch in the Caribbean and on the Wild Coast, 1580-1680* (Assen, 1971); E. Sluiter, 'Dutch maritime power and the colonial status quo, 1585-1641', *Pacific Historical Review*,

XI (1942), pp. 29-41.

31. K. R. Andrews, 'Caribbean rivalry and the Anglo-Spanish peace of 1604', *History*, LIX (1974), pp. 1-17; R. D. Hussey, 'America in European diplomacy, 1597–1604', *Revista de Historia de América*, XLI (1956), pp. 1-30 – *cf*. pp. 24 and 29-30 in particular; J. den Tex, *Oldenbarnevelt*, II (Cambridge, 1973), p. 386.

32. *Resolutiën der Staten Generaal van 1576 tot 1609*, XIV: *1607-1609*, ed. H. H. P. Rijperman (the Hague, 1970), pp. 377-9.

33. P. Gerhard, *Pirates on the West Coast of New Spain, 1575-1742* (Glendale, 1960), pp. 101-34. The first Dutch attack on the Spanish Pacific was the 'trading mission' of Joris van Spilsbergen, sent by the States-General in 1615. The journal of the expedition refers to the Spaniards throughout as 'the enemy'! (An English translation appeared as *The East and West Indian Mirror*, ed. J. A. J. Villiers [Hackluyt Society, London, 1906], pp. 11-160.)

34. For a general survey of the expansion of Dutch trade, *cf*. C. R. Boxer, *The Dutch Seaborne Empire 1600-1800* (London, 1965). For the expansion of the East India trade, *cf*. Algemeen Rijksarchief (the Hague), *Kolonialische Archief* 4389, 'Schepen voor de Generale Vereenigde Nederlandsche Geoctroyeerde Oostindische Compagnie nac d'Oostindies uytgevoeren'.

35. Archives générales du Royaume (Brussels), *Secrétairerie d'Etat et de Guerre* 185 fo. 24, King Philip III to the Archduke Albert, 4 Feb. 1621. Later on, the Count-Duke of Olivares was to claim that the Truce had not been renewed by Spain 'solely for the cause of religion': see the *voto* of 1628 cited in note 25 above. This was quite untrue: see J. I. Israel, *art. cit.*, p. 39. On the expiration of the Truce see the admirable study of J. J. Poelhekke, *'t Uytgaen van den Treves. Spanje en de Nederlanden in 1621* (Groningen, 1960). It is interesting to note that at exactly the same time Spain's solicitude for the fate of the English Catholics diminished: A. J. Loomie, 'Olivares, the English Catholics, and the peace of 1630', *Revue belge de Philologie et d'Histoire*, XLVII (1969), pp. 1154-66.

36. The basic study on Dutch Brazil is by C. R. Boxer, *The Dutch in Brazil, 1624-1654* (Oxford, 1957). Pernambuco contained about 50 per cent of the population of the entire colony and produced about 60 per cent of its sugar.

37. Archivio di Stato, Venice, *Senato*: dispacci Spagna 74, unfol., T. Contarini to the Doge and Senate, 2 Oct. 1638. On the gains

216

and losses accruing to Portugal from the Union with Spain, *cf.* S. B. Schwarz, 'Luso-Spanish relations in Habsburg Brazil, 1580-1640', *The Americas*, XXV (1968), pp. 33-48. The English discerned somewhat earlier, in the 1590s, that Brazil was a weak but lush part of the empire of the Spanish Habsburgs. *Cf.* K. R. Andrews, *Elizabethan Privateering*, pp. 133 and 201-13.

38. In 1636 the Dutch wanted 5 million crowns but Spain would only offer 2 million; in 1638 Spain did offer 5 million but by then it was not enough. A. Waddington, *La République des Provinces-Unies, la France et les Pays-Bas espagnols de 1630 à 1650*, I (Paris, 1895), pp. 343-6; A. Leman, *Richelieu et Olivares: leur négociations secrètes de 1636 à 1642 pour le rétablissement de la paix* (Lille, 1938), p. 55.

39. A. Leman, *op. cit.*, p. 126; J. J. Poelhekke, *De vrede van Munster* (the Hague, 1948), p. 65. As early as 1632-3 Brazil had been almost the only point at issue in the peace talks then under way: *cf.* L. P. Gachard, *Actes des Etats-Généraux de 1632*, I (Brussels, 1853), pp. 96, 108, 124, 159; II (Brussels, 1866), pp. 665-8, 677-8, 680-1.

40. On the falling Indies receipts *cf.* A. Domínguez Ortiz, 'Los caudales de Indias la política exterior de Felipe IV', *Anuario de Estudios Americanos*, XIII (1956), pp. 311-89. There is a growing volume of evidence, as yet unsynthesized, that the critical period for the collapse of the Spanish economy was 1625-30. *Cf.* G. Anes Alvarez and J.-P. le Flem, 'Las crisis del siglo XVII: producción agricola, precios e ingresos en tierras de Segovia', *Moneda y crédito*, XCIII (1965), pp. 3-55; C. J. Jago, 'Aristocracy, war and finance in Castile, 1621-65: the titled nobility and the house of Béjar during the reign of Philip IV' (Cambridge University Ph.D. thesis, 1969), chs. 4 and 7; M. Weisser, 'Les marchands de Tolède dans l'économie castillane, 1565-1635', *Mélanges de la Casa de Velásquez*, VII (1971), pp. 223-36; F. Ruiz Martín, 'Un testimonio literario sobre las manufacturas de paños en Segovia por 1625', in *Homenaje al profesor Alarcos*, II (Valladolid, 1967), pp. 1-21.

41. On the main revolts there is a clear and concise exposition (with bibliography) by J. H. Elliott, 'Revolts in the Spanish Monarchy', in *Preconditions of Revolution in Early Modern Europe*, ed. R. Forster and J. P. Greene (Baltimore and London, 1970), pp. 109-30. The 'Green Banner' revolts with which Professor Elliott does not deal, are covered by A. Domínguez Ortiz, *Alteraciones andaluzas* (Madrid, 1973).

42. Figures from G. Parker, *The Army of Flanders*, p. 295, based on the audited accounts of the army Paymaster. Slightly lower figures were put forward by the vanquished Spanish commander as an explanation for his defeat: Bibliothèque Royale (Brussels), MS. 12428-9 fo. 328. 'Memorial . . . sobre materia de hacienda' (20 September 1644) gives a receipt of 4.7 million crowns in 1640, 4.5 million in 1641, 3.4 million in 1642 and only 1.3 million in 1643.

43. Bibliothèque Publique et Universitaire (Geneva), MS. Favre 39 fos. 88-9, Don Luis de Haro to the Marquis of Velada, 17 Nov. 1643. So few of Haro's letters have survived that this one, giving vent to his personal views, is particularly important.

44. Talks between Spain and the Dutch went on almost continuously at an informal level, but formal negotiations took place in 1621-2, 1627-9, 1632-3, 1635, 1638-9, 1640-1 and (of course) 1644-8. They are all mentioned in the first chapter of J. J. Poelhekke, *De vrede van Munster* (the Hague, 1948). There were also semi-continuous talks about peace between France and Spain from 1636 until 1659.

45. *Colección de Documentos Inéditos para la Historia de España*, LXXXII (Madrid, 1884), pp. 138-9, Count of Fuensaldaña to the king, 17 Sept. 1645; Archivo General de Simancas, *Estado* 2065, unfol. apostil of Philip IV to a report by the 'junta de estado', 3 January 1646; *Correspondencia diplomática de Francisco de Sousa Coutinho durante a sua embaixada em Holanda, 1642-1650*, ed. E. Prestage and P. de Azevedo, II (Coimbra, 1926), p. 256.

46. Quoted by M. A. S. Hume in *Cambridge Modern History*, IV (Cambridge, 1906), p. 659.

47. On Holland's objections to the cost of the war in 1646-7, *cf.* the documents cited by Poelhekke, *De vrede van Munster*, pp. 307ff.

48. *The Lord George Digby's Cabinet* (London, 1648: 68 pages of documents and commentary) and *Eenighe extracten uyt verscheyde missiven gevonden in de Lord Digby's Cabinet* (also London, 1646). These are discussed by P. Geyl, *The History of the Low Countries: Episodes and Problems* (London, 1965), pp. 75 and 246.

49. The policy of the Prince of Orange and his family is discussed by P. Geyl, *Orange and Stuart, 1641-1672* (London, 1969), ch. 1, and by J. J. Poelhekke, *De vrede van Munster*, ch. 5.

50. *Cf.* Poelhekke, *op. cit.*, ch. 7 (quotation from p. 256).

51. Charnacé to Richelieu, 2 Jan. 1634, quoted Waddington, *La République des Provinces-Unies*, I, p. 221. The influence of Charnacé and the French was crucial in aborting the peace talks of 1632-3 between Spain and the Dutch: cf. M. G. de Boer, *Die Friedensunterhandlungen zwischen Spanien und den Niederlanden in der Jahren 1632 und 1633* (Groningen, 1898).

52. *Cf.* M. de Jong, 'Holland en de Portuguese restauratie van 1640', *Tijdschrift voor Geschiedenis*, LV (1940), pp. 225-53; C. van de Haar, *De diplomatieke betrekkingen tussen de Republiek en Portugal, 1640–1661* (Groningen, 1961); and J. Pérez de Tudela, *Sobre la Defensa Hispana del Brasil contra los Holandeses, 1624-1650* (Madrid, 1974).

53. In fact Zealand was cheated: the great fleet was badly delayed by storms and arrived late at Recife with many of its soldiers dead and the rest mutinous for lack of pay. On 19 April 1648 and again on 19 Feb. 1649 the surviving Dutch troops were routed by the Portuguese on the heights of Guararapes outside Recife. These defeats sealed the fate of Dutch Brazil, and that in turn led to the loss of Dutch Angola. *Cf.* C. Moreira Bento, *As batalhas dos Guararapes* (Recife, 1971), text and maps; W. J. van Hoboken, 'De West-Indische Compagnie en de vrede van Munster', *Tijdschrift voor Geschiedenis*, LXX (1957), pp. 359-68; W. J. van Hoboken, 'Een troepentransport naar Brazilie in 1647', *Tijdschrift voor Geschiedenis*, LXII (1949), pp. 100-9.

54. Feltham, *op, cit.*, pp. 91-2.

3. The Dutch Revolt and the Polarization of International Politics

(Originally published in *Tijdschrift voor Geschiedenis*, LXXXIX [1976], pp. 429-44.)

1. G. N. Clark, *The Seventeenth Century* (London, 1929); 2nd edn. (London, 1945), p. 98.

2. H. J. C. von Grimmelshausen, *Der Abenteurliche Simplicissimus Teutsch* (1669), ed. A. von Keller (Stuttgart, 1862-3), I, 3, chs. 4 and 5: 'Von dem Teutschen Helden, der die gantze Welt bezwingen und zwischen allen Völkern Fried stifften werden' and 'Wie er die Religionen miteinander vereinigen und in einen Model glessen wird'.

3. Report of Gaspar van Vosbergen to the States-General in 1625, quoted in G. W. Vreede, *Inleiding tot eene Geschiedenis der Nederlandsche Diplomatie*, I (Utrecht, 1856), p. 1. See also the view of Christopher Hill, *Puritanism and Revolution* (London, 1958), p. 127: 'The Dutch Revolt played a similar part in the politics and thought of the early seventeenth century to that of the Spanish Civil War in the 1930s, only for a longer period.'

4. J. Meerman, quoted Vreede, *op. cit.* For a more extended analysis of why the Dutch Revolt succeeded, see ch. 2 above.

5. G. Groen van Prinsterer, *Archives ou Correspondance inédite de la Maison d'Orange-Nassau*, 1ère série II (Leiden, 1835), p. 397; Brederode to Count Louis, 11 Aug. 1565. For a fuller discussion of the connection between the Dutch Revolt and the Ottoman naval offensive in the Mediterranean *cf.* G. Parker, *The Dutch Revolt* (London, 1977), p. 286, n. 46.

6. *Cf.* Parker, *op. cit.*, p. 290, n. 19.

7. Information from W. Hahlweg, *Der Augsburger Reichstag von 1566* (Neukirchen, 1964), pp. 197-209; J. V. Polišenský, *Nizozemská Politika a Bílá Hora* (The Bohemian War and Dutch Policy, 1618-20) (Prague, 1958), pp. 94-6; N. Mout, *Bohemen en de Nederlanden in de 16e eeuw* (Leiden, 1975), pp. 28-9; B. Chudoba, *Spain and the Empire, 1519-1643* (Chicago, 1952), pp. 134-8.

8. The early contacts between Protestantism and the Turks were noted by Ranke. For more recent surveys *cf.* S. Fischer-Galati, *Ottoman Imperialism and German Protestantism, 1521-55* (Oxford, 1959), *passim*, and K. M. Setton, 'Lutheranism and the Turkish peril', *Journal of Balkan Studies*, III (1962), pp. 133-68. *Cf.* the letters of the Landgrave of Hesse to William of Orange in Groen van Prinsterer, *Archives* (*cf.*, for example, II, pp. 70-3).

9. F. Strada, *De la Guerre Civile de Flandre*, II (Brussels, 1712), p. 343. Although Strada *may* have fabricated the story, the evidence points towards authenticity. The Duke of Naxos certainly possessed direct contact with Antwerp, where he had lived for about nine years as a junior partner in one of the city's Portuguese banks. Since several Marranos were prominent in the Antwerp consistory in 1566, and since they would have been known to Miques personally, the additional information provided by Strada (possibly from documents destroyed at Naples in 1943) must be taken seriously. *Cf.* on the Duke of Naxos: C. Roth, *The House of Nasi: the Duke of Naxos* (Philadelphia, 1948), pp. 58-62; and P. Grunebaum-Ballin, *Joseph Naci, Duc de Naxos* (Paris, 1968), p.

140 (the Duke was probably taken by Christopher Marlowe as the model for his *Jew of Malta*). On the Antwerp Marranos, the latest word is by B. A. Vermaseren, 'De Antwerpse koopman Martin Lopez en zijn familie', *Bijdragen tot de Geschiedenis*, LVI (1973), pp. 3-79.

10. E. Charrière, *Négociations de la France dans le Levant*, III (Paris, 1853), p. 61 ('L'homme du prince d'Orange qui est chez Micques . . .'), and Grunebaum-Ballin, *op. cit.*, p. 61.

11. H. Inalcik, 'The origin of the Ottoman-Russian rivalry and the Don-Volga canal (1569)', *Annales de l'Université d'Ankara*, I (1946-7), pp. 47-110; A. N. Kurat, 'The Turkish expedition to Astrakhan in 1569', *Slavonic and East European Review*, XL (1960-1), pp. 7-23; A. C. Hess, 'The Moriscos: an Ottoman fifth column in sixteenth-century Spain', *American Historical Review*, LXXIV (1968), pp. 1-25 (especially pp. 14-16); on the ways in which the Ottomans gained information about Spanish affairs, see N. H. Biegman, *The Turco-Ragusan Relationship According to the Firmāns of Murad III (1575-95)* (Paris-the Hague, 1967), ch. 6, and Biegman, 'Ragusan spying for the Ottoman empire', *Türk Tarih Kurumu Belleten*, XXVII (1963), pp. 237-49.

12. N. M. Sutherland, *The Massacre of St Bartholomew and the European Conflict 1559-72* (London, 1973), p. 133 onwards; plus two older studies apparently not consulted by Dr Sutherland: P. J. van Herwerden, *Het Verblijf van Lodewijk van Nassau in Frankrijk* (Assen, 1932), ch. 5, and J. C. Devos, 'Un projet de cession d'Alger à la France en 1572', *Bulletin philosophique et historique*, LXXVIII (1953-4), pp. 339-48.

13. Groen van Prinsterer, *Archives*, IV, p. 396, Orange to Count John of Nassau, 7 May 1574. The letter continued: 'And if the poor inhabitants of this country, abandoned by the whole world, still wish to persevere in their struggle . . . it will cost the Spaniards a good half of Spain, both in men and in goods, before they manage to make and end of us.' Orange was right.

14. Charrière, *Négociations de la France*, III, pp. 477-82; Stephen Gerlach, *Tage-Buch* (Frankfurt, 1674), p. 51 (on contact of Porte and Beza in March 1574; Gerlach was the chaplain of the Imperial ambassador at Constantinople). See also p. 31 above.

15. Hess, 'The Moriscos', pp. 19-21.

16. L. Didier, *Lettres et négociations de Claude de Mondoucet, resident de France aux Pays-Bas (1571-74)*, II (Paris, 1892), pp.

338-9, letter of 23 Oct. 1574: 'On account of this disaster which has occurred at Tunis,' Mondoucet argued, Philip II would seek a settlement in the Netherlands, 'in order to be able to turn all his resources and troops against the Turks and offer a more spirited resistance there, since the war in the Mediterranean is more important to Spain.' On 13 Nov. 1574 the provincial government in North Holland was informed of the fall of Tunis which would mean, they surmised, 'that the pressure of Spain on these provinces will be diminished'. (Rijksarchief, Noord Holland, *Archief van de Gecommitteerde Raden*, 131 fo. 84; reference kindly communicated by Mr A. C. Duke.)

17. C. Roth, *The House of Naxos*, p. 61; Gerlach, *Tage-Buch*, pp. 327-8; J. A. Goris, 'Turksche kooplieden te Antwerpen in de XVIe eeuw', *Bijdragen tot de Geschiedenis*, XIV (1922), pp. 30-8. The first Dutch ambassador to the Porte only arrived in 1612: D. M. Vaughan, *Europe and the Turk* (Liverpool, 1954), pp. 145-6.

18. *Calendar of State Papers Foreign in the Reign of Elizabeth, 1586-88*, pp. 508-9: petition to the Sultan by Ambassador William Harborne, 9 November 1587. See also S. A. Skilliter, *William Harborne and the Trade with Turkey: Secret Agent 1578-81* (Oxford, 1978), and H. G. Rawlinson, 'The embassy of William Harborne to Constantinople, 1583-88', *Transactions of the Royal Historical Society*, 4th series, V (1922), pp. 1-27.

19. *The Somers Collection of Tracts*, ed. W. Scott, I (London, 1809), pp. 164-70: 'Advice' of Lord Burghley. On the negotiations which led up to the treaty between England and the Dutch *cf.* C. H. Wilson, *Queen Elizabeth and the Revolt of the Netherlands* (London, 1970), pp. 79-85.

20. Archive du Ministère des Affaires Etrangères, Paris, *Correspondance de Hollande*, IV, fos. 177-178v, 'Maladies de l'estat de Hollande' (Aug. 1587: part of the papers of the Earl of Leicester). The anti-Dutch alliance of Philip II even extended to the Baltic where King Stephen Bathory of Poland threatened to cut off Dutch trade with Danzig unless they made peace with Spain: L. Boratynski, 'Esteban Batory, La Hansa, y la sublevación de los Países Bajos', *Boletín de la Real Academia de la Historia*, CXXVII (1951), pp. 451-500. For an assessment of the feasibility of the Armada campaign, see ch. 7 above.

21. Details on the Spanish payments from Parker, *The Dutch Revolt*, pp. 226-7; details on the papal assistance from I. Cloulas, 'L'armée pontificale . . . pendant la seconde campagne en France de Alexandre Farnèse (1591-2)', *Bulletin de la Commission royale*

Notes

d'Histoire, CXXVI (1960), pp. 83-102; and A. de Mosto, 'Ordinamenti militari delle soldatesche dello stato romano nel secolo XVI', *Quellen und Forschungen aus Italienische Archiven und Bibliotheken*, VI (1904), pp. 72-133 (*cf.* p. 102).

22. Details on German aid in B. Vogler, 'Le rôle des Electeurs palatins dans les guerres de religion en France, 1559-92', *Cahiers d'Histoire*, X (1965), pp. 51-85, and C. P. Clasen, *The Palatinate in European History, 1555-1618* (Oxford, 1966), pp. 5-19. England's aid during these years is described by H. A. Lloyd, *The Rouen Campaign, 1590-92* (Oxford, 1973), pp. 81-103, and C. G. Cruickshank, *Elizabeth's Army* (Oxford, 1966), pp. 236-51.

23. On the Emden occupation (which was made permanent in 1599), *cf.* J. den Tex, *Oldenbarnevelt, II: Oorlog 1588-1609* (Haarlem, 1962), pp. 437-41; on the Dutch subsidies to Henry IV, *cf. ibid.*, pp. 63-99.

24. J. H. H. Siccama, *Schets van de Diplomatieke Betrekkingen Tusschen Nederland en Brandenburg, 1596-1678* (Utrecht, 1867), pp. 12-13.

25. F. Boersma, 'De diplomatieke reis van Daniel van der Meulen en Nicholaes Bruyninck naar het Duitse leger bij Emmerik, Augustus 1599', *Bijdragen en Mededelingen betreffende de Geschiedenis der Nederlanden*, XXXIV (1969), pp. 24-66.

26. Siccama, *op. cit.*, p. 40.

27. D. Buisseret, *Sully* (London, 1968), p. 82, gives the annual subsidies, which averaged 2 million livres. This sum represented about 10 per cent of Henry IV's total income – a generous effort. On Dutch efforts to prevent the peace of Vervins and to expedite regular payment of the subsidy, *cf.* S. Barendrecht, *François van Aerssen, Diplomaat aan het Franse Hof (1598-1613)* (Leiden, 1965), chs. 3 and 8-10. On the significance of Philip II's preoccupation with France, *cf.* Parker, *The Dutch Revolt*, ch. 6.

28. J. Heringa, *De Eer en Hoogheid van de Staat. Over de plaats der Vereenigde Nederlanden in het Diplomatieke Leven van de 17e eeuw* (Groningen, 1961), pp. 252-3. The Dutch consulates that were opened in the Mediterranean during the seventeenth century are listed in H. Waetjen, *Die Niederländen im Mittelmeergebiet zur Zeit ihrer hochsten Machtstellung* (Berlin, 1909), pp. 111-13.

29. E. van Reyd, *Historie der Nederlandtscher Oorlogen . . . tot den Jare 1601* (Leeuwarden, 1650), p. iii.

223

30. L. van Aitzema, *Saken van Staet ende Oorlog*, I (Amsterdam, 1669), p. 1103. Texts for most of the treaties are printed in this work and may be conveniently found by consulting the index of each volume under 'Accoord' and 'Tractaet', or under the name of each country.

31. van Aitzema, *op. cit.*, I, p. 146: treaty with the King of Algiers, July 1622.

32. Francis Bacon, *Certaine Miscellany Works* (London, 1629), p. 32.

33. 330,551 florins of 60 *kreizers* (or 33.3 *pattards*; the Dutch florin was worth 20 *pattards*) were paid for the war in Friuli by the Spanish ambassador to the Imperial court, Don Balthasar de Zúñiga, between Mar. 1616 and Jan. 1617. In all, between July 1608 and Feb. 1617 Zúñiga spent 1,482,392 florins of 60 *kreizers*, much of it in pensions and bribes (51,478 florins to the Cardinal-Elector of Cologne, 22,500 to Cardinal Khlesl, chief adviser of the Emperor Matthias, and so on); *cf.* Archivo General de Simancas (Spain), *Contaduría Mayor de Cuentas, 3a época*, no. 669, audited accounts of Zúñiga. Zúñiga's predecessor, Don Guillén de San Clemente, spent a further 600,000 florins during his embassy between 1599 and 1608; more still was sent from Spain to finance a detachment of Spanish troops fighting at Philip III's expense in Hungary: *cf.* marqués de Ayerbe, *Correspondencia Inédita de Don Guillén de San Clemente* (Zaragoza, 1892), pp. 315-99.

34. Chudoba, *Spain and the Empire*, pp. 225-48. There is much new material in P. Brightwell, 'Spain and the Origins of the Thirty Years' War' (unpublished Cambridge University Ph.D. thesis, 1967).

35. Figures from D. Albrecht, *Die Deutsche Politik Papst Gregors XV* (Schriftenreihe zur bayerischen Landesgeschichte no. 53), p. 13 n. 28. The total cost of papal aid to the Catholic cause in 1618-23 (763,000 *scudi*) should be compared with the total cost of papal aid to the Emperor in 1595-6 during the war in Hungary (600,000 *scudi*: *cf.* de Mosto, *op. cit.*).

36. Detailed figures in D. Albrecht, 'Zur Finanzierung des Dreissigjährigen Krieges. Die Subsidien der Kurie für Kaiser und Liga, 1618-35', *Zeitschrift für Bayerischen Landesgeschichte*, XIX (1956), pp. 534-67, and *Die Auswärtige Politik Maximilians von Bayern, 1618-35* (Göttingen, 1962), pp. 37-42 and 198-200.

37. Archivo General de Simancas, *Contaduría Mayor de Cuentas*,

3a época, no. 949, audited accounts of Nicolas Vizente Escorza, *Pagador General de Alemaña* (in florins of 60 *kreizers* or 33.3 *pattards*):

Apr. 1635 – Apr. 1637 803,564
Apr. 1637 – Sept. 1640 (sic) 2,673,382
Mar. 1640 – Aug. 1641 865,944
Aug. 1641 – Mar. 1643 997,094

Unfortunately I have not yet been able to find any further accounts of the 'Spanish treasury in Germany'.

38. The existence of an 'international' was suggested (and christened) by the Dutch historian A. A. van Schelven, 'Der Generalstab des politischen Calvinismus in Zentraleuropa zu Beginn des Dreissigjährigen Krieges', *Archiv für Reformationsgeschichte* (1939), pp. 117-41. Two important members of the 'General Staff' have been the subject of major biographies since van Schelven: H. Sturmberger, *Georg Erasmus Tschernembl: Religion, Libertät und Widerstand* (Linz, 1953); F. H. Schubert, *Ludwig Camerarius (1573-1651). Eine Biographe* (Kallmünz, 1955). For some perceptive remarks on the central European members of the 'international' (and much more besides), *cf.* R. J. W. Evans, *Rudolf II and his World* (Oxford, 1973), pp. 5-42. See also R. Kleinman, 'Charles Emanuel I of Savoy and the Bohemian election of 1619', *European Studies Review*, V (1975), pp. 3-29.

39. E. Wrangel, *De Betrekkingen Tusschen Zweden en de Nederlanden . . . Voornamelijk Gedurende de 17e eeuw* (Leiden, 1901), ch. 1; P. Geyl, *Christofforo Suriano, Resident van de Serenissime Republiek van Venetië in den Haag, 1616-23* (the Hague, 1913), chs. 1-3; J. G. Smit, ed., *Resolutiën der Staten-Generaal*, n.f. III (R.G.P. grote serie 152, the Hague, 1975), resolutions 816, 817, 1000. News of the proposal to send Dutch troops to Savoy reached Spain and provoked the Council of War to declare that the Twelve Years' Truce would be broken if any aid was sent, (Archivo General de Simancas, *Guerra Antigua* no. 808, unfol., *consultas* of 16, 26 and 28 Dec. 1616). In the end, no aid was sent. *Cf.* also L. Pearsall Smith, *The Life and Letters of Sir Henry Wotton*, 2 vols. (Oxford, 1907), pp. 111-12, 152-6, 180-3.

40. J. V. Polišenský, *Nizozemská Politika a Bílá Hora* (Prague, 1958): this study reveals how little *political* contact there was between Bohemia and the States-General before 1618; J. V. Polišenský, *Anglie a Bílá Hora* (The Bohemian War and British Policy) (Prague, 1949). Both these books have useful English summaries. See also F. A. Yates, *The Rosicrucian Enlightenment* (London, 1972), *passim* (e.g. p. 90).

41. See the promises quoted in S. R. Gardiner, *Letters and Other Documents Illustrating the Relations between England and Germany*, II (London, 1868), p. 7 (Dudley Carleton to Secretary of State Naughton 13 Sept. 1619 new style); figures for Dutch aid from Polišenský, *Nizozemská Politika*, p. 335. The States-General's Staat van Oorlog, however, allocated over 1,000,000 florins to Bohemia (*cf.* Algemeen Rijksarchief, the Hague, *Raad van State*, nos. 1499 and 1500, *Sub annis* 1618-21).

42. See T. K. Rabb in A. Soman (ed.), *The Massacre of St Bartholomew; Reappraisals and Documents* (the Hague, 1974), p. 254. The tentacles extended further at times, even to Moscow and Constantinople. See F. L. Baumer, 'England, the Turk and the common corps of Christendom', in *American Historical Review*, L (1944-5), pp. 26-48. In the 1630s the Orthodox church leaders tried to establish a rapport with the Calvinists at Geneva and Leiden. See B. F. Porshnev, 'Les rapports politiques de l'Europe occidentale et de l'Europe orientale à l'époque de la guerre de trente ans', in *Rapports du XIe Congrès des Sciences Historiques*, IV (Stockholm, 1960), pp. 136-63; and P. G. Westin, *Negotiations about Church Unity, 1628-34: John Durie, Gustavus Adolphus, Axel Oxenstierna* (Uppsala, 1932), pp. 57-60. For the abortive efforts of the Calvinists of Hungary (advised by the ubiquitous Jan Amos Comenius) to form an alliance with England and the Dutch Republic in the 1650s, see L. Makkai, 'The Hungarian Puritans and the English Revolution', *Acta historica* (Budapest), V (1958), pp. 13-44.

43. Although the distinguished Czech historian, J. V. Polišenský, referred to the years 1621-5 as the 'Dutch period' of the Thirty Years' War (*The Thirty Years' War* [London, 1971], ch. 5), the German historian F. H. Schubert has made out a convincing case for regarding the Calvinist exiles from the Palatinate as the driving force in the polarization of European politics during the 1620s: *cf.* his biography of Camerarius (n. 38 above), and his articles 'Die pfälzische Exilregierung im Dreissigjährigen Krieg. Ein Beitrag zur Geschichte des politischen Protestantismus', *Zeitschrift für Geschichte des Oberrheins*, CII (1954), pp. 575-680, and 'Die Niederlande zur Zeit des Dreissigjährigen Krieges im Urteil des Diplomatischen Korps im Haag', *Historisches Jahrbuch*, LXXIV (1955), pp. 252-64. In his latest book, Polišenský appears to accept this view: *Documenta Bohemica Bellum Tricennale Illustrantia, 1. Der Krieg und die Gesellschaft in Europa, 1618-48* (Prague, 1971), pp. 109-15.

44. On the limitations of the Dutch diplomatic service, *cf.* M. A. M. Franken, 'The general tendencies and structural aspects of

the foreign policy and diplomacy of the Dutch Republic in the latter half of the seventeenth century', *Acta Historiae Neerlandicae*, III (1968), pp. 1-42.

45. The *Staten van Oorlog* are to be found in ARA *Raad van State*, 1499 and 1500; the Portuguese intervention is described by M. de Jong, 'Holland en de Portuguese restauratie van 1640', in *Tijdschrift voor Geschiedenis*, LV (1940), pp. 225-53, and C. van de Haar, *De Diplomatieke Betrekkingen Tussen de Republiek en Portugal, 1640-61* (Groningen, 1961), ch. 3; the abortive efforts to send aid to the 'revolutie in Catalogne' are chronicled in van Aitzema, *Saken van Staet ende Oorlog*, II, p. 729. *Cf.* also J. H. Elliott, *The Revolt of the Catalans* (Cambridge, 1963), p. 538. On the nature of Dutch foreign policy at this time, *cf.* the perceptive analysis of E. H. Kossmann, *In Praise of the Dutch Republic; Some Seventeenth-century Attitudes* (London, 1963), pp. 3-8.

46. van Aitzema, *Saken*, I, p. 905.

47. R. Hackluyt, 'Discourse of Western Planting' (1584), in E. G. R. Taylor (ed.), *The Original Writings and Correspondence of the Two Richard Hackluyts* (London, 1935), p. 249. For the nature of the maritime conflict between England and Spain, *cf.* K. R. Andrews, *Elizabethan Privateering: English Privateering during the Spanish War, 1585-1603* (Cambridge, 1964).

48. J. de Laet, *Iaerlijck Verhael van de Verrichtingen der Geoctroyeerde West-Indische Compagnie* (1644), ed. S. P. L'Honoré Naber and J. C. M. Warnsinck, I (the Hague, 1931), p. 2. See also J. I. Israel, 'A conflict of empires: Spain and the Netherlands 1618-1648', *Past and Present*, LXXVI (1977), pp. 34-74.

49. B. Keen, 'The Black Legend revisted', in *Hispanic-American Historical Review*, XLIX (1969), pp. 703-19; J. G. van Dillen, 'De West-Indische Compagnie, het Calvinisme en de politiek', *Tijdschrift voor Geschiedenis*, LXXIV (1961), pp. 145-71.

50. W. Voorbeijtel Cannenburg (ed.), *De Reis om de Wereld van de Nassausche Vloot, 1623-6* (the Hague, 1964), p. xx. The fleet was instructed to continue the contacts made by Spilsbergen with the Indians of Chile (*ibid.*, p. xix).

51. Dierick Ruiters, *Toortse de Zee-Vaert* (Flushing, 1623), ed. S. P. L'Honoré Naber (the Hague, 1909), p. 35. On the Jews in Spanish America, *cf.* L. García de Proodián, *Los Judíos en América. Sus Actividades en los Virreinatos de Nueva Castilla y Nueva Granada en el Siglo XVII* (Madrid, 1966), pp. 93-4; and J. A. Gonsalves da

Spain and the Netherlands

Mello, *Tempo dos Flamengos. Influência da ocupação Holandesa na Vida e na Cultura do Norte do Brasil* (Rio de Janeiro, 1947), pp. 268-70 and 290-311 (from 1636 the Dutch authorities permitted a synagogue, rabbi and Jewish printing press in Recife). See also Israel, 'Spain and the Dutch Sephardim, 1609-60', *Studia Rosenthaliana*, XII (1978), pp. 1-61.

52. In matters of espionage, a charge like this is always hard to substantiate. It may therefore be of interest to note the case of one known Dutch spy in Spanish America: Adriaan Rodríguez.

In his *Toortse der Zee-Vaert* of 1623, Dierick Ruiters (who had lived in South America between 1617 and 1621) drew attention to the large number of Jews resident there, who might serve as allies of the Dutch. Although he mentioned no names, one of these discontented Jews was undoubtedly Adriaan Rodríguez, living in Callao, the principal port of Peru. Rodríguez was a Portuguese Jew who had taken refuge in Leiden in Holland, working as a carpenter. In 1599 he set sail as a ship's carpenter aboard the fleet of Van Noort, which was to circumnavigate the globe, but his ship was wrecked off Peru. Rodríguez and twenty-five other Dutch survivors were kept in prison (although Rodríguez was allowed out on parole and did some carpentry) until 1604, when he was repatriated (via Seville) as part of a general exchange of prisoners-of-war. Rodríguez found conditions more attractive in the New World, however, and as soon as the Twelve Years' Truce was signed he set sail from the Netherlands for Callao again.

It may well be that from this point onwards Rodríguez was acting as a spy, a 'sleeper' in the best spy-story tradition, waiting for the day when he could be useful. Certainly when in May 1624 the fleet of Jacques L'Hermite arrived off Callao, they had with them full reports of the garrisons, batteries and treasure in the port provided by Rodríguez. Moreover, when Rodríguez's room was searched, letters to him from Prince Maurice were found, while under torture he revealed detailed knowledge of the composition and movements of the Dutch fleet.

However, Rodríguez may only have been recruited for Dutch espionage in 1623, since two more spies arrived in Lima in that year direct from Holland. In matters of espionage, where complete secrecy is essential, it is often almost impossible to establish the truth. Rodríguez was only discovered (and thus granted a sort of immortality) because some Spaniards from Callao were captured by the L'Hermite fleet and later released; when they got back to Callao, they denounced Rodríguez – presumably because they had heard his name mentioned on the Dutch fleet. They also testified to the impressive organization and preparation that had gone into the operation against Callao; they knew that the Dutch had intended to free the Negro slaves in Peru and arm them with the special weapons brought from Holland for the purpose. Only an unexpectedly swift reaction by the Spanish viceroy cheated L'Hermite of his prize.

The story has been reconstituted from: W. Voorbeijtel Cannenburg, *De Reis om de Wereld van de Nassausche Vloot, 1623-26* (the Hague, 1964), pp. cxv-cxvi; G. Lohmann Villena, *Las Defensas Militares de Lima y Callao* (Seville, 1964), p. 50; Archivo Histórico Nacional, Madrid, *Inquisición legajo* 1647, no. 7 (the confession of Rodríguez) and *libro* 1030 fos. 296-303 (a report on his case). For other evidence of Marrano-Dutch collusion in South America, see G. Lohmann Villena, 'Una incógnita despejada: la identidad del judío portugues, autor de la "Discriçión general del Piru"', *Revista de Indias*, CXIX-CXXII (1970), p. 317 and n. 8, pp. 384-5 and notes 174-5; J. A. Gonsalves de Mello, *Tempo dos Flamengos. Influência de Ocupação Holandesa na Vida e na Cultura do Norte do Brasil* (Rio de Janeiro, 1947), pp. 290-311; A. Domínguez Ortiz, *Los Judeoconversos en España y América* (Madrid, 1971), pp. 250-3; and J. I. Israel, 'The Portuguese in seventeenth-century Mexico', *Jahrbuch für Geschichte Latein Amerikas*, XI (1974), pp. 12-32.

53. The standard account of the Dutch assaults on Brazil is C. R. Boxer, *The Dutch in Brazil, 1624-54* (Oxford, 1954). On Bahía itself, *cf.* T. de Azevedo, *Povoamento da Cidade do Salvador* (Bahía, 1969): the city had a white population of around 8000 in 1624 (p. 156). *Cf.* also J. Pérez de Tudela, *Sobre la Defensa Hispana del Brasil contra los Holandeses, 1624-50* (Madrid, 1974). On the Dutch attack on Peru, *cf.* G. Lohmann Villena, *Las Defensas Militares de Lima y Callao* (Seville, 1964), part I, ch. 2.

54. *Cf.* Boxer, *op. cit.*, and *Salvador de Sá and the Struggle for Brazil and Angola, 1602-86* (London, 1952). A perceptive short study is also to be recommended: E. Sluiter, 'Dutch maritime power and the colonial status quo, 1585-1641', in *Pacific Historical Review*, XI (1942), pp. 29-41.

55. Lohmann Villena, *op. cit.*, p. 93. On the Dutch and Peru in general *cf.* P. Gerhard, *Pirates on the West Coast of New Spain, 1575-1642* (Glendale, Ill., 1960), ch. 3. The Spaniards had always feared an alliance between the Dutch and the Araucanian Indians. One of the best reflections of this fear was written by the great luminary of the Golden Age, Quevedo, in 1635-6: D. A. Fernández-Guerra y Orbe (ed.), *Obras de Don Francisco de Quevedo Villegas*, I (Madrid, 1946), pp. 407ff. (*La Hora de Todos*, ch. 36, 'Los de Chile y los Holandeses', and 39, 'La isla de los monopantos'.)

56. N. Steensgaard, *The Asian Trade Revolution of the Seventeenth Century* (Chicago, 1974), pp. 131-41. Steensgaard effectively refutes the rival theory of M. A. P. Meilink-Roelofsz, 'Aspects of Dutch colonial development in Asia in the seventeenth century', in J. S. Bromley and E. H. Kossmann (eds.), *Britain and the Netherlands in Europe and Asia* (London, 1968), pp. 56-82 (*cf.* pp. 70-1).

57. K. W. Goonewardena, *The Foundation of Dutch Power in Ceylon, 1638-58* (Amsterdam, 1959), pp. 6-22.

58. T. Raychaudhuri, *Jan Company in Coromandel, 1605-1690* (the Hague, 1962), pp. 15, 22-5; Chang T'ien Tsî, *Sino-Portuguese Trade from 1514 to 1644* (Leiden, 1934), p. 118.

59. A special Japanese word was coined for Dutch studies (*rangaku*), and it came as a sad shock when the *rangaku* scholars discovered in 1853 that Dutch, the only European language that they knew, was not spoken by the entire world outside Japan. *Cf.* G. K. Goodman, *The Dutch Impact on the Japanese, 1640-1853* (Leiden, 1967), pp. 1-25; A. Hyma, *The Dutch in the Far East, a History of the Dutch Commercial and Colonial Empire* (Ann Arbor, 1942), ch. 6; and C. R. Boxer, *The Christian Century in Japan, 1549-1650* (Berkeley, 1951).

60. *Cf.* the quotation in K. Ratelband (ed.), *De Westafrikaanse Reis van Piet Heyn, 1624-1625* (the Hague, 1959), pp. xxxiii-xxxix (from Spranckhuysen's funeral oration of 1629).

61. Adriaen Valerius, *Nederlandtsche Gedenck-Clanck* (Haarlem, 1626; re-edited Amsterdam, 1942), p. 176.

62. C. P. Hooft, *Memorien en Adviezen van Cornelis Pieterszoon Hooft*, I (Utrecht, 1871), p. 182.

63. J. W. Smit, 'The Netherlands and Europe in the seventeenth and eighteenth centuries', in J. S. Bromley and E. H. Kossmann, *op. cit.*, p. 16. In preparing this chapter I wish to acknowledge invaluable suggestions made by Mr André Carus and Dr Hugo Soly.

4. The 'Military Revolution, 1560-1660' – a Myth?

(Originally published in the *Journal of Modern History*, XLVII [1976], pp. 195-314.)

1. Michael Roberts, *The Military Revolution, 1560-1660* (Belfast, 1956); reprinted in a slightly amended form in M. Roberts, *Essays in Swedish History* (London, 1967), pp. 195-225, with some additional material on pp. 56-81. For examples of how the 'military revolution' has been accepted by other scholars *cf.* G. N. Clark, *War and Society in the Seventeenth Century* (Cambridge, 1958), and again in *New Cambridge Modern History*, V (Cambridge, 1964), ch. 8. Compare the approach of C. W. C. Oman, *A History of the Art of War in the Sixteenth Century* (London, 1937). I am grateful to the following for their helpful suggestions concerning the preparation of this chapter: Mr Brian Bond, Dr Peter Burke, Professor John Hale, Professor H. G. Koenigsberger, Mrs Angela Parker, Dr Ian Roy and Professor John Shy. I would also like to thank the 'subject' of this paper, Professor Michael Roberts, for his help over many years and for his encouragement to publish.

2. Roberts, *Essays*, p. 217.

3. On the whole, troops did not dress alike in most armies until the later seventeenth century. It was the 1650s before the English and Swedish armies adopted uniform; the French did not do so until the 1660s. Before that, the troops dressed as they (or their commander) wished, carrying only distinguishing marks such as a feather, a scarf or a sash of the same colour to mark them out from the enemy. Not surprisingly there were a fair number of cases of units from the same army attacking each other in the confusion of battle. *Cf.*, for the introduction of uniforms, C. Nordmann, 'L'armée suédoise au XVIIe siècle', *Revue du Nord*, LIV (1972), pp. 133-47 (at p. 137); L. André, *Michel le Tellier et l'organization de l'armée monarchique* (Paris, 1906), pp. 339-42; and Geoffrey Parker, *The Army of Flanders and the Spanish Road, 1567-1659. The logistics of Spanish victory and defeat in the Low Countries' Wars* (Cambridge, 1972), pp. 164-5.

4. On the reorganization of the Dutch army by Prince Maurice and his cousin, William-Louis, *cf.* W. Hahlweg, 'Aspekte und Probleme der Reform des niederländischen Kriegswesen unter Prinz Moritz von Oranien', *Bijdragen en Mededelingen betreffende de Geschiedenis der Nederlanden*, LXXXVI (1971), pp. 161-77;

231

and M. D. Feld, 'Middle-class society and the rise of military professionalism. The Dutch Army, 1589-1609', *Armed Forces and Society*, I (Aug. 1975), pp. 419-42. Both authors stress that, although classical precedents were closely studied by the Nassau cousins (especially outstanding successes like the battle of Cannae in 216 BC), their relevance to military conditions in the Netherlands was also carefully evaluated.

5. There were a few centres of instruction like the 'academia militaris' of John of Nassau at Siegen (1617-23), and courses of obvious military utility such as mathematics and fencing were added to the curricula of a number of colleges and schools; but when one remembers the central place of war in seventeenth-century society the lack of more formal education in military matters is somewhat surprising.

6. Professor Roberts commented on the proliferation of studies on the 'law of war' in the seventeenth century (*Essays*, pp. 216-17); the basic principles, however, already affected the conduct of wars in the Middle Ages; *cf.* M. H. Keen, *The Laws of War in the Late Middle Ages* (London and Toronto, 1965).

7. In England alone, between 1470 and 1642 a total of at least 164 English and 460 foreign books were published. *Cf.* M. J. D. Cockle, *A Bibliography of Military Books up to 1642* (London, 1900; reprinted 1957), and H. J. Webb, *Elizabethan Military Science: the Books and the Practice* (Wisconsin, 1965). For many years, Venice appears to have been the centre of printed military culture: between 1492 and 1570, some 67 new titles on military matters were published in the city, compared with about 64 in the whole of the rest of Europe (J. R. Hale, 'Printing and the military culture of Renaissance Venice', *Mediaevalia et Humanistica*, N. S. VIII [1977], 21-62). It is interesting to note that scarcely any work dealt with naval warfare (*ibid.*, p. 49).

8. On the influence of the Italian wars upon Europe's military history *cf.* P. Pieri, *Il Rinascimiento e la crisi militare italiana*, 2nd ed. (Turin, 1952) and M. E. Mallett, *Mercenaries and their Masters. Warfare in Renaissance Italy* (London, 1974), especially chs. 7 and 9. The points at which the European 'military revolution' tended to follow Italian precedents are indicated *seriatim* in the notes below; *cf.* note 20 for the linguistic inheritance.

9. The 'countermarch' was devised by William-Louis of Nassau, and a diagram showing what was involved was sent to Count Maurice on 8 Dec. 1594: *cf.* a facsimile of this on p. 6 of J. B. Kist's *Commentary* to J. de Gheyn, *The Exercise of Armes* (New

York, facsimile edition, 1974). Professor Maury Feld has claimed that the countermarch turned an army into 'a unit of continuous production' and the soldiers into some sort of assembly-line workers, and that this constituted a major tactical improvement. In theory, this is true; but, as noted above, there were, in practice, serious technical limitations. (*Cf.* M. D. Feld, 'Middle-class society', *art. cit.* in note 4. This important and interesting article was kindly brought to my attention by Professor P. David Lagomarsino of Dartmouth College.)

10. It is incorrect to say that 'a Spanish army of 12,000 men would have four units' (Roberts, *Military Revolution*, p. 7); although Professor Roberts omitted this passage from the second edition of his paper, he still overestimated the size of the Spanish units on active service (*Essays*, pp. 59-60 and 62). It now appears that the Swedish army, also, did not have regiments of uniform size (Nordmann, 'L'armée suédoise', p. 137 n. 23), and that there was no fixed ratio of pike to 'shot' in the army of Gustavus Adolphus – it all depended on the availability of weapons at the time of recruitment.

11. Take, for example, the peacetime muster of the four Spanish *tercios* in the Netherlands, held on 12 May 1571. There were 50 companies (an average of 12 per *tercio*) and 7509 men (an average of 150 men – 9 of them officers – per company). Of the 7509 men, 596 (9 per cent) were musketeers and 1577 arquebus-men, a total of 30 per cent 'shot'. (Archivo General de Simancas, *Estado*, leg. 547 fo. 99 *bis*, 'Relación sumaria de los soldados que se pagaron'.)

12. The *escuadrón* was also a common tactical unit in the Dutch army, *eo nomine*; *cf.* J. W. Wijn, *Het krijgswezen in den tijd van prins Maurits* (Utrecht, 1934), p. 424. For the Swedish equivalent *cf.* A. Åberg. 'The Swedish Army, from Lützen to Narva', in M. Roberts (ed.), *Sweden's Age of Greatness, 1632-1718* (London, 1972), pp. 265-87, at p. 282.

13. G. Parker, *The Army of Flanders*, pp. 167-72, and the sources there quoted. It seems that Spain and Sweden were far ahead of the field in the provision of religious care for their troops. There were even Jesuit priests aboard the Dunkirk privateers after 1623 (*cf.* E. Hambye, *L'aumônerie de la flotte de Flandre au XVIIe siècle*, Louvain, 1967) and every soldier aboard the Spanish Armada of 1588 received a leaden medallion with the Virgin on it (and several of these have been found by nautical archaeologists excavating the Armada wrecks off Ireland). The Swedish Army in Germany had an 'ecclesiastical consistory' under an Almoner-General and every soldier was issued with a Lutheran prayer-

book (Nordmann, *art. cit.*, p. 136).

14. J. X. Evans, *The Works of Sir Roger Williams* (Oxford, 1972), p. 15. *Cf.* the confirmation of Sir Francis Bacon in 1624 that 'the great Secret of the Power of Spaine . . . will be found, rather to consist in a Veterane Army (such as vpon several Occasions and Pretensions, they haue euer had on foot, in one part or other of Christendom, now by the space of [almost] sixscore yeares) than in the strength of the Dominions and Prouinces.' (Quoted *apud* Evans, *op. cit.*, p. cxli.)

15. Parker, *op. cit.*, pp. 32-5.

16. G. E. Rothenburg, *The Austrian Military Border in Croatia, 1522-1747* (Urbana, Ill., 1960), chs. 3-5; E. Heischmann, *Die Anfänge des Stehenden Heeres in Oesterreich* (Vienna, 1925), *passim.*

17. R. A. Newhall, *Muster and Review: a Problem of English Military Administration, 1420-1440* (Cambridge, Mass., 1940); P. Contamine, *Guerre, état et société à la fin du moyen âge. Etudes sur les armées du roi de France, 1337-1494* (Paris, the Hague, 1972); C. T. Allmand, *Society at War. The Experience of England and France during the Hundred Years' War* (Edinburgh, 1973); M. E. Mallett, *Mercenaries and their Masters: Warfare in Renaissance Italy* (London, 1974).

18. Garrard served in the Burgundian regiment of the baron de Chevreux in the Netherlands for fourteen years; Williams served in the Spanish *tercio* of Julian Romero from 1574 until 1578; Barwick mentions his Spanish service but does not indicate how long it lasted. All three put their experience to good use in their writings: *cf.* H. J. Webb, *Elizabethan Military Science*, pp. 44-50. There was, of course, a vigorous debate throughout most of the sixteenth century between the 'Ancients' (who believed that Greece and Rome had provided exemplars to be copied in all spheres save religion) and 'Moderns' (their opponents, of whom the three writers above are examples). *Cf.* also Hahlweg, 'Aspekte und Probleme', *art. cit.* in note 4.

19. F. Redlich, *The German Military Enterpriser and his Workforce*, I (Wiesbaden, 1964), pp. 157-62 for examples.

20. Sir Roger Williams stressed the point to readers of his *Discourse of Warre* (1590): 'Some will condemnde mee for my strange names of fortifications, they ought to pardon me: for my part, I knowe no other names than are given by the strangers,

because there are fewe or none at all in our language.' (*Works*, ed. Evans, p. 41). In the Netherlands, Simon Stevin's manual of fortification – *Stercktebouwing* (1594) – carried foreign military terms in the margin with an explanation in the text; while a popular account of the Dutch Revolt, Emanuel van Meteren's *History of the Low Countries* (the Hague, 1612), contained a special glossary of foreign military words ('*Vreemde Krijghs-vocabulen*'). In every modern army, many of the current officers' titles (captain, sergeant etc.) and some of those now obsolete (e.g. 'reformado', an officer who is temporarily without a unit to command) appear to have come from Spanish or Italian to France, the Netherlands, and England. *Cf.* J. Herbillon, *Eléments espagnols en Wallon et dans le Français des anciens Pays-Bas* (Liège, 1961). It seems likely, however, that many of these military terms came to Spanish from Italian first: J. Terlingen, *Los Italianismos en español desde la formación del idioma hasta principios del siglo XVII* (Amsterdam, 1943). There is no full analysis of the Spanish words loaned to Flemish and Dutch although there is a sketchy introduction by C. F. A. van Dam, 'De Spaanse woorden in het Nederlandsche', in *Bundel . . . aangeboden aan Prof. Dr C. G. N. de Vooys* (Groningen, 1940), pp. 86-103.

21. Van den Valckert's painting of Captain Burgh's militia company hangs – like Rembrandt's more famous picture of the company of Captain Hans Banning Cocq, done in 1642 – in the Rijksmuseum, Amsterdam. There is a reproduction of the portion which clearly shows de Gheyn's book on p. 37 of Kist's *Commentary* to the facsimile edition of de Gheyn cited in note 9. Dr Kist establishes beyond all doubt the influence of Johan II of Nassau on the composition of the *Wapenhandelingen* (pp. 14-15) and he describes the measures taken in 1599 to standardize armament in the Dutch army. For a little more information on the first English edition of de Gheyn, *cf.* Anna E. C. Simoni, 'A present for a prince', in *Ten Studies in Anglo-Dutch Relations*, ed. J. A. van Dorsten (Leiden and London, 1974), pp. 51-71.

22. Roberts, *Military Revolution*, p. 7, and *Essays*, p. 202.

23. M. A. Ladero Quesada, *Castilla y la conquista del reino de Granada* (Valladolid, 1967), p. 127. For a general assessment of the importance of artillery to Europe, *cf.* C. M. Cipolla, *Guns and Sails in the Early Phase of European Expansion, 1400-1700* (London, 1965). However the demise of the old-style castles did not occur overnight. In many areas where artillery could not easily be brought in, medieval fortifications retained their value. *Cf.* H. M. Colvin, 'Castles and government in Tudor England', *English Historical Review*, LXXXIII (1968), pp. 225-34.

24. J. R. Hale, 'The early development of the bastion: an Italian chronology, *c.* 1450 – *c.* 1534', in *Europe in the Later Middle Ages*, ed. J. R. Hale, J. R. L. Highfield and B. Smalley (London, 1965), pp. 466-94.

25. G. Dickinson (ed.), *The 'Instructions sur le Faict de la Guerre' of Raymond de Beccarie de Pavie, sieur de Fourquevaux* (London, 1954), p. 58; *The Works of Sir Roger Williams*, p. 33.

26. G. Parker, *The Army of Flanders*, pp. 7-11 and notes. The same was true for many of the wars of the Middle Ages. The Hundred Years' War was, according to a recent study, 'character-ized more by sieges than by any other form of martial exercise' (C. T. Allmand, *Society at War*, p. 7; *cf.* also pp. 6-9 and 104-22).

27. *Cf.* the policy of Sir Humphrey Gilbert, commander of Queen Elizabeth's forces in Ireland in 1579 and a veteran of the Low Countries Wars: 'He further tooke this order infringeable, that when soever he made any ostyng, or inrode, into the enemies Countrey, he killed manne, woman, and child, and spoiled, wasted, and burned, by the grounde all that he might: leavying nothing of the enemies in saffetie, which he could possiblie waste, or consume . . . The killing of them by the sworde, was the waie to kill the menne of warre by famine, who by flight oftentymes saved them selves from the dinte of the sworde.' (Quoted from Thomas Churchyard's *Generall Rehearsall of Warres* of 1579 by J. T. Johnson, *Ideology, Reason, and the Limitation of War. Religious and secular concepts, 1200-1740* [Princeton, N. J., 1975], pp. 141-2. Dr Johnson points out that this is an early application of the counter-revolutionary doctrine that 'if revolutionaries live among the people like fish in water, the way to kill the fish is to dry up the water'.)

28. Military geography also affected military theory. It is true that Londoño, Valdes, Escalante and the other Spanish writers of the period who dealt with war said very little about battles; but this was because after 1559 Spain fought very few wars in which battles were necessary. At least two of the wars in which she was engaged were little more than extended guerilla actions: in New Galicia and in Chile. It is therefore no surprise to find that the first European manual of guerilla warfare was written by a Spaniard, Bernardo de Vargas Machuca, who had fought long years in Chile. His *Milicia de las Indias* of 1599 described jungle warfare with operational units of 20 or 30 men under a *caudillo* (leader) who knew not only how to lead and how to fight but also how to cure sores and wounds inflicted deep in the forest (most of his remedies involved the use of tobacco as a pain-killer), which

vegetable seeds to take on the march to sow over the winter and harvest in the spring, and so on. The Indians of Chile never fought battles, Vargas Machuca observed, because they had learned from bitter experience that they always lost them! (For an account of the similar guerilla war on the northern frontier of Spanish America *cf.* P. W. Powell, *Soldiers, Indians and Silver: the Northward Advance of New Spain, 1550-1600* [Berkeley, 1969].)

29. F. Lot, *Recherches*, pp. 21 and 56. Even where cavalry continued to play a decisive role in battles, as in the French religious wars, its character and composition (as well as its tactics) were entirely different from those of the fifteenth-century *gendarmerie. Cf.* R. Puddu, *Eserciti e monarchie nazionali nei secoli XV – XVI* (Florence, 1975), pp. 35-6.

30. R. Bean, in an article of 1973, advanced a similar argument but failed to provide convincing evidence. *Cf.* the telling criticisms of Professors David Ringrose and Richard Roehl in *Journal of Economic History*, XXXIII (1973), pp. 203-31.

31. J. Vicens Vives, 'Estructura administrativa estatal en los siglos XVI y XVII', in *XIe congrès internationale des sciences historiques. Rapports*, IV (Stockholm, 1960), pp. 1-24; I. A. A. Thompson, 'The Armada and administrative reform', *English Historical Review*, LXXXII (1967), pp. 698-725; G. N. Clark, *The Seventeenth Century*, chs. 6 and 7; J. A. Maravall, *Estado moderna y mentalidad social*, 2 vols. (Madrid, 1972), *passim*, and especially 513-85.

32. The classic account of the organization of war by military middlemen is F. Redlich, *The German Military Enterpriser and his Workforce*, 2 vols. (Wiesbaden, 1964). For military contracting in early modern Spain, see I. A. A. Thompson, *War and Government in Habsburg Spain, 1560-1620* (London, 1976).

33. For some uses to which these copious military records can be put, *cf.* for the sixteenth century G. Parker, *The Army of Flanders and the Spanish Road*; for the eighteenth century A. Corvisier, *L'armée française de la fin du XVIIe siècle au ministère de Choiseul. Le Soldat*, 2 vols. (Paris, 1964); and for the nineteenth century E. Le Roy Ladurie and P. Dumont, 'Quantitative and cartographical exploitation of French military archives, 1819-1826', *Daedalus* (spring, 1971), pp. 397-441.

34. For some examples from the Army of Flanders *cf.* G. Parker, *op. cit.*, chs. 2 and 3.

35. *Cf.* Parker, *op. cit.*, ch. 3. However for a reminder that roads were not the only brake on military mobility *cf.* J. Milot, 'Un problème opérationnel du XVIIe siècle illustré par un cas regional', *Revue du Nord*, LIII (1971), pp. 269-90, which argues that until 1700, at least, tactics dictated that armies on active service had to march as a single formation (which might be 50,000 strong). No existing road network could cope with a horde like that, and most of the troops had to plough their way through trees and scrub just like their predecessors in earlier centuries.

36. P. Contamine, 'Consommation et demande militaires en France et en Angleterre, XIIIe – XVe siècles' (paper given at the *Sesta settimana di studia* at the *Istituto internazionale di storia economica*, Prato, 3 May 1974), pp. 26-7.

37. Esteban de Ibarra, Spanish secretary of war; quoted Parker, *op. cit.*, p. 134.

38. 'Declaration' of Thomas Wilkes, 22 July 1587, printed in H. Brugmans (ed.) *Correspondentie van Robert Dudley, graaf van Leycester*, II (Utrecht, 1931), p. 402. For further information on mutinies, see ch. 5 above.

39. For a brief survey of the financial organization of the European states during this period see G. Parker, 'The emergence of modern finance in Europe', in C. M. Cipolla (ed.) *The Fontana Economic History of Europe*, II (London, 1974), pp. 560-82.

40. In France, A. Corvisier has suggested that one man in six was called up during the war of the Spanish succession (*L'armée française*, I, p. 65). The calculation of 'military participation ratios' before 1700 is extremely hazardous since we cannot be sure of the exact size either of the army or of the total population which it defended; and there is also the problem of 'foreign' troops serving in 'national' armies. But there are some interesting calculations in A. Corvisier, *Armées et sociétés en Europe de 1494 à 1789* (Paris, 1976), p. 127, but these almost all come from the eighteenth century.

41. See the attempt to establish the costs of the Low Countries Wars in ch. 10 below.

5. Mutiny and Discontent in the Spanish Army of Flanders, 1572-1607

(Originally published in *Past and Present*, LVIII [1973], pp. 38-52.)

1. M. Bloch, *Les caractères originaux de l'histoire rurale française*, I (Paris, 1960), p. 175; R. Pillorget, *Les mouvements insurrectionnels de Provence entre 1596 et 1715* (Paris, 1975), pp. 379-80; Y. Bercé, *Histoire des Croquants. Etude des soulèvements populaires au XVIIe siècle dans le sud-ouest de la France* (Geneva, 1974), p. 682.

2. For recent studies of these two areas, see: I. Gutiérrez Nieto, *Las comunidades como movimiento antiseñorial* (Barcelona, 1973 – on the revolt of the 'comuneros' in 1520-1), and A. Domínguez Ortiz, *Alteraciones andaluzas* (Madrid, 1973 – on popular revolts in Andalusia between 1647 and 1652); and R. M. Dekker, 'Oproeren in de provincie Holland, 1600-1750: frequentie en karakter, relatie met de conjonctuur en repressie', *Tijdschrift voor Sociale Geschiedenis*, IX (1977), pp. 299-329, and P. M. Crew, *Calvinist Preaching and Iconoclasm in the Netherlands, 1544-1569* (Cambridge, 1977).

3. G. Parker, *The Army of Flanders and the Spanish Road, 1567-1569. The logistics of Spanish victory and defeat in the Low Countries' Wars* (Cambridge, 1972), pp. 207-10.

4. Agrippa d'Aubigné, *Histoire universelle* (2nd edn., Paris, 1626), III, col. 527 (writing of the Croquant revolts of the 1590s in France). For an appreciation of the same problem in a later period see N. Gash, 'After Waterloo: British society and the legacy of the Napoleonic Wars', *Transactions of the Royal Historical Society*, 5th series, XXVIII (1978), pp. 145ff.

5. B. de Mendoza, *Comentarios de lo sucedido en las guerras de los Países-Bajos* (B.A.E. edition, Madrid, 1948), p. 513 gives the classic, eye-witness account. However there is some evidence that the mutiny began *before* the battle, at least among some Spanish units: see J. S. Coonan, 'War and the "County community" during the Dutch Revolt: the case of Gelderland' (in press).

6. The normal mutiny hierarchy was as follows: an *electo* and between three and five councillors; a sergeant-major and two adjutants for the infantry and a governor for the cavalry; one or

more secretaries; a treasurer and, inevitably, a chaplain-in-chief. The title *electo* (or *eletto* for the Italian units) may owe something to the office of *eletto del popolo*, the man chosen by the freemen of certain Italians towns to represent them in the municipal government.

7. In many English peasant revolts it was the village officials (reeves, bailiffs or constables) who led their villages in rebellion, but there were also 'natural leaders' who had no official position. *Cf.* C. S. L. Davies, 'Les révoltes populaires en Angleterre, 1500-1700', *Annales E.S.C.*, XXIV (1969), pp. 24-60 (at pp. 44-5) and *ibid.*, 'Peasant revolts in France and England: a comparison', the *Agricultural History Review*, XXI (1973), pp. 122-34.

8. Examples taken from the Archivo General de Simancas (hereafter AGS), Estado 558, fo. 51, petition of the mutinous Spaniards at Antwerp, 23 May 1574, and Estado 559, fo. 118, petition of the mutinous *tercio de Italia*, 4 Jan. 1575.

9. These figures come from the full list of mutiny settlements in G. Parker, *The Army of Flanders and the Spanish Road, 1567-1659*, pp. 290-2.

10. Details of these reforms are given in *ibid.*, pp. 161-73.

11. References in *ibid.*, p. 200, n. 2 for the character of the mutineers. For the condemnations of their motives, *cf.* A. Rodríguez Villa, 'Correspondencia de la Infanta Archduquesa Doña Isabella . . .', *Boletín de la Real Academia de la Historia*, XLVII (1905), p. 356, Infanta Isabella to the duke of Lerma, 2 Nov. 1602; G. Bentivoglio, *The History of the Wars of Flanders*, English edn. (London, 1678), part I, book viii, pp. 109-10.

12. A copy of this Ordinance, the only one known to exist today, is conserved in the Vatican Archives, Nunziatura Fiandra, III, fos. 206-7, 'Ordinanze fatte del eletto e consiglieri dei Italiani e Valloni alli 23 di agosto, 1593'. A translation of most of it was printed by L. van der Essen, *Les Italiens en Flandre au XVIe et au XVIIe siècle* (Brussels, 1926) – with the date '1599'.

13. AGS, *Contaduría Mayor de Cuentas, 2a época*, nos. 79 and 875/4 gives details of the 10,000 *escudos* raised in 88 instalments by the mutineers of Aalst between July and October 1576 as contributions from the villages around their fortified stronghold.

14. This was especially true of the Spanish infantry, who could 'lawfullie refuse to assault, vntill the flankes [i.e. the artillery on

the bastions overlooking the town walls] be taken away'. *Cf.*
Sir Roger Williams, *A Briefe Discourse of Warre*, printed in John X.
Evans (ed.), *The Works of Sir Roger Williams* (Oxford, 1972), p.
22. At the siege of Alkmaar in 1573 the Spanish troops twice
refused the order to assault the town because the 'flankes' were
not yet silenced: see G. Parker, *The Dutch Revolt* (London, 1977),
p. 162.

15. Bentivoglio, *History of the Wars of Flanders*, pp. 109-10.

16. AGS, Estado 558, fos. 45 and 48, flysheets of the mutineers of
Antwerp, 17 and 23 May 1574. A common slogan of later in-
surrections was TODO Y EN ORO ('all and in gold'). For the
same phrase – 'all, all, all' – used by English mutineers in the
garrison of Tournai in 1515, see C. G. Cruickshank, *The English
Occupation of Tournai* (Oxford, 1971), p. 73.

17. Detailed references in Parker, *op. cit.*, pp. 200-2. The banner
of the mutineers of Diest in 1600, which was covered with religious
slogans and symbols picked out in gold on a blue damask background, is described in H. Haestens, *La nouvelle Troye, ou
mémorable histoire du siège d'Ostende* (Leiden, 1615), pp. 56-7.
On the use of emblems in civilian revolts at this time, *cf.* the
banners of the Croquants of Perigord in 1594 (G. Walter, *Histoire
des paysans de France* [Paris, 1963], p. 208) and the *bonnets rouges*
of the vigilantes of the Burgundian countryside at the same time
(H. Drouot, *Mayenne et la Bourgogne, 1587-1596: contribution à
l'histoire des provinces françaises pendant la Ligue*, 2 vols. [Paris,
1937], II, p. 289).

18. The urge to be 'somebody' as a possible motive for civilian
revolts is given full attention by R. Mandrou, 'Vingt ans après, ou
une direction de recherches fécondes: les révoltes populaires en
France au XVIIe siècle', *Revue historique*, CCXLII (1969), pp.
29-40 (*cf.* pp. 36-40 in particular), and by G. A. Williams, *Artisans
and Sans-culottes: popular movements in France and Britain during
the French Revolution* (London, 1968), pp. 46-7. See also the
account of the British naval unrest of 1797 in G. E. Manwaring
and B. Dobrée, *The Floating Republic. An account of the mutinies
at Spithead and the Nore in 1797* (London, 1935). The petitions of
the Spithead mutineers in particular bear a striking resemblance
in both tone and content to those of the Spaniards in 1574-5
discussed above. So did their behaviour: 'The men conducted
themselves with a degree of prudence and decency which I
thought them incapable of,' wrote one officer.

19. Archivo de la Casa de los Duques de Alba (Madrid), *caja* 33,

fo. 156, Hernando Delgadillo to Juan de Albornoz, 9 July 1574.

20. Motley's account of the 'Spanish Fury' is one of the most moving passages of *The Rise of the Dutch Republic* (London, 1882 edn.), pp. 635-44. The sources quoted in his copious footnotes may be augmented by the documents printed by P. Genard, 'La furie espagnole. Documents pour servir à l'histoire du sac d'Anvers en 1576', *Annales de l'Académie royale d'archéologie de Belgique*, XXXII (1876), pp. 1-728.

21. Further information on individual mutinies may be found in L. de Torre, 'Los motines militares en Flandes', *Revista de Archivos, Bibliotecas y Museos*, XXV (1911)–XXXII (1915) – seven articles which describe each mutiny from 1570 until 1596 – and G. Wymans, 'Les mutineries militaires de 1596 à 1606', *Standen en Landen*, XXXIX (1966), pp. 105-21. Both these authors relied almost exclusively on chroniclers for their data, and this has led them to errors of fact and emphasis. Only one mutiny has been studied in depth from documentary sources – the great mutiny at Hoogstraten, 1602-5: L. M. G. Kooperberg, 'Een muiterij in den Spaanischen tijd', *Bijdragen voor Vaderlandsche Geschiedenis en Oudheidkunde*, 5th ser., V (1918), pp. 113-72. The Spanish documents which detail the participants in each mutiny and their dues are recorded in G. Parker, *Guide to the Archives of the Spanish Institutions in or concerned with the Netherlands, 1556-1706* (Brussels, 1971), p. 81.

22. There are no proper studies of the first three series of disorders. Information may be gleaned from, respectively: C. G. Cruickshank, *Elizabeth's Army*, 2nd edn. (Oxford, 1966), pp. 168-72; E. Heischmann, *Die Anfänge des Stehenden Heeres in Oesterreich* (Vienna, 1925); and F. Redlich, *The German Military Enterpriser and his Workforce, 14th-17th centuries*, 2 vols. (Wiesbaden, 1964) – e.g. I, pp. 257-8 and 506. See also B. Sastrow, *Social Germany in Luther's Time* (London, 1902), pp. 218-19, for an account of a mutiny among a unit of *Landsknechten* at Augsburg in 1547.

23. See *Rikskansleren Axel Oxenstiernas Skrifter och Brevväxling, Förra Afdelningen*, VIII (Stockholm, 1894): nos. 169, 170, 244, 293-5 (letters of Oxenstierna to field commanders, 6 Mar., 22 Apr. and 15 May 1633) and pp. 682-3 (Memorial sent by Oxenstierna to the Swedish *råd*, 13 May 1633) about the *confoederatio* of the army; *Senare Afdelningen*, VI (Stockholm, 1893), nos. 145, 146, and 149 (letters of Marshall Johan Banér to Oxenstierna, 29 and 30 Oct. and 5 Nov. 1635) about the '*alteration*' organized and led by '*der sämptlichen officieren von der gantzen armée*'. There were,

of course, numerous mutinies by Swedish troops before the re-
forms of Gustavus Adolphus: *cf.* Roberts, *The Early Vasas*
(Cambridge, 1967), p. 258; C. Nordmann, 'L'armée suédoise au
XVIIe siècle', *Revue du Nord*, LV (1972), p. 135.

24. J. Maciszewski, 'La noblesse polonaise et la guerre contre
Moscou, 1604-18', *Acta poloniae historica*, XVII (1968), p. 44; T.
Korzon, *Dzieje wojen i wojskowiósci w Polsce*, III (Warsaw, 1923),
pp. 41-9.

25. See the explicit recognition of this truth by the Spanish marquis of Castañeda at the Council of State of Philip IV in 1632:
Parker, *Army of Flanders*, p. 206.

26. See I. Gentles, 'The arrears of the parliamentary army at the
end of the first civil war', *Bulletin of the Institute of Historical
Research*, XLVIII (1975), pp. 52-63; J. S. Morrill, 'Mutiny and
discontent in English provincial armies, 1645-1647', *Past and
Present*, LVI (1972), pp. 49-74; and C. H. Firth, *Cromwell's
Army* (London, 1962), chs. 12 and 14.

27. E. P. Thompson, 'The moral economy of the English crowd in
the eighteenth century', *Past and Present*, L (1971), pp. 76-136 at p.
119.

6. Lepanto (1571): the Costs of Victory
(Originally published in the *Mariner's Mirror*, LXIV
[1978], pp. 13-21.)

The following abbreviations are used in the notes to this chapter:

AGS	Archivo General de Simancas (Spain).
AGS CMC 2a	*Ibid.*, Contaduría Mayor de Cuentas, *segunda época*, with *legajo* number.
AGS E.	*Ibid.*, sección de Estado, with *legajo* and folio.
AGS GA	*Ibid.*, sección Guerra Antiqua, with *legajo* number.
BM Eg	British Museum, Department of Manuscripts, Egerton Manuscripts.
BPU Favre	Bibliothèque Publique et Universitaire, Geneva, Collection Edouard Favre, with volume and folio number.
CODOIN	*Colección de Documentos Inéditos para la Historia de España*, 112 volumes, Madrid, 1842-92.

1. For details of the treaty of the League and the Lepanto campaign in general, see L. Serrano, *Correspondencia diplomática entre España y la Santa Sede durante el Pontificado de San Pio V*, 4 vols. (Madrid, 1914), vols. 3-4, and *La Liga de Lepanto entre España, Venecia y la Santa Sede (1570-73)*, 2 vols. (Madrid, 1919). For Sessa's estimate see M. Brunetti and E. Vitale, *La Corrispondenza da Madrid dell' ambasciatore Leonardo Donà (1570-1573)* (Venice-Rome, n.d.), I, pp. 342-3, letter of 1 Aug. 1571. The duke's figure is corroborated by another estimate, made in Madrid at roughly the same time, which suggested a cost of three million *escudos* for the six months, BPU Favre 62, fos. 12-31, 'Relación de lo que es menester', 15 July 1571.

2. BPU Favre 62, fos. 38-47, 'Vilanco de las galeras, naos y infantería que servieron el año pasado 1571', and fos. 33-35v., 'Relación que han dado los oficiales de Su Magestad del gasto que se ha hecho en la armada', 14 Nov. 1571.

3. BPU Favre 62, fos. 68-68v., letter of a Treasury official to [?] Don Juan de Zúñiga, 18 Mar. 1571: 'Ya hemos embiado un tanteo o juizio en el qual lo que era arbitrio lo alargavamos quanto era possible en favor de su magestad, y quiças mas de lo que sufria el honesto sino se tuviera por çierto que venecianos havien de yr tan rotos en esto como despues ha parecido . . .'

4. This general agreement does not mean that the allies did not argue interminably about how to apportion costs. Disagreement, however, centred not on Spain's estimate but on a number of Venetian galleys which were lost at sea before they reached the Grand Fleet (16 in all), and on a further squadron (11 galleys and three galeasses) which only arrived on 30 Oct. The Venetians wanted the cost of these to be shared by Spain, Spain refused. The allies were still arguing in spring 1573 when the Venetians made a separate peace with the Sultan and thereby forfeited all claim to full compensation: BPU Favre 62, fos. 61-6, 'La respuesta que se dio al scripto de los señores venecianos sobre las quentas del año de 71', 15 Oct. 1572.

5. Brunetti and Vitale, *Corrispondenza*, I, pp. 180, 204, 228-9, 348.

6. The 31 galleys of Naples and the 11 of Sicily, plus the three of Stefano de Mari and Bendineli Sauli whose retainers were also assigned on Neapolitan revenues; BPU Favre 28, fos. 83, 98, 101, two letters of Philip II to the duke of Sessa, 27 Dec. 1576; H. G. Koenigsberger, *The Government of Sicily under Philip II of Spain* (London, 1951), p. 128; AGS CMC 2a, leg. 814, account of Juan Morales de Torres, 'Pagador General del Armada y

Exercito de Su Magestad', for money received 1 June 1571 to 4 Jan. 1578, items 11, 12, 141.

7. A statement of the debts owed to the infantry and the sailing ships of the Fleet on 1 Feb. 1572, drawn up by the *Contador* Diego Garcia de Pradilla, makes no mention either of the *tercios* of Naples and Sicily or of the Italian regiments of Sigismondo Gonzaga and the count of Sarno; it also ignores the five *compañías sueltas*: José-María Gárate Córdoba, ed., *Los Tercios de España en la ocasión de Lepanto* (Madrid, 1971), p. 266. (This book was kindly brought to our notice by Dr Henry Kamen of the University of Warwick.) For the *compañías sueltas*, Francisco-Felipe Olesa Muñido, *La organización naval de los estados mediterráneos y en especial de España durante los siglos XVI y XVII*, 2 vols. (Madrid, 1968), II, p. 834. Sforza's *coronelía*, however, seems to have been paid by the *Pagador General* Morales, AGS CMC 2a, leg. 814, item 5.

8. E. Alberi, *Le relazioni degli ambasciatori veneti*, 15 vols. (Florence, 1839-52): series I vol. 6, p. 385 (Spain 1572), vol. 5, p. 12 (Naples 1563), p. 15 (Sicily 1563); for Milan, AGS E. leg. 1240, fo. 2, leg. 1244, fo. 17. The variations in these proportions, as they can be traced from the defence budget for 1566 (Koenigsberger, *op. cit.*, p. 54), through Lepanto and the Armada (Santa Cruz's estimates, 1586, printed in C. Fernández Duro, *La Armada Invencible*, 2 vols. [Madrid, 1884-5] pp. 250-319) to the Union of Arms in 1626 (J. H. Elliott, *The Revolt of the Catalans* [Cambridge, 1963], p. 205), provide an interesting reflection of the changing balance of the Monarchy as its interests moved from the Mediterranean to the Atlantic and northern Europe.

	1566	1571	1586	1626
Spain		63.8%	68%	73.2%
Naples		22.5%	20.5%	14.3%
Sicily	11%	10%	5.8%	5.4%
Milan		3.7%	5.5%	7.1%

9. Koenigsberger, *Government of Sicily*, pp. 54, 129-30; AGS E. leg. 450, n.f., 'Relación del dinero que se deve en el Armada de Su Majestad', 10 Sept. 1574, puts at about 150,000 *escudos* the money owed for victuals and munitions procured by the duke of Terranova for Tunis and for the Fleet. For the donative, Brunetti and Vitale, *Corrispondenza*, I, p. 271 and AGS CMC 2a, leg. 814, items 9, 25, 31, 77. Unfortunately, the Paymaster's accounts do not specify with any consistency the ultimate source of his receipts, nor are they directly concerned with the regular appropriations of the galleys and *tercios* of either Naples or Sicily.

10. Brunetti and Vitale, I, pp. 207, 267. Naples also paid the 1000 Italians raised in the Romagna in 1574 by *Coronel* Stefan Motino, for example, AGS CMC 2a, leg. 814, item 139.

11. Serrano, *Correspondencia diplomática*, III, pp. 350-1. Spanish ministers not only insisted publicly on their utter financial dependence on the papal grants, they also intended that as far as possible no other resources should be diverted to the financing of the League; Brunetti and Vitale, I, pp. 199-200, 213, 255, 257. Their private correspondence suggests that these were not solely bargaining positions: *cf.* Don Juan de Zúñiga to the King, 7 Mar. 1570, 'No comenzandole [the League] Su Beatitud con conceder la Cruzada era imposibilitar el effecto; porque sin esta gracia y otras muchas V. Md. aun no podia atender a la defensa de sus estados, quanto mas emprender . . . guerras', Serrano, *Liga de Lepanto*, I, p. 58.

12. Brunetti and Vitale, I, pp. 90, 335. The Pope's sudden decision to renew all three concessions at once, after years of waiting, was too much for the King's confessor Fray Bernardo de Fresneda; with that indelicacy for which he was famous, he blurted out to the Papal envoy who brought the news, 'His Holiness has demonstrated the truth of a proverb we have here in Castile – that the constipated die of diarrhoea *(los estíticos mueren de cámaras)*'; quoted by L. P. Gachard, *Don Carlos et Philippe II* (2nd ed., Paris, 1867), p. 275 n. 1.

13. As the current instalments of the *subsidio* did not expire until 1574, and the *excusado* was granted too late to be collected in 1571, the real importance of the concession lay in this easing of credit: Brunetti and Vitale, I, pp. 199, 207, 267, 277, 335, and I. Cloulas, 'Le "subsidio de las galeras", contribution du clergé espagnol à la guerre navale contre les Infidèles de 1563 à 1574', *Mélanges de la Casa de Velásquez*, III (1967), pp. 289-326, at p. 302.

14. For varying estimates of the yield of the 'Three Graces', *cf.* Cloulas, *op. cit.*, pp. 289, 290 n. 3, 300-2; J. Goñi Gaztambide, *Historia de la Bula de la Cruzada en España* (Vitoria, 1958), p. 508; M. Ulloa, *La Hacienda real de Castilla en el reinado de Felipe II* (Rome, 1963), p. 384; F. Braudel, *La Méditerranée et le monde méditerranéen à l'époque de Philippe II*, 2 vols. (Paris, 1966), II, p. 379; Brunetti and Vitale I, pp. 90, 311, 335; C. Douais, ed., *Depêches de M. de Fourquevaux, ambassadeur du roi Charles IX en Espagne, 1565-1572*, 3 vols. (Paris, 1896-7), II, pp. 258, 357; AGS GA, leg. 88, fo. 357, 'Relación de lo que monta al subsidio y excusado', Madrid, 30 Oct. 1578 *(Subsidio* 350,000 ducats,

Excusado 271,149); GA leg. 1299, n.f., 'Relación de lo que toca el dinero de las consignaciones', Lisbon, 9 June 1582 ('Three Graces' 1583, 952,247 ducats).

15. We have no direct figures for the exact cost to Venice, but the cost of the Venetian arsenal, the crews, and the rations of the galleys alone was over 600,000 ducats in 1594, and over 700,000 in 1602; more Venetian warships were mobilized in 1571 than in either of the later years. (*Cf.* R. Romano, 'Economic aspects of the construction of warships in Venice in the sixteenth century', in B. S. Pullan, *Crisis and Change in the Venetian Economy in the Sixteenth and Seventeenth Centuries* [London, 1968], pp. 59-87, on p. 80.) See also J. R. Hale, 'Men and weapons: the fighting potential of sixteenth-century Venetian galleys', *War and Society*, I (1975), pp. 1-23.

16. F. Besta, *Bilanci generali della Repubblica di Venezia* (Milan, 1912), p. 241.

17. We have no evidence for the yield of the *décimo al clero* in the 1570s, but it produced only 40,000 ducats in 1602, 30,699 ducats in 1621 and 17,270 in 1633; F. Besta, *op. cit.*, pp. 368 and 473.

18. Information in this paragraph is based on the excellent article of R. Romano in B. S. Pullan, *Crisis and Change*, pp. 59-87.

19. Brunetti and Vitale, *Corrispondenza*, I, p. 348.

20. Cloulas, pp. 296, 318, 320, and 306 n. 1 for Nov. 1562; 'Memoria de las galeras que son de Su Magestad', 1567, AGS GA, leg. 3142, n.f.; Brunetti and Vitale, I, p. 228, letter of 11 Mar. 1571, for the fifteen new galleys, p. 237 for 17 Mar. 1571, p. 298 for the galleys left in Spain; AGS E. leg., 450, n.f., 'Las Galeras que se haze quenta que se podran juntar en Italia en la Armada de Su Majestad', and AGS GA leg. 80, fo. 143, 'Las galeras que ay en la costa despaña a xx de febrero de 1575', for 1574; BPU Favre 28, fos. 83-83v, Philip II to the duke of Sessa, 27 Dec. 1576, and fos. 155-6, same to same, 28 June 1577, for 1576 and 1577.

21. The actual number of soldiers in Philip II's pay at Lepanto remains uncertain. It is worth noting, therefore, that of the conflicting contemporary figures, that used in the 14 November estimate is the highest. Don John of Austria reported only 22,000 at the end of August: CODOIN, III, p. 15.

22. Douais, *Dépêches de Fourquevaux*, II, pp. 306-7, 325, 343, 350, 362; Brunetti and Vitale, I, pp. 137, 187, 212-13, 260, 283, 310.

23. Gárate Córdoba, *Tercios de España*, pp. 112-13.

24. Olesa Muñido, *Organización naval*, II, pp. 802, 834, 840.

25. Gárate Córdoba, p. 262 document 26, 'Relación del reparti-miento que se hizo de los bajeles y artillería y esclavos que se tomaron de los Turcos en la Victoria de la Batalla de los 7 de octubre 1571', 18 Oct. 1571. For the value of these prizes, *ibid*. p. 268 document 29, 'En lo que se tasaron las cuatro galeras que rindio el Marqués de Santa Cruz, mi Señor, a Su Majestad, año 1572'.

26. One observer in Madrid did in fact think, for a time, that the preparations in 1571 were largely defensive and that the king was not contemplating any immediate offensive action, Brunetti and Vitale, I, p. 257. For 1563: Archives Générales du Royaume, Brussels, *Audience* 475, fos. 84, Courtewille to Viglius, 24 May 1563, quoting Erasso's estimate of cost; for 1566: CODOIN vol. 30, p. 54, Erasso to Don García de Toledo, 31 Dec. 1565, Koenigs-berger, *Government of Sicily*, p. 54; and Bibliothèque Royale, Brussels, Ms. 17437-50, fos. 292-3, 'Relation des provisions que Sa Majesté Catholique ha ordonné'. Anticipated extraordinary expenditure for 1565 was 825,000 *escudos* (748,000 ducats), AGS Diversos de Castilla leg. 46, fo. 90 'Relación de las rentas encave-cadas y arrendadas para 1565'.

27. BPU Favre 28, fos. 97-101v, Philip II to the Duke of Sessa, 27 Dec. 1576; AGS GA, leg. 79, f. 93, Juan Delgado on 'Los puntos de lo que escrive Don Juan Canoguera de Cerdeña'. Between 1572 and 1577 extraordinary expenditure averaged around 900,000 *escudos* a year, see AGS CMC 2a, leg. 814.

28. For a very forceful statement of the view that the League would actually save the king money, see Serrano, *Correspondencia diplomática*, III, pp. 324-9, Fray Luis de Torres to Philip II, 4 May 1570: 'Haziéndose esta liga . . . puede V. Md. disminuir la costa que tiene en sus estados . . .' and so on. Since writing this paper, similar conclusions have been reached independently by F. Ruiz Martín, 'Las finanzas de la Monarquía hispánica y la liga santa' (to be published as part of the proceedings of the Venice Lepanto Symposium).

7. If the Armada had Landed
(Originally published in *History*, LXI [1976], pp. 358-68.)

1. J. L. Motley, *History of the United Netherlands, 1584-1609*, II (London, 1869), p. 488.

2. A[rchivo] G[eneral de] S[imancas], Spain, Estado 165/174-5, Instructions of Philip II for the duke of Parma, to be opened when he had come aboard the Armada, 1 Apr. 1588; and Estado 165/176-7, Philip to Parma, 3 Apr. 1588, minute. (There is an English précis of these fascinating documents in M. A. S. Hume, ed., *Calendar of letters and state papers relating to English affairs, preserved principally in the archives of Simancas*, vol. IV [London, 1899], pp. 250-2.) The chances of a Catholic rising are discussed by A. J. Loomie, 'The Armada and the Catholics of England', *Catholic Historical Review*, LIX (1973), pp. 395-403.

3. The Dutch and the Armada is a subject covered by J. B. van Overeem, 'Justinus van Nassau en de Armada (1588)', *Marine-blad*, LIII (1938), pp. 821-31. This article was not used by G. Mattingly, *The Defeat of the Spanish Armada* (London, 1959), which still remains the standard work.

4. W. Raleigh, *History of the World*, vol. 1 (London, 1614), pp. 304-8, a fascinating exercise in counterfactual history.

5. In fact Parma was deceived: the king assured him that 6000 Spanish troops aboard the fleet would be placed under his command and would take part in the invasion, but Medina Sidonia was under strict orders not to release any of his men until after the English fleet had been destroyed. See Hume, *op. cit.*, pp. 188 and 248.

6. Williams in J. X. Evans, ed., *The Works of Sir Roger Williams* (Oxford, 1972), p. 14 (in a work published in 1590); Leicester in H. Brugmans, ed., *Correspondentie van Robert Dudley, graaf van Leycester . . . 1585-88*, III (Utrecht, 1931), pp. 284-6 (in a letter to Burghley dated 15 November 1587).

7. Paolo Rinaldi, quoted by L. van der Essen, *Alexandre Farnèse, prince de Parme, gouverneur-général des Pays-Bas*, V (Brussels, 1937), p. 295.

8. See ch. 10 below.

9. AGS, Estado 1262/26 and 54 (musters of the troops in Lombardy) and Estado 594/192 (muster of the same units in the Netherlands). For more about the journey from Lombardy to the Low Countries see G. Parker, *The Army of Flanders and the Spanish Road, 1567-1659. The logistics of Spanish victory and defeat in the Low Countries' Wars* (2nd edn., Cambridge, 1975), chs. 2 and 3.

10. AGS, *Contaduría Mayor de Cuentas, 2a época* 23, unfol., 'Cuenta y relación jurada de Gabriel de Alegría', paymaster for Spanish subsidies to the League, 1587-90; G. Parker, *op. cit.*, pp. 293-4; Instituto de Valencia de Don Juan, Madrid, *envío* 101 fo. 99-100, report of Mateo Vázquez to the king, 31 Jan. 1587, about raising 7 million ducats for the Armada. The king later informed the *Cortes* that the entire campaign had cost 10,000,000 ducats but this no doubt included money sent to the Netherlands (see this figure in *Actas de las Cortes de Castilla*, vol. X, pp. 239 and 287, and vol. XI, pp. 235 and 321). On the French dimension, see E. H. Dickerman, 'A neglected aspect of the Spanish Armada: the Catholic League's Picard offensive of 1587', *Canadian Journal of History*, LVII (1974), pp. 18-23.

11. AGS, Estado 2218/161, Philip II to Parma, 25 Oct. 1587.

12. Parker, *op. cit.*, pp. 293-4.

13. This remarkable new evidence has been produced by the nautical archaeologists whose excavation of several Armada wrecks since 1965 has revolutionized our knowledge of the great fleet. No historian can afford to neglect their findings. See the preliminary reports of Colin Martin, *Full Fathom Five: Wrecks of the Spanish Armada* (London, 1975), especially pp. 203-24, and Robert Sténuit, *Treasures of the Armada* (Newton Abbot, 1973).

14. Sir Thomas Wilson, quoted by L. Boynton, *The Elizabethan Militia* (London, 1976), p. 126.

15. We should not be surprised at this. Philip II knew the southeast of England quite well at first hand (he had spent almost two years there as king-consort). He also possessed maps and charts, and could have consulted the detailed publication of Lucas J. Waghenaer, *De Spieghel der zeevaerdt* ('the mariner's mirror', 2 vols., Leiden, 1584-5) which gave the depths of the sea and the configuration of the coast around Kent. What is remarkable (as one of my students, Mr Stephen Davies, has pointed out to me) is

the failure of the English government to foresee that the Armada would probably aim for north-east Kent, as previous invaders – the Romans, the Saxons and the Danes – had done before. This was well known to antiquaries like William Camden (see his description of Kent in *Britannia*, published in 1590). The 'antiquated and decayed' fortifications of Rochester and Canterbury are both illustrated in J. Speed, *The Theatre of the Empire of Great Britaine* (London, 1611), details from the map between pp. 6-7.

16. H. A. Lloyd, *The Rouen Campaign, 1590-1592* (Oxford, 1973), p. 182.

17. A. Fletcher, *Tudor Rebellions* (London, 1970), p. 149 (quoting a contemporary chronicle). For evidence that the defences of the Home Counties had not changed since Wyatt's day, see H. B. Wheatley and E. W. Ashbee, *The Particular Description of England, 1588 . . . by Wm. Smith* (London, 1879). The survey was commissioned by the worried government of Elizabeth early in 1588.

18. Parker, *op. cit.*, pp. 241-2.

19. On Yorke, see Lloyd, *op. cit.*, p. 59; on Williams, Evans, *op. cit.*; on Stanley, Parker, *op. cit.*, pp. 214-15, and A. J. Loomie, *The Spanish Elizabethans* (New York, 1963), pp. 129-81.

20. J. R. Scott, 'Pay-list of the Kentish forces raised to resist the Spanish Armada', *Archaeologia Cantiana*, XI (1877), pp. 388-91.

21. P[ublic] R[ecord] O[ffice], London, *State Papers* 12/213/45, Sir Thomas Scott to Lord Burghley, 6 August 1588.

22. B. H. St. J. O'Neil, *Castles and Cannon: a Study of Early Artillery Fortifications in England* (Oxford, 1960), pp. 65-79.

23. PRO, *State Papers* 12/212/40, Scott to Burghley, 23 July 1588. See also Boynton, *Elizabethan Militia*, pp. 146-8. Initially the government followed the advice of Scott: on 18 July it ordered all forces in Kent to move to the sea-shore to prevent a landing (G. Scott Thomson, ed., 'The Twysden Lieutenancy Papers, 1583-1668', *Kent Records Society*, X (1926), pp. 70-1, letter of the Privy Council to Lord Cobham).

24. There were also anti-government riots in some places in 1587 as a result of the economic crisis. See J. D. Gould, 'The crisis of the export trade, 1586-87', *English Historical Review*, LXXI (1956), pp. 212-22.

25. See the excellent study of W. Maltby, *The Black Legend in England. The development of anti-Spanish sentiment, 1558-1660* (Durham, N. C., 1971), pp. 76-87.

26. C. Z. Wiener, 'The Beleaguered Isle. A study of Elizabethan and early Jacobean anti-Catholicism', *Past and Present*, LI (1971), pp. 27-62, at p. 55.

27. *Ibid.*, p. 49. Defeatism seems to have continued into the 1590s in some quarters. In 1596, William Holland, a Sussex clerk, stated 'that he thought yt best that yf the Spaniards should come yt ware best to yield to them'. He was indicted for treason. (See J. S. Cockburn, ed., *Calendar of Assize Records: Sussex indictments, Elizabeth I* [London, 1975], p. 344: reference kindly communicated by my pupil, Mr Robert A. Houston.)

28. K. Roberts, *Pavane* (London, 1968), pp. 7-8. This passage was brought to my attention by my student, Miss Susan P. Mills.

29. Haus-, Hof- und Staatsarchiv, Vienna, *Belgien*, Repertorium P, Abteilung C, 43, fos. 1, 3, letters of the Spanish negotiators at Bourbourg to Parma, 6 and 7 Aug. 1588. It was clear that even the negotiators did not know the real destination of the Armada.

30. *Cabala sive Scrinia Sacra* (3rd edn., London, 1691), 2, p. 37, Buckhurst to the Queen, 27 May 1587. See also G. Parker, *The Dutch Revolt* (London 1977), chs. 5 and 6.

31. N. Japikse, *Resolutiën der Staten-Generaal van 1576 tot 1609*, V (the Hague, 1921), pp. 565-7; VI (the Hague, 1922), pp. 57-8, 181-2, and 252-3. See also A. M. van der Woude, 'De Goudse magistraat en de strijd tegen de koning', *Bijdragen voor de Geschiedenis der Nederlanden*, XIII (1958), pp. 101-7.

32. Historians are coming to recognize these positive achievements. See Peter Pierson, 'A commander for the Armada', the *Mariner's Mirror*, LV (1969), pp. 383-400, and I. A. A. Thompson, 'The appointment of the duke of Medina Sidonia to the command of the Spanish Armada', *Historical Journal*, XII (1969), pp. 197 216.

8. Corruption and Imperialism in the Spanish Netherlands: the Case of Francisco de Lixalde, 1567-1612
(Originally published in *Tijdschrift voor Geschiedenis*, LXXXIX [1976], pp. 429-44.)

1. A. W. Lovett, 'Francisco de Lixalde: a Spanish Paymaster in the Netherlands (1567-1577)', *Tijdschrift voor Geschiedenis*, LXXXIV (1971), pp. 14-23. The bundles containing Lixalde's account are listed in G. Parker, *Guide to the Archives of the Spanish Institutions in or concerned with the Netherlands, 1556-1706* (Brussels, 1971), pp. 88-9. A copy of Lixalde's printed *tanteo*, with some holograph corrections by the Paymaster, is to be found in the library of the Archivo General de Simancas (it was formerly in the section AGS, CMC – *Contaduría Mayor de Cuentas* – *2a época, legajo* 55). No other copy of the *tanteo* appears to have survived; however, a Latin translation which was sent to the Elector Augustus of Saxony has been published: F. Rachfahl, *Le Registre de Franciscus Lixaldius, trésorier-général de l'armée espagnole aux Pays-Bas de 1567 à 1576* (Brussels, 1902). Despite this formidable bulk, Dr Lovett's statement that 'Lixalde's papers were preserved intact' (*art. cit.*, 31-2) is certainly untrue: *of.* Instituto de Valencia de Don Juan, *envío* 24 fo. 358, 'Relación' of a letter from members of the Tribunal examining Lixalde's accounts, 10 Feb. 1582, referring to 'un libro q[ue] dizen sus herederos les falto en el saco de Anvers [1576] en el qual havia de tener assentado lo que recibia y pagava, y en las species de monedas'. *Cf.* also AGS CMC 2a/55, unfol., *medio y concierto* with Lixalde's heirs, 27 Sep. 1612, p. 2: 'haviendose llevado [to Antwerp] los libros que los contadores del exercito tenian de lo pagado [by Lixalde] . . . los rebeldes los rompieron y quemaron.'

2. However the appointment was not, perhaps, quite as 'brusque' as Dr Lovett suggests (*art. cit.*, p. 15). Lixalde had served in Philip II's treasury in England from 1555 until 1560, dealing mainly with the pensions and wages of the household personnel of the 'king of England'. He was praised by the Count of Feria, Spanish ambassador in England as 'onbre [= hombre] de bien y de mucha fidelidad y diligençia' (AGS, Estado 8334/185, Feria to the king, 25 Nov. 1560). Lixalde was proposed as Paymaster-General of the new Army of Flanders on 27 Dec. 1566, four months before he left Spain: BM (= British Museum) Addl. (= Additional Manuscript) 28,386/11-12, 'Relacion de las personas q[ue] ha pareçido al Consejo [of Finance] q[ue] seran a proposito para oficiales del exerçito'. Candidates for the other senior administrative posts in

the army were also proposed: all of those eventually chosen were on this list. (Dr Lovett's statement – p. 15 and n. 4 – that 'Alonso del Canto' became one of the two *contadores del Sueldo* is incorrect and should be amended to read 'Alonso de Alameda'.)

3. Lovett, *art. cit.*, p. 22. Dr Lovett incorrectly states that Lixalde 'continued as financial head of the army until a short time before his death' (p. 20). Actually he continued in office until he died (14 Apr. 1577) and indeed, according to one document, even afterwards: 'Fran[cis]co d[e] Lixalde. Pagador general q[ue] fue . . . hasta fin de Abril d[e] jUdlxxvij a[ño]s, no embarga[n]te q[ue] fallescio a los xiiij d[e]l d[ic]ho mes' ('F. de Lixalde, late paymaster-general . . . until the end of April, 1577, not withstanding the fact that he died on the fourteenth of the said month' (!): AGS CMC *2a época*/79 – *cubierta* of the first bundle).

4. The wording of the agreement is unequivocal: 'que no se prosigan sus quentas y las dio por fenecidas . . . pagando 13,000 d[ucado]s dentro de ocho meses' (AGS CMC 2a/55 . . . *Medio y concierto*, quoted by Lovett, *art. cit.*, p. 23n.).

5. Lixalde had his *tanteos* (81 pages) printed expressly to substantiate this claim.

6. Details from BM Addl. 28,387/166-89, papers on the Lixalde case sent to Cardinal Espinosa; Archives Municipales, Besançon, Ms Granvelle 27/204-9, statement of F. de Ibarra; duquesa de Alba, *Documentos escogidos del Archivo de la Casa de Alba* (Madrid, 1891), pp. 90-9.

7. Evidence presented on oath to a commission of enquiry in Antwerp on 4-5 Dec. 1577: Stadsarchief, Antwerp, Certificiatieboek 38/164-74, printed by P. Genard, *Les poursuites contre les fauteurs de la Furie Espagnole ou du Sac d'Anvers de 1576* (Antwerp, 1880), pp. 6-21.

8. AGS CMC 2a/29, unfol., statement of Lixalde's lawyer, 27 Oct. 1611: 'el d[ic]ho pagador nunca desconto la d[ic]ha limosna'. He had been arguing this since 1603. Actually Lixalde was not the first Spanish paymaster to serve in the Netherlands; Garcia de Portillo held the office from 1552 until 1559. He did deduct the *limosna* (*cf.* AGS CMC 1a/1491).

9. *Ibid.*, statement of the *Fiscal de la contaduría*, 22 Nov. 1603 in reply to the *petición* of Lixalde's lawyer dated 22 May 1603.

10. The existence of the prior order is noted on the facsimile.

('Nota: . . . una copia autentica de una orden que el duq[ue] de
alua dio . . . en prim[er]o de noviembre de 1552 . . . por donde
consta la antigüedad q[ue] ay p[ar]a descontarse esta limosna.'
This order of the duke of Alva at the siege of Metz is presently
located in AGS CMC 1a *època*/1491.) The idea of providing free
medical care for soldiers in return for a small deduction from their
monthly wage soon spread to other countries. The system was
introduced into Elizabethan Ireland in 1600: *cf.* H. J. Webb,
Elizabethan Military Science: the Books and the Practice (Wisconsin, 1965), pp. 152-3 and 213-14. For the admission by Lixalde
himself that he had given money to the hospital, *cf.* his printed
tanteo, folio 48. A Treasury official had written *ojo* – look! – by the
side of the entry.

11. AGS CMC 2a/44, *cuenta* of Martín de Unceta, including a
cargo of 5003 *escudos* deducted from wages in *limosna* for the
hospital.

12. AGS CMC 2a/1, unfol., *pliegos de asiento* (wage-sheets) of
individual soldiers (e.g. Juan Coloma, 'descuento del ospital, 2
escudos'; Andrés de Carrión, 'baxa por el ospital, 1 escudo 13', and
so on). This is the most telling evidence of all against Lixalde:
irrefutable proof that he did in fact deduct the *limosna* from a
number of soldiers. There is another piece of evidence in Archivo
de la Casa de Alba, *caja* 30/105, Don Gonzalo de Braçamonte to
Alva, 30 Oct. 1567: 'V[uestra] Ex[cellenci]a manda se quitten dos
reales por soldado destas dos pagas para un ospital que se aze
en Malinas [Mechelen].'

13. *Cf.* G. Parker, *The Army of Flanders and the Spanish Road,
1567-1659* (Cambridge, 1972), p. 193 and n. 2.

14. AGS CMC. 2a/29, unfol., accounts of wages paid to the
Spanish infantry with the *limosna* added in the margin by an
official of the *contaduría* (*cf.* the example printed as a facsimile).
The total of the *limosna* was later reduced to 93,621 *reales*, or
about 10,000 ducats (and a fine of 40,000 ducats).

15. AGS CMC 2a/55, unfol.: (a) the text of the *medio y concierto*
gives Lixalde's original claim as 112,929 *escudos*, the figure in his
printed *tanteo*; (b) the document entitled 'Francisco de Lixalde:
relación del estado de su quenta' gave a gross receipt of 23,308,012
escudos and a gross expenditure of 23,308,655 *escudos*. This result
was the fruit of thirty-one years of constant auditing: from 1581
until 1590 by the special *Tribunal de las Cuentas de Flandes*, from
1590 until 1612 by the *Contaduría Mayor de Cuentas*.

16. In 1612 Juan Bautista de Lixalde claimed to have spent 50,000 *escudos* on the case (AGS CMC 2a/55, declaration of 10 Mar. 1612) but ten years later (a decade with no further legal action) he estimated the total cost at 60,000 (AGS, Estado 2139/9, petition of Juan Bautista de Lixalde, Apr. 1622).

17. *Cf.* note 1 above, and the text of the *medio y concierto*.

18. 'Quando la d[ic]ha quenta se feneçiese y en ella se le hiçiese alcanze por grueso q[ue] fuese, no se podia estender a cobrar de sus bienes mas de lo que montase la haz[ien]da q[ue] dexo [el Pagador]': *cf. medio y concierto*, p. 3.

19. CMC 2a/55, *medio y concierto* of 27 Sept. 1612 – the king prudently retained the right to lay claim to any further property found to have been left by Lixalde. AGS Consejos y Juntas de Hacienda 511, unfol., contains a *consulta* of the Council of Finance of 15 May 1612 informing the king that Juan Bautista de Lixalde had proposed a settlement 'out of court' and advising the king to accept it.

20. AGS CMC 2a/28, unfol., fragments of Navarette's accounts and personal fortune, calculated in 1581-2; BM Addl. 28,387/196, Count of Olivares to Espinosa, undated but 1567, suspending Navarette from office; on Alva and Albornoz *cf.* Parker, *Army of Flanders*, p. 114 and n.

21. Dr Lovett (p. 16) states that Inspector-General Carvajal 'died early in 1568'. Although he cites a document in support, there must be something wrong since Carvajal continued to sign official orders and draw his pay until 28 June 1569 when he resigned (AGS CMC 2a/79, *pliego de asiento* of Carvajal). Nor is it true to say that Lixalde regretted the *Veedor*'s departure: Carvajal declared on 29 June 1569 that he had never been able to perform his duties properly because Lixalde had persistently refused to admit his deputies to the Military Treasury (autograph declaration in AGS CMC 2a/55). Finally Dr Lovett's major source on the duties of the *Veedor* (BM Addl. 28,366/127-38 'undated and anonymous') was in fact written by Esteban de Ibarra and sent to the king's secretary on 7 May 1578 (*ibid.*, f. 125).

22. From a tract of 1599, quoted by D. B. Quinn, 'Ireland and sixteenth-century European expansion', *Historical Studies*, I (1958), pp. 20-32 (at p. 30).

23. On the powers and activities of one tribunal in Spanish America *cf.* J. H. Parry, *The Audiencia of New Galicia in the*

sixteenth century (Cambridge, 1948), especially pp. 38-9, 81 and 123-4. On the commissions of enquiry in the New World, *cf.* G. Céspedes del Castillo, 'La visita como institución indiana', *Anuario de Estudios Americanos*, III (1946), pp. 984-1025.

24. Quotations from J. H. Elliott, *The Revolt of the Catalans* (Cambridge, 1963), p. 13, and L. Paris, *Négociations, lettres et pièces diverses relatives au règne de François II* (Paris, 1841), p. 66.

25. On the Indians, quotations from Juan de Matienzo, a jurist (1567), and Pedro de Feria, bishop of Chiapa in Mexico (1585); they are cited along with a wealth of other fascinating material in J. H. Elliott, 'The discovery of America and the discovery of Man', *Proceedings of the British Academy*, LVIII (1972), pp. 101-25 (at pp. 109 and 111). On the Italians, letter from the Spanish Governor of Milan to the king, Feb. 1570, quoted by H. G. Koenigsberger, 'The statecraft of Philip II', *European Studies Review*, I (1971), pp. 1-21 (at p. 9).

26. E. S. Arnoldsson, *La leyenda negra: estudios sobre sus origenes* (Stockholm, 1960), chs. 2 and 3.

27. C. Piot, *Correspondance du Cardinal de Granvelle*, IV (Brussels 1884), p. 93 (Morillon to Granvelle, 28 Jan. 1572); Duke of Berwick y Alba, *Epistolario del III duque de Alba*, II (Madrid, 1952), pp. 367-71 (Alva to the king, 5 May 1570: 'No hay en todos los Estados hombre de quien se pueda hacer cabeza; . . . es gente mediana y poco menos que mediana'); AGS Estado 545 fo. 69, Alva to the king, 9 July 1570 ('estos estados . . . hanse de governar desde ay y no de aqui').

28. *Colección de Documentos Inéditos para la Historia de España*, XXXIII, p. 84, Alva to the king, 6 Jan. 1568: 'Si V. M. mira bien lo que hay que hacer, verá que es plantar un mundo nuevo.' It seems likely that Alva had in mind the sort of 'New World' created by Spain in America.

29. On the divided opinions concerning Spanish policy in the Indies *cf.* J. H. Parry, *The Spanish Theory of Empire in the Sixteenth Century* (Cambridge, 1940); and L. Hanke, *The Spanish Struggle for Justice in the Conquest of America* (Philadelphia, 1949).

30. A. W. Lovett, 'Some Spanish attitudes to the Netherlands (1572-1578)', *Tijdschrift voor Geschiedenis*, LXXXV (1972), pp. 17-30. *Cf.* also the penetrating thesis of P. D. Lagomarsino, *Court factions and the formation of Spanish policy towards the Netherlands (1559-1567)* (Cambridge University Ph.D. thesis, 1973), ch.

8, and M. Herrero García, *Ideas de los Españoles en el siglo XVII* (Madrid, 1966), pp. 417-55. Favourable comments by Spanish writers on the Netherlands, and indications of a good rapport between the two nations, have been collected by: E. Gossart, *Les Espagnols en Flandre. Histoire et Poésie* (Brussels, 1914); J. Brouwer, *Kronieken van Spaansche soldaten, uit het begin van den tachtigjarigen oorlog* (Zutphen, 1933); J. Lefèvre, 'La compénétration hispano-belge aux Pays-Bas catholiques pendent le 17e siècle', *Revue belge de Philologie et d'Histoire*, XVI (1937), pp. 599-621.

31. It is true that, in later years, genuine efforts were made by the Spanish central government to control abuse in the Netherlands. There was a special commission of enquiry established in Madrid from 1581 until 1590 to audit all accounts involving Spanish money sent to the Netherlands. From 1594 until 1602 another commission, the *Tribunal de la Visita*, sat in Brussels publicly hearing evidence against over 200 members of the duke of Parma's administration who were accused of fraud. Most of them were found guilty. (*Cf.* J. Lefèvre. 'Le Tribunal de la Visite [1594-1602]'. *Archives, Bibliothèques et Musées de Belgique*, IX [1932], pp. 65-85.) In the seventeenth century a special *Sala de Cuentas* was created in Brussels (1609-15 and 1619-1706) but it was only allowed to audit minor accounts. All these bodies were staffed by Spaniards, however; the government never consented to set Netherlanders above Spaniards. Corruption and cheating therefore continued to characterize the Spanish regime in the Netherlands right until the end in 1706.

9. The Decision-making Process in the Government of the Catholic Netherlands under 'the Archdukes', 1596-1621
(Originally published in the *English Historical Review*, XCI [1976], pp. 242-54.)

1. *Cf.* R[ijks] A[rchief] G[hent], R[aad] v[an] Vl[aanderen], 180, act of acceptance for an *aide* voted by the estates of Flanders, 26 Mar. 1591.

2. A[lgemeen] R[ijksarchief, or Archives Générales du Royaume] B[russels], Aud[ientië], 1783/3, unfol., 'Mémoire de ce que son Excellence a proposé à Messieurs des Finances', 21 Mar. 1592; ARB SGR [= Geheime Raad, Spaanse tijdperk], 170, apostil to a request from the estates of Cambrai and Cambrésis, 11 Sept.

1598. For a study of the financial organization of one province, *cf.* J. Craeybeckx, 'De Staten van Vlaanderen en de gewestelijke financien in de XVIe eeuw. Het verzet tegen Alva's tiende penning', *Handelingen der Maatschappij voor Geschiedenis en Oudheidkunde te Gent*, new series IV, 2 (1949-50), pp. 78-119.

3. RAG RvVl., 180, act of 26 Mar. 1591 mentioned above; ARB RvF., 44/10-14, I. Verreycken and S. van Steelandt ('commis pour oyr les comptes du receveur général des aydes de Flandres') to Council of Finance, 9 Jan. 1595; *ibid.* 477, unfol., Memorandum from Desmarez, accountant of the Audit Office of Gelderland, 30 July 1605. *Cf.* also J. Dhondt in *Estates or Powers. Essays in the Parliamentary History of the Southern Netherlands* (ed. W. Blockmans, Paris-Leuven, 1977), pp. 131-68.

4. L. P. Gachard, *Actes des Etats-Généraux de 1600* (Brussels, 1849), pp. 681-90: Memorandum of the States-General, 14 Oct. 1600, with apostils of the archdukes, 31 Oct. The treasurer of war was responsible for the pay of the troops raised in the Netherlands.

5. ARB Aud., 185/208, Parma to Philip II, 15 Nov. 1580; A. L. P. de Robaulx de Soumoy, *Mémoires de Frédéric Perrenot, sieur de Champagney, 1573-1590* (Brussels, 1860), pp. 273 and 291-3. In the interests of efficiency and better co-ordination, the Council of Finance proposed in Nov. 1580 that all sources of revenue, whether provisions from Spain or taxes from the Netherlands, should be handled by the *Recette générale des Finances*; all the troops would receive payment from this source via the treasurer of war. Neither Parma nor Philip II gave the plan serious consideration.

6. Ottavio Gonzaga was charged with the *superintendencia del dinero del exercito* in 1578-80 (*cf.* references to his office in A[rchivo] G[eneral de] S[imancas], *Contaduría Mayor de Cuentas, 2a época*, 75, accounts of Ysuardo Capelo). The first person to hold the official post of *superintendente de hacienda* was Esteban de Ibarra (1594-6) (*cf.* AGS E[stado], 2310/304-6, Mateo de Urquina to Philip III, 15 Jan. 1621; and AGS S[ecretarías] P[rovinciales], 2580/50-1, 'La instrucción para lo de la hazienda', 21 Aug. 1595). For the decreasing volume of 'deniers venans des coffres du roy' to the *Recette générale des Finances*, *cf.* Archives départmentales du Nord, Lille, série B, 2770, 2776, 2782, 2788, 2794, 2800, 2806, 2812, 2818, 2824, 2830 and 2836. The distinction between payments *por via de finanças* and payments *por via del ejército* was underlined by Geoffrey Parker, *The Army of Flanders and the Spanish Road, 1567-1659. The logistics of Spanish victory and defeat in the Low Countries' Wars* (Cambridge, 1972), ch. 6.

7. ARB Aud., 1224/140-144v, Instruction for the Cardinal-Infante, 10 Oct. 1632, articles 13-22. On the Privy Council, see also P. Alexandre, *Histoire du Conseil Privé dans les anciens Pays-Bas* (Brussels, 1894-5).

8. V. Brants, *Les ordonnances monétaires du XVIIe siècle, 1598-1700* (Brussels, 1914), pp. 2-7; ARB Aud., 620/213, Council of Finance to Archduke Albert, 12 Dec. 1598; *ibid.* 621/7, Albert to Council, 1 Jan. 1599; ARB RvF., 168, unfol., Council of Finance to Albert, 17 Aug. 1599.

9. AGS E., 620, unfol., Don Balthasar de Zúñiga to Philip III, 22 Nov. 1602; AGS E., 622/188-9, Juan de Gauna (until 1605 the archdukes' principal commercial adviser) to Philip III, 1 Feb. 1603; V. Brants, *Receuil des Ordonnances des Pays-Bas. Règne d'Albert et Isabelle, 1598-1621*, I (Brussels, 1909), pp. 203-10, Placard of 5 Apr. 1603. The king's councils in Castile also had to endorse policies made by others; *cf.* the crisp reminder sent by Philip III to his Spanish Council of Finance in 1601: 'When I order a despatch to be made, the council is not required to know how or with what advice I have decided upon it, for this is not its concern; [it is there] only to fulfil the orders sent it in my name.' (Quoted P. L Williams, 'Philip III and the restoration of Spanish government, 1598-1603', *English Historical Review*, LXXXVIII (1973), p. 767.)

10. ARB SGR., 172, unfol., 'Liste des personnes pour servir d'eschevins en la ville de Lessines pour le Saint Jehan 1588'; *ibid.* J. le Louchier (bailiff of Lessines in Hainaut) to Privy Council, 12 June 1600. *Cf.* also J. M. Goris, 'Het Herentalse stadsmagistraat, 1600-1715', *Taxandria. Tijdschrift van de koninklijke geschied-en oudheidkundige kring van de Antwerpse Kempen*, new series, XXXVII (1965), pp. 7-12; R. Boumans, *Het Antwerps stadsbestuur vóór en tijdens de Franse overheersing. Bijdrage tot de ontwikkelings-geschiedenis van de stedelijke bestuursinstellingen in de Zuidelijke Nederlanden* (Bruges, 1965), pp. 13-15.

11. *Cf.* ARB Aud., 1845/3 and 1917/2, correspondence of the central government with the Great Council of Mechelen, 1593-1621; and ARB SGR., 643-4, requests presented 1580-1621. *Cf.* also J. Lefèvre, 'Le Grand Conseil sous Albert et Isabelle, 1598-1621', *Handelingen van de koninklijke kring voor oudheidkunde, letteren en kunst van Mechelen*, LIII (1949), pp. 130-49; H. de Schepper, 'Regeringsbeslissingen in bestuurzaken, 16e-18e eeuw: de benoeming van hoge magistraten en ambtenaren, *c.* 1550-*c.* 1650, in *De besluitvorming, vroeger en nu*, ed. J. Gilissen and H. de Schepper (Brussels, 1975), pp. 71-104.

12. ARB Aud., 624/375-6, instructions for Willem van Grysperre (Privy Councillor), 4 Sept. 1600. *Cf.* also ARB SGR., 143, unfol., closed letter to the attorney-general of Luxemburg, 3 Jan. 1600; *ibid.* 784, unfol., closed letter to the council of justice in Mons, 9 Nov. 1606; AGS SP., *libro* 1420/327, 'appoinctement' of the Privy Council, 9 Dec. 1604. The Privy Council in Scotland behaved in much the same way. Even after the creation of a supreme court (the 'College of Justice') in 1532, the Council issued 'letters of precognition' which took over a case being heard in another court. See G. Donaldson, *Scotland: James V to James VII* (Edinburgh, 1965), pp. 287-91.

13. ARB Grote Raad van Mechelen, Memoriaalregister 153/8, closed letter to Great Council, 9 Nov. 1600, and judgement of the Council, 18 Nov. *Cf.* also RAG RvVl., 190, unfol., Council of Flanders to Privy Council, 31 July 1608.

14. ARB SGR., 783-5 contain requests and minutes of orders for 'staet ende surceancie', 1596-1619; *ibid.* 716-24 contain those for 'atterminatie ende respijt', 1595-1620; *ibid.* 906-46 those for 'abolitie' and 'gratie ende remissie', 1596-1621; and *ibid.* 1425 those for 'rehabilitatie', 1584-1621.

15. The Privy Councillors regarded themselves as 'juges ordinaires d'icelle nostre cour' (ARB Aud., 1293, unfol., commission for M. de Vuldere *et al.*, 5 Aug. 1606). For examples of this view in practice *cf.* the following cases judged by the Privy Council: suit of Ann of Egmont versus Charles Count of Egmont (Knight of the Golden Fleece and therefore an *escroe*) for debt, Oct. 1600 (ARB OGR [=Geheime Raad, Oostentijkse tijdperk], 677/96v-7); suit of Martin von Hohenstein (secretary of state for German affairs and therefore an *escroe*) versus Ludwig Biglia, colonel of German infantry, for debt, 1600 (ARB SGR., 216, unfol.); suit of Johan van Steenweghe, woodseller, versus Lamoral de Tassis, postmaster-general and therefore an *escroe*, for debt, 1621 (ARB OGR., 677/352 verso); and many, many more. See also H. de Schepper, 'De Grote Raad van Mechelen, hoogste rechtskollege in de Nederlanden?', *Federatie van kringen voor oudheidkunde en geschiedenis. XLIIIe Congres Sint-Niklaas-Waas 1974. Annalen* (St Niklaas, 1975), pp. 129-31.

16. ARB SGR., 776, unfol., contains requests with apostils and minutes of letters concerning cases brought to the Privy Council directly by outsiders (i.e. by non-*escroes*) 1600-19; ARB OGR., 677 contains the verdicts of the Council in such cases, 1591-1626.

17. ARB OGR., 677/57, judgement of the Privy Council, 7 Oct.

1596; *ibid.* fo. 163v-4, judgement of 14 Nov. 1607. On the general situation of the Church and the interference of the government's law-courts in ecclesiastical cases, *cf.* A. Louant, *Correspondance d'Ottavio Mirto Frangipani, premier nonce de Flandres, 1596-1606*, III (Rome-Brussels-Paris, 1942), 14; J. Lefèvre, *Documents relatifs à la juridiction des nonces et internonces aux Pays-Bas pendant le régime espagnol, 1596-1706* (Brussels, 1942), pp. 15 and 22; H. J. Elias, *Kerk en Staat in de Zuidelijke Nederlanden onder de regering der Aartshertogen Albert en Isabella, 1598-1621* (Antwerp-Leuven, 1931), pp. 241-50.

18. AGS E., 620, unfol., Albert to Philip III and Balthasar de Zúñiga to Philip III, both 6 Mar. 1602. On military justice in general, *cf.* L. van Meerbeeck, *Inventaire des archives des tribunaux militaires* (Gembloux, 1939), pp. 16-20, and R. Aubert, 'Les débuts de la surintendance de la justice militaire dans les Pays-Bas espagnoles', *Miscellanea historica in honorem Leonis van der Essen*, I (Leuven, 1947), 491-505. The military jurisdiction of the Privy Council was limited to two fields: surveillance of certain personal suits between civilians and soldiers, and hearing appeals against sentences pronounced by *Netherlands* military judges (i.e. concerning 'native' troops). *Cf.* ARB SGR., 216, abovementioned suit of Martin von Hohenstein against Colonel Ludwig Biglia, and of the lord of Alsdorp against Colonel Bentinck (1600); *ibid.* closed letter to Ferdinand de Boisschot (auditor-general), 24 Sept. 1601; ARB Aud., 621/300-1, Council of State to Cardinal Andrew of Austria, acting Governor-General, 21 June 1599; *ibid.* 1897/1, unfol., Cardinal Andrew to the Council of State, 14 June 1599.

19. On the competence of the Council of State, *cf.* ARB Aud., 1191/23, dossier on a controversy with the Council of Finance, Mar.-Apr. 1596; *ibid.* 620-4, 1842/1-2 and 1897/1-5, correspondence of the Council of State with the Archdukes; *ibid.* 783, minutes of the meetings of the Council of State, 1604-6.

20. AGS E., 581/81, 'Memorial tocante al govierno de las financas de Su Magestad Catholica en los sus estados de Flandes', s.d. [1579-80?] ARB Aud., 783, *ut supra*; *ibid.* 1175/2, unfol., instruction for the Council of State, 2 Aug. 1595; *ibid.* 1124/247v-8, secret instruction for the Cardinal-Infante, 19 Oct. 1632; A. L. P. de Robaulx de Soumoy, *Considérations sur le gouvernement des Pays-Bas*, II (Brussels, 1872), p. 60.

21. J. Lefèvre, 'Le Ministère espagnol de l'Archiduc Albert, 1598-1621', *Bulletin de l'Académie royale d'archéologie de Belgique*, I (1924), pp. 203-5 and 224; C. H. Carter, 'Belgian "autonomy"'

under the Archdukes, 1598-1621', *Journal of Modern History*, XXXVI (1964), pp. 245-54.

22. *Cf.* H. de Schepper, article 'Richardot', in *National Biografisch Woordenboek*, I (Brussels, 1964), cols. 771-2.

23. ARB Aud., 783, *Notules* of the Council of State, 1590-6 and 1604-6; ARB OGR., 622-3, 'Registres des appointements extenduz', 1591-1612; ARB RvF., 44, 'Depesches de Finances', 1595. A brief glance at these representative samples of the records left by the three councils gives a clear impression of their differing activities.

24. ARB Aud., 1897/1, unfol., Council of State to Archduke Andrew, 3 May 1599: 'Avons jugé convenir de faire dresser lesd. lettres en temps pour les envoyer à Vostre Altèze, afin qu'elle les veuille signer et les nous renvoyer pour les encheminer.' *Cf.* also *ibid.* 623/356v, Council to Archdukes, 14 July 1600.

25. A. Louant, *Correspondance . . . Frangipani*, III p. 465 n. 4 and 486-7, Frangipani to Aldobrandino, 8 May and 27 Aug. 1604. *Cf.* J. Lefèvre, 'Le Ministère espagnol . . .', pp. 202-24, *passim*.

26. A[rchivo] S[egreto] V[aticano], Fondo Borghese, series II, no. 115, fo. 79v, nuncio Bentivoglio to Cardinal Borghese (Papal secretary of state), 1 Mar. 1608; A. Louant, *op. cit.* III, pp. 825-6, 'Trattato delli amotinati', 1602-3; Erycius Puteanus, *Relationi fatte dall'Illmo. e Revmo. Signor Cardinal Bentivoglio in tempo delle sue Nunziature di Fiandra e di Francia*, II (Cologne, 1629), pp. 1-75; ARB Aud., 917-22, a set of dossiers concerned with the nomination of abbots, 1596-1621.

27. A. Louant, *op. cit.* III, p. 244 and note, Frangipani to Aldobrandino, 12 May 1601.

28. J. Lefèvre, *Ambrosio Spinola et la Belgique, 1601-1627* (Brussels, 1947), p. 33; J. den Tex, *Oldenbarnevelt*, II (Haarlem, 1962), pp. 530-1 and 542-9; ARB Aud., 1366, 'Papiers concernans la négotiation . . . en matière de la paix, faicte en Hollande ès années 1606 et 1607'; *Colección de Documentos Inéditos para la Historia de España*, XLII and XLIII, *passim*; ASV, Fondo Borghese, series II, nos. 100, 111 and 114-15, correspondence of nuncio Bentivoglio to Borghese, 1607-9. The Brussels government was also largely excluded from the decision on whether or not to renew the Truce in 1621: P. Brightwell, 'The Spanish system and the Twelve Years Truce', *English Historical Review*, LXXXIX (1974), pp. 270-94.

Spain and the Netherlands

29. A. Louant, *Corr. Frangipani*, III, 437, 450-1, 456 and 460-1, letters of nuncio Frangipani to Aldobrandino, 25 Oct. 1603, 3 Jan. 1604, 7 Feb. 1604 and 27 Mar. 1604; Oesterreichisches Staatsarchiv, Vienna, H[aus-], H[of- und] St[aats]a[rchiv] Belgien, [Bestände des Repertoriums] P[Abteilung] C, Fasz, 44, unfol., instructions to Arenberg, Richardot and Verreycken 12 Apr. 1604; J. Cuvelier, 'Les préliminaires du traité de Londres . . .', *Revue Belge de Philologie et d'Histoire*, II (1923), pp. 505-8. See also A. Loomie, 'Philip III and the Stuart succession in England, 1600-1603', *idem*, XLIII (1965), pp. 492-514.

30. ASV, Fondo Borghese, series II, nf. 111/121 and 114/50, letters of nuncio Bentivoglio, 4 Oct. 1608 and 14 Feb. 1609. *Cf.* W. J. M. van Eysinga, *De wording van het Twaalfjarig Bestand van April 1609* (Amsterdam, 1959), p. 74.

31. ARB Secrétairerie d'Etat et de Guerre, 176/27, Philip III to Albert, 24 Oct. 1598; ARB Aud., 620/200-1, 226v and 236v-7, letters of the marquis of Havré (councillor of Finance) to Albert, 5, 19, and 24 Dec. 1598; AGS E., 615/42, Andrew of Austria to Philip III, 5 Dec. 1598, *cf.* J. H. Kernkamp, *De handel op den vijand, 1572-1609*, II (Utrecht, 1939), pp. 227-8 and 233-4.

32. V. Brants, *Recueil des Ordonnances*, I, pp. 262-3, placard, 12 Mar. 1605; ARB Rk., 20.492/32v, account of *Audiencier* Verreycken, 1605; *ibid.* registers 23.576-23.579, *passim*, accounts of licence dues, 1606-10; AGS E., 2225, unfol., Philip III to Albert, 19 Sept. 1605: 'It is an order, I repeat it.' *Cf.* J. H. Kernkamp, *op. cit.* II, 310-12; E. Stols, *De Spaanse Brabanders of de handelsbetrekkingen der Zuidelijke Nederlanden met de Iberische Wereld, 1598-1648*, I (Brussels, 1971), pp. 13 and 35.

33. J. Lefèvre, 'La correspondance des gouverneurs-généraux à l'époque espagnole', *Archives, Bibliothèques et Musées de Belgique*, XXI (1950), pp. 33-7; RAG RvVl., 180-216, *passim*, correspondence of the Council of Flanders with the central government, 1590-1621; ARB Rk., portfeuilles 782-96, *passim*, correspondence of the Audit Office (*Rekenkamer*) of Brabant with the government, 1597-1622.

34. ARB Aud., 1840/2-3 and 1895/3, *passim*, Requests sent in to the government, 1596-1621; *ibid.* 1783/1, unfol., Privy Council to Parma, 21 Apr. 1588; and placard (21 Apr. 1588) in C. Verlinden and J. Craeybeckx, *Prijzen- en lonenpolitiek in de Nederlanden in 1561 en 1588-9. Onuitgegeven adviezen, ontwerpen en ordonnanties* (Brussels, 1962), pp. 115-20, *Cf.* J. Gilissen, 'Essai statistique de la législation en Belgique de 1507 à 1794', *Revue du Nord*, XL (1958), pp. 431-5.

35. ARB Aud., 2780, unfol., apostil of 14 Dec. 1596 to a Request; HHStA Belgien, P. C., Fasz. 11 fo. 415, apostils to a memorandum from the envoy of the duke of Lorraine (Charles III 'le Grand'), 22 Jan. 1600.

36. ARB Aud., 1898/1, unfol., Privy Council to Archduke Albert, 4 July 1601; ARB SGR., 1398, unfol., apostil of 30 July 1599 to a letter of the Council of Luxemburg to Archduke Andrew, 20 July 1599; RAG RvVl., 180-216, correspondence of the Council of Flanders, 1590-1621; ARB Rk., portefeuilles 782-96, correspondence of the Audit Office of Brabant, 1597-1622; ARB SGR., 643-6, 649, 653 and 655-7, closed letters to the provincial Councils of Justice, 1580-1621. *Cf.* M. R. Thielemans, R. Petit and R. Boumans, *Inventaire des archives du conseil d'Etat* (Brussels, 1954), p. xxii.

37. ARB RvF., 529, unfol., Licence Office at Antwerp to Council of Finance, 10 Apr. 1598, and apostil, 4 May 1598; ARB SGR., 175, unfol., apostil of 20 Jan. 1600 and dossier of Jan. 1600; ARB RvF., 354, unfol., archdukes to lord of Bousies, governor of Landrecies, 8 Apr. 1609, and attached dossier. Example of recommendation: ARB Aud., 1901/1, unfol., P. Peckius, ambassador in France, to B. de Robiano (Treasurer-General of Finance), 24 Sept. 1607.

38. ARB Rk., portefeuilles 782-96, correspondence of Council of Finance with the Audit Office of Brabant and of the Audit Office with regional collectors, 1596-1622.

39. ARB Aud., 622/234, archdukes to the Council of Luxemburg, 20 Sept. 1599; RAG RvVl., 187, unfol., archdukes to Council of Flanders, 27 Sept. 1606; R. Fruin and H. T. Colenbrander, *Geschiedenis der Staatsinstellingen in Nederland tot de val der Republiek* (the Hague, 1922), p. 64.

40. ARB SGR., 143, unfol., closed letter to Council of Luxemburg 22 Apr. 1596 (compare placard of 7 Feb. 1587 in Aud., 1146, unfol.). See also Aud., 202/1, unfol., Council of Flanders to Archduke Ernest, 19 Feb. 1594 (compare placard of 8 Feb. 1594, Koninklijke Bibliotheek, Brussels, *Kostbare Werken*, no. LP. 2530A). There is an obvious parallel here with the powers and practice of the French *parlement de Paris*.

41. ARB RvF., 5, unfol., Parma to L. Verreycken, 4 Feb. 1589, and 'Addition et esclaircissement des instructions des Finances', 27 Dec. 1603; ARB OGR., 623, unfol., 'appoinctements' in the Privy Council, 30 Apr. 1604; A. Gaillard, *Le Conseil de Brabant*.

Histoire, organisation, procedure, II (Brussels, 1901), pp. 62-3.

42. ARB SGR., 776, unfol., closed letter to the magistrates of Ieper, 21 July 1600; *ibid.* 1223, unfol., same to the *parlement* of Dôle in Franche-Comté, 27 Aug. 1604; *ibid.* 175, unfol., same to the magistrates of Kortrijk, 7 Nov. 1609.

43. *Placcaetbouck . . . van Vlaanderen*, ii, 594-7; ARB SGR., 182, unfol., request with apostil, 28 Apr. 1599; *ibid.* 175, unfol., requests with apostils, 7 and 20 July 1599.

44. V. Brants, *Les ordonnances monétaires*, pp. 2-65. *Cf.* ARB Aud., 1897/3, unfol., Council of State to Albert, 6 Jan. 1602; *ibid.* 1918/1, unfol., Council of State to Council of Brabant, 23 Mar. 1602; RAG RvVl., 186, unfol., Council of Flanders to Privy Council, 24 Dec. 1605; *ibid.* 192, unfol., same to Albert, 24 Jan. 1609.

45. This article is a much expanded version of H. de Schepper, 'De besluitsvorming in de regering van de Katholieke Nederlanden rond 1600', *Nederlands archievenblad*, LXXVII (1973), pp. 174-85. A full-length study of the Collateral Councils in the Catholic Netherlands between 1579 and 1609 by Hugo de Schepper will be published by the Koninklijke Academie voor Wetenschappen, Letteren en Schone Kunsten van Belgie. Klasse der Letteren (meanwhile see his unpublished doctoral dissertation, in Dutch, University of Leuven, 1972).

10. War and Economic Change: the Economic Costs of the Dutch Revolt

(Originally published in *War and Economic Development. Essays in Memory of David Joslin*, ed. J. M. Winter [Cambridge, 1975], pp. 49-71.)

1. I am very grateful to Mrs A. M. Parker, Dr R. M. Price, Dr H. Soly, Professor Charles Wilson and Dr J. M. Winter for supplying me with helpful suggestions and comments about this paper.

2. N. Froumenteau, *Le secret des finances de France* (Paris, 1581); T. K. Rabb, 'The effects of the Thirty Years' War on the German economy', *Journal of Modern History*, XXXIV (1962), pp. 40-51.

3. For Holland: F. Snapper, *Oorlogsinvloeden op de overzeese*

handel van Holland, 1551-1719 (Amsterdam, 1959). For 'Belgium':
C. Verlinden, 'En Flandre sous Philippe II: durée de la crise
économique', *Annales E.S.C.*, VII (1952), pp. 21-30, and J. A.
van Houtte, 'Onze 17e eeuw "Ongelukseeuw"?', *Mededelingen
van de Koninklijke Vlaanse Akademie*, XV (1953), no. 8.

4. Francisco Gómez de Quevedo y Villegas, *La Hora de Todos*,
ch. 36 (written in 1635-6). *Cf. Biblioteca de Autores Españoles*,
XXIIII, p. 409.

5. Although even here there have been some doubting voices: *cf.*
S. H. Steinberg, *The Thirty Years' War and the Conflict for European Hegemony* (London, 1967), p. 107 – 'None of the campaigns
fought on its ['Belgium's'] soil between the arrival of Alva and the
departure of Marlborough had any appreciable effect on the
steady growth of its towns.'

6. Abundant details are to be found in H. van der Wee, *The
Growth of the Antwerp Market and the European Economy*, II, pp.
245-62 and 269-80.

7. H. E. de Sagher *et al.*, *Receuil de documents relatifs à l'histoire
de l'industrie drapière en Flandres*, 2e partie, II (Brussels, 1961),
pp. 244-5 (collapse of Dixmuide's production), pp. 271-2 (Eecke);
III (Brussels, 1966), *sub art.* Menin, 'Neuve Eglise et Poperinghe'.
It was the same story with the linen industry: E. Sabbe, *De
Belgische vlasnijverheid* (Bruges, 1943), pp. 300-17.

8. Archivo General de Simancas, Estado 589 fo. 120, Alexander
Farnese, duke of Parma, to Philip II, 31 Dec. 1585 ('no haviendo
sembrado ni en Brabante ni en Flandes'), and Archives Générales
du Royaume, Brussels, *Audience* 189, ff. 85-91, Parma to Philip II,
12 Jan. 1587.

9. J. Verbeemen, 'De werking van economische factoren op de
stedelijke demografie der XVIIe en der XVIIIe eeuw in de
Zuidelijke Nederlanden', *Revue Belge de Philologie et d'Histoire*,
XXXIV (1956), pp. 680-700 and 1021-55; on p. 695.

10. On the remarkable recovery of Antwerp, *cf.* the rich and
perceptive article of W. Brulez, 'Anvers de 1585 à 1650', *Vierteljahr-
schrift für Sozial- und Wirtschaftsgeschichte*, LIV (1967), pp.
75-99. *Cf.* also F. J. Smolar, 'Resiliency of enterprise: economic
crises and recovery in the Spanish Netherlands in the early
seventeenth century', in *From the Renaissance to the Counter-
Reformation*, ed. C. H. Carter (London, 1965), pp. 247-68.

Spain and the Netherlands

11. E. Stols, *De Spaanse Brabanders, op de Handelsbetrekkingen der Zuiderlijke Nederlanden met de Iberische wereld, 1598-1648* (Brussels, 1971), bijlage 1; W. Brulez, *De firma della Faille en de internationale handel van Vlaamse firma's in de 16e eeuw* (Brussels, 1959), pt II, *cf.* p. 574; H. Pohl, 'Die Zuckereinfuhr nach Antwerpen, durch Portugiesische Kaufleute während des 80-jährige Krieges', *Jahrbuch für Geschichte von Staat, Wirtschaft und Gesellschaft Lateinamerikas*, IV (1967), pp. 347-73.

12. J. Craeybeckx, 'Les industries d'exportation dans les villes flamandes au XVIIe siècle, particulièrement à Gand et à Bruges', *Studi in onore di Amintore Fanfani*, IV (Milan, 1962), pp. 411-67; J. Bastin, 'De Gentse lijnwaadmarkt en linnenhandel in de 17e eeuw', *Handelingen der Maatschappij voor Geschiedenis en Oudheidkunde te Gent*, XXI (1967), pp. 131-62; E. Coornaert, *Un centre industriel d'autrefois. La draperie-sayetterie d'Hondschoote, XIVe-XVIIIe siècles* (Paris, 1930).

13. D. van Rijssel, *De Gentse Huishuren tussen 1500 en 1795* (Brussels, 1967), pp. 56-7 and 73-95.

14. R. Weston, *A discours of husbandrie used in Brabant and Flanders, showing wonderful improvement of Land there* (London, 1650), p. 2.

15. *Cf.* G. Parker, *The Army of Flanders and the Spanish Road, 1567-1659* (Cambridge, 1972), pp. 143-5 for the financial cost of the Spanish army to the Netherlands; for population loss in the south, *cf.* J. de Smet, 'Les dénombrements de la population dans la châtellenie d'Ypres (1610 et 1615 à 1620)', *Bulletin de la commission royale d'histoire*, XCVI (1932), pp. 255-332, and J. Verbeemen, 'L'évolution démographique d'une ville wallonne: Mons (1283-1766)', *L'intermédiaire des généalogistes*, LV (1955), pp. 23-5.

16. Archivo General de Simancas, Estado 2037 fo. 11, *consulta* of the Council of State, 14 Apr. 1623, *voto* of Don Fernando Girón.

17. Archivo General de Simancas, Estado 634 fo. 19, Instruction of Philip III for Don Rodrigo Niño y Lasso, envoy to the Netherlands, spring 1604.

18. I. A. A. Thompson, *War and government in Habsburg Spain 1560-1620* (London, 1976), p. 103, estimates annual recruiting at 9000 per year in wartime; for some detailed figures *cf.* G. Parker, *The Army of Flanders*, pp. 42-3 and 278-9. Of course the burden of recruiting grew heavier as the population of Castile declined (from c. 1600 onwards).

19. Quoted by M. Herrero García, *Ideas de los Españoles del siglo XVII* (2nd edn., Madrid, 1966), p. 420.

20. Archivo General de Simancas, Estado 575 fo., 134, Philip II to Don John of Austria, 16 Mar. 1578 (minute).

21. Clearly the financial provisions sent to the Army of Flanders were an important channel by which the treasure of the Spanish Indies was transferred to northern Europe. Treasure figures from J. H. Elliott, *Imperial Spain (1469-1716)* (London, 1963), p. 175 (the original figures of E. J. Hamilton converted into ducats); expenditure in the Netherlands from G. Parker, *The Army of Flanders*, pp. 293-6; expenditure in the Mediterranean from Archivo General de Simancas, *Contaduría Mayor de Cuentas*, 2a *época* 814 (account of Paymaster-General Juan Morales de Torre).

22. J. Vicens Vives, 'The decline of Spain in the 17th century', in *The Economic Decline of Empires*, ed. C. M. Cipolla (London, 1970), p. 154; N. Salomon, *La campagne de Nouvelle Castille à la fin du XVIe siècle d'après les 'Relaciones topográficas'* (Paris, 1964), pp. 234-5 and 250-1.

23. J. Vicens Vives, 'The decline of Spain in the 17th century', pp. 149-50; F. Braudel, *La Méditerranée et le monde méditerranéen à l'époque de Philippe II* (2nd edn., Paris, 1966), I, p. 449 note 6; A. Castillo, 'Population et richesse en Castille, 1550-1600', *Annales E.S.C.*, XX (1965), pp. 710-33. Although some Castilian wool continued to be exported to Italy and to England after 1572, the quantities were not sufficient to offset the lost market of the Low Countries.

24. J. Lynch, *Spain under the Habsburgs*, II (Oxford, 1969), p. 182; P. Bakewell, *Silver Mining and Society in Colonial Mexico, Zacatecas 1546-1700* (Cambridge, 1971), p. 232.

25. C. R. Boxer, *The Portuguese Seaborne Empire, 1415-1825* (London, 1969), ch. 5; F. Mauro, *Le Portugal et l'Atlantique au XVIIe siècle, 1570-1670. Etude économique* (Paris, 1960), pp. 440-55.

26. Compare the maps of van Deventer printed by R. Fruin, *Nederlandsche steden in den 16e eeuw. Plattegronden van Jacob van Deventer* (the Hague, 1916-23 – facsimiles of 111 maps) with J. Blaeu, *Tooneel der steden van de Vereenighde Nederlanden met hare beschrijvingen* (Amsterdam, 1649). Of course, exactly the same process had taken place in the South Netherlands, as a comparison

of the same two sources shows: *cf.* C. Ruelens, *Atlas des villes de la Belgique au XVIe siècle* (2 vols., Brussels, 1884) and J. Blaeu, *Tooneel der steden van 's Konings Nederlanden met hare beschrijvingen* (Amsterdam, 1649).

27. Figures taken from the *Staten van Oorlog* of the Dutch Republic, summarized conveniently in Algemeen Rijksarchief, the Hague, *Raad van State*, 1499 and 1500.

28. R. M. Dekker, 'Oproeren in de provincie Holland 1600-1750: frequentie en karakter, relatie met de conjunctuur en repressie', *Tijdschrift voor Sociale Geschiedenis*, IX (1977), pp. 299-329; G. Parker, 'The emergence of modern finance' in C. M. Cipolla, ed., *The Fontana Economic History of Europe*, II (London, 1974), pp. 572-4.

29. J. G. van Dillen, 'Amsterdam in Bredero's tijd', *De Gids*, XCIX (1935), part II, p. 311; van Dillen, *Bronnen tot de Geschiedenis van het bedrijfsleven en het Gildewezen van Amsterdam*, I (The Hague, 1929), pp. xvii and xxxvi; van Dillen, *Het oudste aandeelhoudersregister van de Kamer Amsterdam der Oost-Indische Compagnie* (the Hague, 1958), pp. 60-1; W. J. van Hoboken, 'The Dutch West India Company: the political background of its rise and decline', in J. S. Bromley and E. H. Kossmann, *Britain and the Netherlands*, I (1960), pp. 41-61.

30. van Dillen, *Bronnen*, I, pp. xxxii-xxxvi; L. van Nierop, 'De Bruidegoms van Amsterdam van 1578 tot 1601', *Tijdschrift voor Geschiedenis*, XLVIII (1933), pp. 337-59, XLIX (1934), pp. 136-60 and pp. 329-44. *Cf.* p. 154.

31. Faber *et al.*, 'Population changes and economic developments in the Netherlands: a historical survey', *Afdeling Agrarische Geschiedenis Bijdragen*, XII (1965), pp. 47-113, especially pp. 53, 75-6, 93-4, 105; A. M. van der Woude, *Het Noorderkwartier* (3 vols., A. A. G. Bijdragen, 1972), I, pp. 154-6.

32. Quoted by P. Geyl, *The Revolt of the Netherlands, 1559-1609* (2nd edn., London, 1958), p. 233. Hooft's writing often harped upon the 'gains' which the war had brought to Holland; *cf.* *Memoriën en Adviezen van Cornelis Pieterszoon Hooft*, I (Utrecht, 1871), p. 186 (from 1617) and pp. 383-4 (1619), and II (Utrecht, 1925), p. 73 (from 1598), pp. 223 (from 1611) and 340 and 345 (from 1616-17). For corroboration from an English source of 1664 (*The Dutch Drawn to the Life*), *cf.* the quotation in C. Wilson, *Queen Elizabeth and the Revolt of the Netherlands* (London, 1970), p. 19. There were costs, however: between 1595 and 1795, at least

a million young men were 'exported' to the East Indies, most of them Dutch, of whom barely one-third ever returned; and over the same period over 590 million florins were exported directly by the company from Europe to Asia. See I. Schöffer, 'Import of bullion and coin into Asia by the Dutch East India Company in the 17th and 18th centuries' (paper given to the Franco-Dutch Conference in Paris, 1976, pp. 5 and 12).

33. W. J. van Hoboken, 'The Dutch West India Company'; C. C. Goslinga, *The Dutch in the Caribbean and on the Wild Coast 1580-1680* (Assen, 1971), pp. 323, 328, 509; S. P. L'Honoré Naber & I. A. Wright, *Piet Heyn en de Zilvervloot* (Utrecht, 1928), pp. *9-*11; I. A. Wright, *Nederlandsche Zeevaarders op de Eilanden in de Caraibische Zee en aan de kust van Columbia en Venezuela gedurende de jaren 1621-1649*, I (Utrecht, 1934), pp. *36-*46.

34. Quoted by I. J. Brugmans, 'De Oost-Indische Compagnie en de welvaart in de Republiek', *Tijdschrift voor Geschiedenis*, LXI (1948), pp. 225-31. Although this actual quotation comes from 1785 it epitomizes a long tradition of similar argument which originated – as far as I can see– in the 1607-9 truce talks. Although he does not wholly accept the Brugmans thesis, Professor C. R. Boxer furnishes a number of quotations and references which suggest that the importance of Dutch colonial trade in the seventeenth and eighteenth centuries has been overrated: *cf.* Boxer, *The Dutch Seaborne Empire* (London, 1965), pp. 86 and 278-81.

35. J. E. Elias, *Het voorspel van den eersten Engelschen oorlog*, I (the Hague, 1920), pp. 61-2. Elias dismisses as exaggerated a calculation of 1636 used subsequently by Professor Brugmans in the article cited above.

36. Evidence of the predominance of Baltic trade in the Dutch economy is abundant. *Cf.* for a sample, A. E. Christensen, *Dutch Trade to the Baltic about 1600* (Copenhagen, 1941); J. G. van Dillen, 'Amsterdam's role in seventeenth-century Dutch politics and its economic background', in J. S. Bromley and E. H. Kossmann *Britain and the Netherlands*, II (Groningen, 1964), pp. 133-47; and J. A. Faber, 'The decline of the Baltic grain trade in the second half of the seventeenth century', *Acta Historiae Neerlandicae*, I (Leiden, 1966), pp. 108-31.

37. Figures from I. J. Brugmans, 'De zoutpilaar van Nederlands economische ontwikkeling' in R. J. Forbes, ed., *Het zout der aarde* (Hengelo, 1968), pp. 53-80, at pp. 66-7; and from the major article – which fully supports my thesis – by J. I. Israel, 'A conflict of empires: Spain and the Netherlands 1618-1648', *Past and Present*,

LXXVI (1977), pp. 34-74, at pp. 58-60. Dr Israel is preparing a study on this subject which will surely replace all previous work, but until his book is in print, see J. A. Alcalá-Zamora y Queipo de Llano, *España, Flandes y el mar del Norte 1618-1639* (Barcelona, 1975).

37. For full details *cf.* J. H. Kernkamp, *Der handel op den vijand, 1572-1609* (2 vols., Utrecht, 1931).

38. This was precisely what Philip II had intended. *Cf.* his letter explaining the purpose of the embargo, Archivo General de Simancas, Estado 2218 fo. 32, Philip II to Parma, 29 Dec. 1585.

39. For German trade: H. Kellenbenz, *Unternehmerkräfte im Hamburger Portugal und Spanienhandel, 1590-1625* (Hamburg, 1954), e.g. pp. 106 and 335; F. Mauro, *Le Portugal et l'Atlantique*, 494. For French trade: P. Deyon, *Amiens – capitale provinciale. Etude sur la société urbaine au 17e siècle* (Paris, 1967), pp. 156-63. For English trade: F. J. Fisher, 'England's export trade in the early seventeenth century', *Economic History Review*, III (1950), pp. 151-61; H. Taylor, 'Price revolution or price revision? The English and Spanish trade after 1604', *Renaissance and Modern Studies*, XII (1968), pp. 5-32, and 'Trade, neutrality and the "English Road", 1630-1648', *Economic History Review*, XXV (1972), pp. 236-60.

40. On Dutch losses through privateering, see H. Malo, *Les corsaires: les corsaires dunquerquois et Jean Bart*, I (Paris, 1913), pp. 333-5, and J. I. Israel, 'A conflict of empires', pp. 46-7. On Dutch privateering successes, see F. Mauro, *Le Portugal et l'Atlantique*, p. 449, and L. de Figueiredo Falcão, *Livro em que se contem toda a fazenda e real patrimonio dos reynos de Portugal* (Lisbon, 1859), pp. 194-6.

41. F. Snapper, *Oorlogsinvloeden op de overzeese handel van Holland, 1551-1719* (Amsterdam, 1959), p. 76. *Cf.* also the views even of Amsterdam merchants that the Truce had been a golden age of profits: J. G. van Dillen, 'De West-Indische Compagnie, het Calvinisme en de politiek', *Tijdschrift voor Geschiedenis*, LXXIV (1961), pp. 145-71.

42. A close analysis of why Spain and the Dutch made a truce confined to Europe in 1609 instead of a general peace, of why the truce was not renewed in 1621 and of why no cease-fire was arranged at the peace conferences of 1627-9 and 1632-3 reveals that in each case the stumbling block was trade with the East and West Indies. The Dutch would not abandon their trading posts

there and the Spaniards would not relinquish their claim to monopoly status.

43. G. Parker, *The Army of Flanders*, pp. 119 and 120 n, quoting E. Crucé, *Le nouveau Cynée* (Paris, 1623), p. 13.

44. For the prosperity of Liège, *cf.* J. Lejeune, *La formation du capitalisme moderne dans la principauté de Liège au XVIe siècle* (Paris-Liège, 1939), and J. Yerneaux, *La Métallurgie liégeoise et son expansion au XVIIe siècle* (Liège, 1939). For the 'gains' of Frankfurt, R. van Roosbroeck, *Emigranten. Nederlandse vluchtelingen in Duitsland, 1550-1600* (Leuven, 1968), pp. 308-17. Of course many other German towns also gained from the arrival of the Dutch refugees, *cf. ibid.* pp. 318-46.

45. H. H. Rowen, *The Low Countries in early modern times* (New York, 1972), p. 179. For Professor Postan's views on war and economic 'gains' *cf.* his brilliant article 'The costs of the Hundred Years' War', *Past and Present*, XXVII (1964), pp. 34-53.

Sources to the figures in chapter ten

Figure 1:

Antwerp: R. Boumans, 'La dépeuplement d'Anvers, 1575-1600', *Revue du Nord*, XXIX (1947), pp. 181-94.

Ath and Avesnes: M. A. Arnould, 'Ath et Avesnes en 1594. Etat démographique de deux villes hennuyères à la fin du XVIe siècle', *Annales du cercle royale d'archéologie d'Ath*, XXVII (1941), pp. 89-101.

Brugse Vrije (Franc de Bruges): K. Maddens, 'Het uitzicht van het Brugse Vrije op het einde van de XVIe eeuw', *Annales de la société d'emulation de Bruges*, XCVII (1960), pp. 31-73.

Evergem: A. de Vos, 'Dertig jaar bevolkingsevolutie te Evergem (1571-1601)', *Handelingen der Maatschappij voor Geschiedenis en Oudheidkunde te Gent*, XIV (1960), pp. 117-29.

Herentals: H. van der Wee, *The Growth of the Antwerp Market and the European Economy* (3 vols., the Hague, 1963), II, p. 262.

Kasselrij Ieper (châtellenie d'Ypres): K. Maddens, 'De krisis op het einde van de XVIe eeuw in de kasselrij Ieper', *Revue Belge de*

Philologie et d'Histoire, XXXIX (1961), pp. 365-90.

Kasselrij Oudenaarde (châtellenie d'Audenarde): J. de Brouwere, 'Les dénombrements de la châtellenie d'Audenarde): 1469-1801', *Bulletin de la Commission royale d'Histoire*, CIII (1938), pp. 513-46.

Land van Aalst (Pays d'Alost): J. de Brouwere, *Demografisches evolutie van het Land van Aalst, 1570-1800* (Brussels, 1968), p. 111.

Leuven (Louvain): H. van der Wee, *The Growth of the Antwerp Market*, II, p. 262.

Mechelen (Malines): J. Verbeemen, 'De demografisches evolutie van Mechelen, 1370-1800', *Bulletin de la cercle archéologique de Malines*, LVII (1953), pp. 63-97.

Mons: J. Verbeemen, 'L'évolution démographique d'une ville wallonne: Mons (1283-1766)', *L'intermédiaire des généalogistes*, LV (1955), pp. 23-5.

Ninove: H. Vangassen, 'De honger van Ninove', *Het Land van Aalst*, V (1953), pp. 213-32.

Schorisse: C. de Rammelaere, 'De bevolkingscijfer in het Land van Schorisse (1569-1796)', *Handelingen der Maatschappij voor Geschiedenis en Oudheidkunde te Gent*, XIII (1959), pp. 53-98.

Turnhout: H. van der Wee, *The Growth of the Antwerp Market*, II, p. 262.

Figure 4:

G. Parker, *The Army of Flanders and the Spanish Road, 1567-1659* (Cambridge, 1972), pp. 293-5, for all years except 1633-4, which are taken from H. Pohl, 'Zur Bedeutung Antwerpens als Kreditplatz im beginnenden 17. Jahrhundert', in *Die Stadt in der europäischen Geschichte, Festschrift Edith Ennen* (Bonn, 1972), pp. 667-86.

Figure 5:

For 1602-19, O. van Rees, *Geschiedenis der staatshuishoudkunde in Nederland tot het einde der 18e eeuw*, II (Utrecht, 1868), pp. 146-7. For 1619-49, G. C. Klerk de Reus, *Geschichtlicher Ueberblick der administrativen, rechtlichen und finanziellen Entwicklung der Niederländisch Ost-Indischen Compagnie* (the Hague-Batavia, 1894), Beilage VI.

Figure 6:

C. R. Boxer, *The Portuguese Seaborne Empire, 1415-1825* (London, 1969), p. 379 for Portuguese figures; for the Dutch: R. Bijlsma, 'De archieven van de Compagnieën op Oost-Indië, 1594-1603', *Verslagen omtrent 's Rijks Oude Archieven*, XLIX (1926), pp. 173-225, and I. Schöffer, 'Import of bullion and coin into Asia by the Dutch East India Company in the 17th and 18th centuries' (Paper delivered to the Franco-Dutch Historical Conference, Paris, 1976), p. 4.

Index

Aalst (Alost), town in Flanders:
  Spaniards sack (1576), 117–18;
  betrayed to Spaniards (1584),
  141
absolutism in early modern
  government, 173–6
administration, see government
Africa, Dutch trade with, 54–6,
  60, 189–90
agriculture: in Netherlands, 184,
  189; in Spain, 189, 198
Alba, duke of, see Alva
Albert, archduke of Austria, see
  archdukes
Albornoz, Juan de, secretary of
  state and war to duke of Alva
  (1567–73), 153–4, 157–8
Algiers, Ottoman dominion:
  Dutch ally with, 69–70, 74
Alkmaar, town in Holland:
  Spaniards besiege (1573), 33,
  47, 49, 240 n.14; fortifications
  of, 48
Alva (Alba), Fernando Alvarez
  de Toledo third duke of
  (1510–82): opinions, 42, 160;
  expedition to Netherlands
  (1567), 22, 28, 207 n.23;
  government of Netherlands
  (1567–73), 28, 30, 34, 46,
  151–63, 191; military methods,
  46, 89, 212 n.5; proposed trial
  of (1574), 158; debts, 200
America: Spanish policy in,
  159–60; Spanish trade with,
  21, 185; Spanish Netherlands'
  trade with, 183; Dutch trade

with, 54–5, 56, 60–2, 78–81,
  179, 189–90, 195–6; stumbling
  block to Dutch-Spanish peace,
  54–6, 60–2; English and
  French attempts to colonize,
  49
Amsterdam, city in Holland,
  189–99
Anabaptists, religious group: in
  Netherlands, 46, 202, 211 n.4
Angola, Portuguese colony in
  Africa: Dutch contacts with,
  56
Anjou, Francis Hercules duke of
  (d.1584): intervention in
  Netherlands, 19, 70–1
*Annales: économies, sociétés,
  civilizations*, French historical
  journal: philosophy of, 12–14,
  42–3
Antwerp, city in Brabant:
  economy and population, 181,
  182, 183, 184, 192, 198;
  fortifications, 48, 140; religion,
  213 n.11; Spanish troops
  mutiny at (1574), 108, 109–10,
  111, 115, 117, 155–6; 'Spanish
  fury' at (1576), 114, 118–19,
  143, 154; Turkish consulate at
  (1581–4), 70; Spaniards capture
  (1584–5), 35, 140
archaeology: importance for
  post-medieval history, 134–5,
  250 n.13
archdukes (Albert, 1559–1621,
  and Isabella, 1566–1633):
  government of Spanish

277